Acclaim for past works by Jamal Khwaja

"Here is a book written with a notable lucidity, characterized by wisdom and tolerance, and remarkable for the range and comprehensiveness of its survey."

— *Prof. I.T. Ramsey, University of Oxford*

"I found it most interesting and informative and very clearly expressed."

— *Prof. C.D. Broad, University of Cambridge*

"I congratulate you on its excellent content and clarity of exposition."

— *Prof. John Wisdom, University of Cambridge*

"His (Mr. Khwaja's) is the most systematic and perhaps pioneering attempt to see Islam in the modern light."

— *Asghar Ali Engineer*

"Khwaja has made a weighty contribution to the debate on the reconstruction of Islam. Khwaja's 'Quest for Islam' is the approach of a philosopher [?]... which laudably takes into account the widened scope and sharpened tools of contemporary (admittedly, mainly British) scholarship."

— *Prof. Christian W. Troll*

"It shows real independent thought."

— **Prof. A.R. Wadia, University of Bombay**

"Jamal Khwaja has carried the insights of Azad to the deepest levels and reexamined and reformulated the basic concepts of Islam in his masterly work, 'Quest for Islam'."

— **Lalit Uniyal**

"The book is … an effort much outside the beaten orbit, born of a vision which aims not at regeneration but at resurrection. Mr. Khwaja's success cannot be overstated."

— **Amrita Bazar Patrika**

Living the Qur'an in Our Times

Composition in geometric *Kufi*. The Arabic phrase
"la ilaha illa Allah" (There is no god except Allah)
has been repeated four times.

Living the Qur'an
in Our Times

Jamal Khwaja

SAGE   www.sagepublications.com
Los Angeles • London • New Delhi • Singapore • Washington DC

First published in 2012 by

SAGE Publications India Pvt Ltd
B1/I-1 Mohan Cooperative Industrial Area
Mathura Road, New Delhi 110 044, India
www.sagepub.in

SAGE Publications Inc
2455 Teller Road
Thousand Oaks, California 91320, USA

SAGE Publications Ltd
1 Oliver's Yard, 55 City Road
London EC1Y 1SP, United Kingdom

SAGE Publications Asia-Pacific Pte Ltd
33 Pekin Street
#02-01 Far East Square
Singapore 048763

Published by Vivek Mehra for SAGE Publications India Pvt Ltd, typeset in 10/13 Berkeley by Tantla Composition Pvt Ltd, Chandigarh and printed at De-Unique, New Delhi.

Library of Congress Cataloging-in-Publication Data Available

ISBN: 978-81-321-1046-0 (HB)

The SAGE Team: Rudra Narayan, Aniruddha De and Nand Kumar Jha

In the name of God, the Beneficent, the Merciful

Also by Jamal Khwaja

Five Approaches to Philosophy

Quest for Islam

Authenticity and Islamic Liberalism

The Call of Modernity and Islam

Essays on Cultural Pluralism

The Vision of an Unknown Indian Muslim

Numerous articles and scholarly essays

"Verily never will Allah change the condition of a people until they change it themselves (with their own souls). But when (once) Allah willeth a people's punishment, there can be no turning it back, nor will they find, besides Him, any to protect."
  Qur'an; 13:11

"Whoever works any act of righteousness and has faith,—His endeavour will not be rejected: We shall record it in his favor."
  Qur'an; 21:94

"Offer in thy heart all thy works to me, and see me as the End of thy love, take refuge in the Yoga of reason, and ever rest thy soul in me."
  Bhagavad Gita; Ch.18, verse 57

"The truth is one, the wise call it by many names."
  The Rig Veda.

"You must be the change you wish to see in the world."
  Mahatma Gandhi (d. CE 1948)

Thank you for choosing a SAGE product! If you have any comment, observation or feedback, I would like to personally hear from you. Please write to me at contactceo@sagepub.in

—Vivek Mehra, Managing Director and CEO,
SAGE Publications India Pvt Ltd, New Delhi

Bulk Sales

SAGE India offers special discounts for purchase of books in bulk. We also make available special imprints and excerpts from our books on demand.

For orders and enquiries, write to us at

Marketing Department
SAGE Publications India Pvt Ltd
B1/I-1, Mohan Cooperative Industrial Area
Mathura Road, Post Bag 7
New Delhi 110044, India
E-mail us at marketing@sagepub.in

Get to know more about SAGE, be invited to SAGE events, get on our mailing list. Write today to marketing@sagepub.in

This book is also available as an e-book.

Contents

Preface*

Who Should Read the Work and Why?

THERE HAS EVER BEEN AN INSCRUTABLE MYSTERY about the origin of man and the cosmos, and the enigma of life and death. This mystery is as baffling today in the age of space travel and computers as it ever was in past millennia. Apart from providing group bonding, morality, and stable relationships, all religions attempt to solve the enigma of life and death and give to the believer an inner peace and equanimity to face the inevitable trials and tribulations of life.

Just as there are several races and languages in the human family, there are several religions. Moreover, every religion has several versions or paradigms within its umbrella. Any particular version or paradigm survives only as long as it fulfills the above need. The moment any particular religion or any particular paradigm of religion loses its power to give unconditional and clear satisfaction to the believer, the religious tradition begins to lose on its "existential appeal" even though its votaries may continue, by sheer force of convention and habit, to go on using the same old words, symbols, and rituals.

I think there would be general agreement that the major religious traditions of the human family did quite well in the past (in varying degrees) when there was very marginal communication among different wings of the human family. They were all scattered, and even when they clashed, the damage to life and property was limited. The human situation today is radically different due to the immense destructive power of modern technology. Moreover, the relative insularity of the different wings of the human family until recent times has now given way to a shrunken global village where votaries of different religions jostle with each other in multicultural workplaces and residential homes all enmeshed in a global economic system. The ancient and medieval separation of different cultures and religions has almost become a fairy tale.

The needs and demands of the present multicultural sovereign states are now powerfully motivating the relatively more intelligent and aware believers (among all religious groups) to distill the essential core of their faith from the total historical mix of secondary beliefs, myths, and customs of their respective groups. This distillation process will enable them the better to focus on the core of the

---

* I have incorporated in this Preface some passages from my essay "The Dream That Failed".

faith and its basic spiritual and moral values, instead of having to carry the entire baggage or social and cultural "padding" of one's tradition. This approach to one's religious and cultural heritage gives hitherto adversarial groups the democratic freedom to forge a consensus on secondary issues—social, economic, cultural—and to enjoy equal rights and opportunities and yet preserve their religious and cultural identity in a mixed free society.

This pragmatic and rational approach to religion is, however, resisted by several quarters, especially the traditionally dominant priests and religious scholars. In the case of Muslims, the strong insistence of Islamic scholar jurists that Islam is a complete code of conduct binding on the believer in every sphere of life, together with their great pride in their glorious past, pushes even highly educated and professionally qualified Muslims into believing that purely social and cultural patterns and modes of dressing and eating, gender segregation, and intracommunity marriage, etc., are integral to being good Muslims. However, to my mind, the deeper concern to reach the essential core of one's spiritual and cultural values would gradually outweigh and marginalize the current concern for outward symbols. The requirements of the modern world will soon make the different religious groups realize that their essential similarities far outweigh their differences. They will also come to realize that tensions and conflicts between human groups spring more from a clash of material interests than from creedal differences. This is a crucial and liberating insight into the human situation.

Foreign policy apart, the USA remains the land of freedom and opportunity in an open society. Individuals and organizations vigorously promote the good, as they see it; separation of Church and state, interfaith understanding, ultraright orthodoxies, ban on abortion, gender equality, plural sexual orientations, social justice, environmental protection, heritage preservation, free enterprise, and whatnot. Outgoing and friendly to all, the common man is busy enjoying his or her affluence, leisure and opportunities for both growth and entertainment. What is, perhaps, most significant for persons like myself is the air of tolerance and the spirit of live and let live in society. Enlightened circles have turned to the idea that religion or faith is a matter of existential choice, not reasoning. Diana Eck, Chomsky, Karen Armstrong, Annemarie Schimmel, the Dalai Lama, Nelson Mandela, Mother Teresa, Pope John Paul, Gandhi, and, last but not least, Abul Kalam Azad all, in their own way, have taught modern man that different organized religions are different roads to a basically common destination. The fundamentalist religious approach, on the other hand, holds that religion is a total code of conduct, and only one code ought to prevail.

The USA was the first and the foremost leader of spiritual pluralism and the separation of Church and state. The founding fathers of the American Constitution were as good, perhaps, better Christians than the vast majority of those who opposed the principled separation of Church and state. This is the great lesson that Muslims have yet to appropriate inwardly as Muslims. At present the very idea of separating the "church" and state creates in numerous Muslims feelings of guilt that this amounts to deserting their faith or becoming indifferent to faith. The present confrontation between American *realpolitik* and the *"jihadi"* version of Islam has produced a blinding haze that has made it difficult for both Muslims and others to see matters in the clear light of reason and the evidence of history.

Religious fundamentalists honestly think that this is a battle between the party of God and the party of the Devil. But the fight is not between good and evil as such, but rather between different ideas of what is good and what is bad. Human ideas about God or about good come into conflict because different individuals and groups occupy different stages of growth and development, and therefore have different viewpoints and material interests. The battle of ideas is, therefore, not a battle between good people and bad people but between good people who have different ideas of what good is. And the right way of discovering the truth is not murder or suicide but dialogue.

Liberal Western scholars who genuinely stress the need for intellectual honesty and empathy in the field of comparative cultural studies are steadily paving the way for fruitful interfaith dialogue on a global scale. Unfortunately, Muslim scholars are still in the grip of religious apologetics as the Christian missionaries once were in the 19th century. Muslims are very resistant to the idea of religious pluralism. However, no religion today can survive unless it genuinely accommodates spiritual pluralism and humanist democracy, implying the corollary of the separation of religion and state.

Is the above view of the nature and purpose of religion too intellectual or philosophical for popular acceptance? Well, the simple fact is that sages and saints of all religions have preached and practiced universal love and compassion rather than fear and hatred of the other. To my mind, the basic approach of the saints and sages will eventually overcome the approach of religious fanatics or power seekers. The present political, economic, and social pressures will eventually give way to the deeper wisdom of the spirit. The road to this happy consummation, however, will be long and bumpy and also require a sound road map.

I hope and trust that the great centers of learning and research in the West and East will engage themselves in impartial critical study of all religions and cultures of the human family. May each one of us cultivate the ability to hear, in the silence of the spirit, one's innermost whisper of his or her soul and find peace and salvation in one's freely chosen way.

The emergence of Islamic terrorism in present times is a negative response of some well-organized and well-funded activists among the larger bewildered Muslim world that finds itself outdistanced and marginalized in a much more industrially advanced secular age. Western *realpolitik*, even at the highest level at the UN, makes them apprehensive about their future. Some strategic blunders of Western powers in the sphere of international relations have led to mutual alienation between Muslim powers and others. However, behind the blood and tears of an agonized Asia and Africa, the process of slow learning through suffering is going on both in the downtrodden East and the affluent West. A new, more equitable balance of power and a new interfaith movement is being born. No racial, territorial, or religious group can now presume that it is divinely destined to preside over humanity forever.

The peoples of the East and the West, the North and the South, irrespective of religious ideology, are waking up to the sordid facts of *realpolitik* down the ages. The heat and dust raised by the "will to power" almost always blocks the vision of the participants, their supporters, and beneficiaries. This is how a substantial section of Muslims even today are hardly able to see and admire the genuine and enduring ideals of the modern West: free inquiry, spiritual autonomy with inner responsibility, freedom of expression and of association, tolerance of dissent, gender equality, cultural pluralism, affirmative action without appeasement, international cooperation without hegemony, and so on. This is also how a section of Jews are unable to admire the prolonged Jewish-Arab cultural efflorescence and fraternity in southern Europe and North Africa for centuries past. This is also how a very large number of modern Christians and other non-Muslims lack the faintest idea of the magnificent contribution of medieval Islam, in its creative period, to world culture. But how long can the mutual alienation between the East and West continue? The death cry of a near collapsing natural environment due to spiraling industrial pollution and irresponsible consumerism has begun to blast the illusion of permanent security and superiority of one tribe, nation, or religion to the other.

The present affluent overlords of the earth can no longer pretend that all is well at the banquet table, and the wine and music will ever go on if they just distribute some cake and Coke among the deprived quarters of the old world. No serious and informed well-wisher of the human family can evade the truth that, if humans are to survive, there must be genuine and total international cooperation and interreligious understanding (at all levels, in all quarters) to resolve all disputes and contentious issues between different wings of the human family. Due to obvious reasons, North America is, indeed, well-qualified to play a responsible leadership role in this tremendous task. But it would be disastrous if the leader behaves like a boss, not only toward developing Asian and African countries, but even while dealing with Britain and the "old" Europe. Is not the "new world" the progeny of the "old world," and shall not the young respect the old, and the old admire the young and find themselves renewed in humanity's march to a destination as yet rather dimly prefigured?

Preface

The present work is addressed to all those who desire to build bridges between minds and hearts that really care for unity in diversity and diversity in unity (in equal measure) and also care to be sure of their facts before they venture to judge themselves or others.

Jamal Khwaja
New Delhi, July 2012

Acknowledgments

THE WORK *LIVING THE QUR'AN IN OUR TIMES* has been sponsored by the New Aligarh Movement (NAM)—a nonpolitical, voluntary association that was established in 1986 at Aligarh, Uttar Pradesh, India. Its objective was to stimulate sympathetic, creative thinking on Islam and to publish literature on religious and cultural issues of the modern age. Its policy was to sponsor creative writing by competent persons but leave them free to express their authentic views. Its founding members were: Professor Riazur Rahman Sherwani, (late) Professor A. A. Suroor, (late) Mr. Ali Ashraf, Mr. Farrukh Jalali, Professor Masoodul Hasan, Professor A. A. Siddiqi, (late) Dr. Nasim Ansari, (late) Professor Mohibbul Hasan, and myself.

The Islamic Vision of Sir Syed (in Urdu), edited by Jamal Khwaja, was the first to be published by NAM. *Living the Qur'an in Our Times* is the second presentation.

My late father, Abdul Majeed Khwaja (d. CE 1962), was the first to teach me the wisdom of the Qur'an. An eminent product of Sir Syed Ahmed Khan's Aligarh Movement in the late 19th century, he was actively associated with the joint Khilafat and Civil Disobedience Movements in the early 20th century, under Gandhiji's leadership. He was also one of the eminent founders of the Jamia Millia Islamia at Aligarh in 1920. It was later shifted to Delhi in 1925, where it functioned under the able and inspiring leadership of Dr. Zakir Husain, the first Muslim President of the Indian republic. It has now blossomed into a Central university.

My father had the rare intellectual insight and moral courage to say openly and repeatedly that, among all the people he had come across in life, he found Gandhiji to be the closest follower of Prophet Muhammad ﷺ. It is a pity he never put his thoughts in writing. I dedicate this work to his fond memory, but I alone am responsible for the views expressed.

I am greatly indebted to Abdullah Yusuf Ali, Muhammad Ali of Lahore, Abul Kalam Azad, Pickthall, and Arberry. I have also learnt much from the writings of H. A. R. Gibb, Fazlur Rahman, Montgomery Watt, Izutsu, and Annemarie Schimmel. Karen Armstrong, in her own inimitable way, has done a lot to promote interfaith understanding. I greatly value the works of (late) Martin Lings, Professor Carl Ernst, and Professor Bruce Lawrence in this respect. However, I have tried to follow my own lights and my own mix of the Cambridge method of linguistic analysis and European religious existentialism in my understanding of the Qur'an.

I have learnt from many sources (that I have not named), but the conclusions I have arrived at are my own and, in all humility, I stand by them.

Throughout my work, I have used Yusuf Ali's monumental English translation of the Qur'an. As regards the transliteration of Arabic/Persian/Urdu words, expressions, and proper nouns, I have not used diacritical marks for the sake of simplicity. All dates refer to the Common Era (CE).

I express my warm thanks to my dear friend, Professor Masoodul Hasan, for his moral support in my task. His intellectual honesty and empathetic understanding of different points of view have helped a large circle in the Aligarh academic community. He carefully read early drafts of the work and gave very valuable advice. Maqbol Ahmad, of Karachi, an engineer by profession, but a voracious reader of books on Islam, patiently read an early draft of my work. His extremely valuable comments and suggestions led to much improvement of the original draft. I am much indebted to him. My very good friends, Professor Aulad Ahmad Siddiqui and Professor Riazur Rahman Sherwani, also favored me with their valuable comments. I cherish the memory of my numerous intellectual chats with (late) Hashim Ali, former Vice Chancellor, Aligarh Muslim University, and author of the work *The Essence of Islam*.

I must thank my young friends, Dr. Luqman Khan, Dr. Sanjay Grover, Azhar Khan, and my granddaughter, Samia, for their loving and unfailing help and assistance in computer-related matters. I also express my loving gratitude to Qadeer Khwaja for bringing to my knowledge variant interpretations of the Qur'anic text concerning the procedure of divorce in Islamic law.

I deeply appreciate the loving interest my son, Rajen Habib, took in the publication of the present work. The comments of the (to me) unknown evaluators of SAGE Publications were very thought provoking. I must thank them and the entire team at SAGE for their constructive suggestions and professionalism.

Last, but not the least, I must express my deep appreciation and affectionate regard for my son, Jawahar, without whose expert guidance the present work might not have been published at all.

Introduction

IT IS AN INTEGRAL PART OF THE ISLAMIC FAITH that the Qur'an is the infallible "Word of God." Yet, the plain fact is that there is woeful disagreement among the faithful over what the revealed texts mean or imply in regard to multiple matters and issues. The air is thick with polemics and apologetics.* The present work analyses the reason or reasons for this state of affairs and suggests a better method of interpreting the Qur'anic texts.

Even if one accepts on faith (as I do) that the Qur'an is a revealed scripture, the proper understanding of the Islamic scripture requires that the believer not only understands the literal meaning of the Arabic text, but also knows the context of the revelation together with (to some extent at least) the "usage" of Qur'anic Arabic. Neglecting any of three basic factors—the text, the context and "usage" of the language of revelation—confuses and will ever mislead both Muslim believers and others.

Many disagreements arise because several Qur'anic texts admit of plural interpretations depending on the individual's level of understanding and the broad conceptual framework he has come to acquire through his exposure to the factual knowledge and "spirit of the times." This is how educated Muslims today (easily and honestly) can explain Qur'anic verses dealing with cosmology or God's creative activity in a way quite different from the way medieval Muslims did when the body of modern science had not emerged. I submit that this approach should be extended to the basic moral and spiritual values enshrined in the Qur'an. In short, the task of interpreting the Qur'an should never end.

Another basic source of disagreement in regard to Qur'anic injunctions is that one does not make a clear distinction between basic "intrinsic" values (spiritual and moral) and the "instrumental" rules† of conduct for promoting the said basic values. It will never be easy to sort out basic moral and spiritual values from the instrumental ones since many Qur'anic prescriptions or injunctions are bound to be mixed. Yet, it is part of essential wisdom that the Muslim believer maintains and continually applies this distinction in judging what is ethically right or wrong.

The following pages are addressed to Western educated Muslims who value the essentials of the great Islamic heritage, but feel emotionally and intellectually

---

* See Appendix 1: Annotated Glossary of Key Concepts.
† See Appendix 1: Annotated Glossary of Key Concepts.

"uneasy" that many unjustifiable beliefs, attitudes, and customs have become a part of the tradition, and that Muslims generally resist the idea of reform and growth in the Islamic value system. In fact, Muslims tend either to suppress their doubts or perplexities, or explain them away by giving rather dubious reasons in defense of the traditional position. This inevitably leads to inner conflicts, unconscious hypocrisy, "surface-faith," and self-alienation. As a result, many Muslims shy away from modernity even when the values in question appeal to them, rationally and emotionally.

The analytical existentialist[‡] approach to the Qur'an (as suggested in this work) should remove inner perplexities and honest doubts of Muslims without their deviating from the essence of the Qur'anic teachings. This will facilitate Muslims in reaching higher levels of inner integration and peace while remaining fully rooted in their traditions. Many followers of other religions are also in the same situation. Using this approach, both Muslims and non-Muslims would promote interfaith and interethnic harmony between all segments of humanity, including those who decry religion for some reason or the other, yet are ethically upright.

All true believers (irrespective of religion) must strive for mutual understanding and accommodation of the interests of the human family as a whole. The modern interfaith movement with its message of complete tolerance, equal respect for all races and religions, and equitable concern for the welfare of the entire human family is the need of the century and, indeed, a need for all times. Muslims in the modern global age should now reflect on Qur'anic texts with full intellectual honesty, without any fear that the traditional religious leadership might accuse them of imitating Western thinking for the sake of material ends or of indulging in political expediency.

The semantic approach[§] to the Qur'an, in a broad sense, was actually practiced in the past by eminent creative Muslim intellectuals and thinkers such as Tabari, Ghazali, Ibn Sina, Ibn Rushd, and Ibn Khaldun, *et al.* But this approach never trickled down to reach the vast majority of the faithful. Qur'anic studies gradually ossified into a rigid and isolated discipline, and Muslim scholars became almost totally cut off from the natural and social sciences of the West. Sufi poets and thinkers, however, were an exception. The Aligarh Movement inaugurated by Sir Syed Ahmed Khan and his associates in the last quarter of the 19th century had this objective in mind. Iqbal and Azad also strove to carry forward the legacy of the Syed, but not much has been done to date. Rather, thanks to Abul Ala Maududi and his activist associates in Pakistan and elsewhere, numerous highly intelligent,

---

‡ See Appendix 1: Annotated Glossary of Key Concepts.
§ See Appendix 1: Annotated Glossary of Key Concepts.

Introduction

educated, and relatively progressive Muslim believers, in different parts of the world, have been bewitched by the slogan of *"Islamization of knowledge"* and of society and state. However, they should not be dubbed as "fundamentalists" in a bad sense, or as terrorists. They are as intelligent and well-meaning as any other group interested in reforming state and society.

I regard the present work as a companion volume to my earlier work, *Quest for Islam* (1977). The focus of the earlier work was on a philosophical analysis of the basic concepts and values of Islam in the light of modern thought. The focus of the present work is on Qur'anic texts in the light of functional linguistic analysis of Scripture and a broad religious existentialism.

Chapter 1 of the work briefly delineates a Qur'anic paradigm of the Islamic faith, as I understand it. Chapter 2 critically analyzes the concept of revelation *(wahy)* in the light of modern thought and discusses some basic issues connected with the Islamic faith that the Qur'an is the "Word of God." Chapter 3 applies the basic principles of elementary semantics and Cambridge linguistic analysis to the proper understanding of Qur'anic texts. Chapters 4 and 5 comprise, mainly, a selection of Qur'anic texts (in English translation) that describe the Qur'anic thought and value system. Chapter 6 deals with some problems that arise when one tries to implement Qur'anic injunctions in the literal sense without reference to any coherent theory of ethical values. Indeed, I have, on purpose, avoided citing prescriptive texts of the Qur'an in this chapter as I wanted to focus the reader's attention on the crucial need to create a balanced and sound rationale for interpreting the moral imperatives of the Qur'an. Chapter 7 is my authentic response to the perennial human situation, as I see it. The extensive notes are an integral part of the main text, and I request the reader to kindly bear with me in this matter.

Before closing, I simply must refer to the work *Interpreting the Qur'an* (2006) by Professor Abdullah Saeed of Melbourne University, Australia. This well-informed, wide-ranging, objective, and balanced study of the Qur'an came to my knowledge much after I had completed my own work. I admire Saeed's approach and the wealth of his background historical information relevant to the subject, and the clarity of his analysis. It seems there is almost total agreement between my own and his method of interpreting the Qur'an.

The Qur'anic paradigm of perennial** Islam, as here stated, may sound strange and even shocking to many good and intelligent Muslim believers as well as other sober and sympathetic students of Islam. In all humility, may I say that, whether one realizes it or not, at this point of time, Muslims all over the world (slowly but steadily and unknowingly) are actually moving in this direction, and further that this is a good thing, indeed. However, God alone knows the full truth,

---

** See Appendix 1: Annotated Glossary of Key Concepts.

and we humans should ever beware of possessing exclusive truth and falling into the pit of spiritual conceit.

Note: Suggested Reading Pattern for the Book

The explanatory notes (pp. 128–178) are meant to develop the theme and the line of the argument in the text. Each note contains some important information or insight. Reading each note along with the text should considerably add to the pleasure and the profit of reading the book. Using two bookmarks, one in each section, would make the process effortless. This arrangement aims to serve the requirements of readers who are hard pressed for time as well as readers who can devote more time for pondering highly complex issues.

1

Perennial Islam: A Qur'an Based Paradigm

Introductory Remarks

BEFORE ATTEMPTING THE TASK, I, in all humility, would like to uncover a long-standing hidden assumption or semantic illusion that has shaped the Muslim mind throughout centuries past. This assumption is as follows: "The word, 'Islam' has only one definitive and incontrovertible meaning, and this definitive meaning is the one which my in-group professes."

It is incontrovertible (for a Muslim) that the standard meaning of the word "Islam" is the one used in the Qur'an. However, the human understanding of what God means by the word "Islam" or any other Qur'anic word or expression is, I submit, a rather different case. Muslims must, indeed, accept the Qur'an as the "Word of God" and Muhammad 🕊* as the "Messenger of God," the cosmos as the "creation of God," and God as the "only Self-Existent, Sovereign Lord of all that exists." However, the believer cannot help understanding or interpreting the exact meaning of the above expressions according to his/her own conceptual level and range of knowledge. Human understanding of the Qur'an is, at bottom, a matter of continual growth in the ongoing historical process. I submit this insight is crucially significant for understanding the issue concerned. The Muslim mind must accept that plural interpretations of Islam are, indeed, inevitable, and it is eminently desirable to accept this *de facto* plurality as natural and permissible. However, the believer must ever strive for conceptual clarity and practice "loving tolerance" of both internal dissent and of other religious traditions.

Perennial Islam, as joyful submission to one Supreme Creator and acceptance of the Qur'an as the "Word of God," revealed to Prophet Muhammad 🕊, is one thing; the surrender to a static *Shariah* conceived as a perfect and total guide for the believer in every walk of life is quite another. To remain rooted

---

* "Peace be upon him" in Arabic.

1

in the perennial spiritual values of the Qur'an, as exemplified in the life and character of the historical Muhammad ☙, the "Seal of the Prophets" is one thing; to hold that this implies that believers should actively strive to become "carbon copies" of the Prophet's actions and lifestyle is quite another. Rootedness in the basic Qur'anic values does not imply a mechanical and unreflective adherence to Qur'anic injunctions without making a distinction between "intrinsic" values and "instrumental" rules. Likewise, genuine reverence and love for the Prophet ☙ does not imply uncritical acceptance of the many miracles or myths found in the popular versions of the Islamic faith, especially the dramatic detailed events and dialogues mentioned in the stories of the Prophet's ☙ journey (meraj) to God's Throne. To deny such myths or miracles in no way diminishes his sublime spiritual status and his authentic mystical experiences or his amazing achievements as an historical figure.

Muslims generally believe that Prophet Muhammad ☙ must have possessed supernatural powers on the ground that earlier prophets performed miracles. Prophet Muhammad ☙ being the greatest, God must have endowed him with similar, if not greater, powers, so it is held to be the case. Muslims commonly cite the Qur'anic verse (54:1) as evidence that Prophet Muhammad ☙ performed the miracle of "splitting the moon" (shaqq ul Qamar). Numerous saints and mystics of Islam are also credited with possessing extraordinary powers through Divine grace. Sufi tombs attract numerous devotees (both Muslim and others) who seek the intervention of the saints in securing various material benefits for themselves.

However, the Qur'an gives no warrant at all for accepting this traditional image of Prophet Muhammad ☙. Indeed, the Qur'an categorically denies that Prophet Muhammad ☙ possessed supernatural powers with the sole exception of the gift of Divine revelation (wahy). The Qur'an is the only miracle, which Prophet Muhammad ☙ claimed to possess.[1]

The process of Qur'anic revelation continued intermittently over a long period of twenty-three years. It is incontrovertible that the revealed contents were closely related to the needs and situational requirements of the Prophet ☙ and the nascent Muslim community and that the Divinely revealed texts were meant to teach and inculcate basic values and principles of conduct and also to address the then prevailing social, economic, and political conditions of the region, apart from providing inner strength and consolation to the Prophet ☙ and consoling him and the nascent Islamic community. It is also incontrovertible that the Prophet ☙ could not but use his own discretion or personal judgment while interpreting and applying the revealed Qur'anic injunctions as also when a novel challenge or situation arose, and no specific guidance was available in the Qur'an. We should also reflect on the fact that the Prophet ☙ freely consulted his close and trusted companions and, on several occasions, he preferred their advice to his own initial judgment. After his passing away, the second Caliph, Umar, introduced many changes and reforms in political, administrative, and legal matters in view of the changed social and economic conditions of time and place. His innovative and rational approach to the polity dating back to the Prophet ﷺ himself even met with some honest and well-meaning criticism, but Umar's sagacity and forceful personality prevailed. Unfortunately, the struggle for ascendancy among the warring tribes and human weaknesses of individuals and rulers conspired to dilute and then to extinguish the high idealism and ethical politics of the Prophet's ﷺ time. It is tragic that close companions of the Prophet ﷺ were ranged on different sides and even resorted to civil war to capture power. Barring a few exceptions, Muslim society fell victim to the politics of violence in place of the politics of consultation and peaceful solution to situational challenges that are an integral part of the human condition, as such. The tragic assassination of Husain, the Prophet's ﷺ grandson, on the field of Karbala in what is now part of modern Iraq, was the tragic finale of the process of moral decay and reign of "*realpolitik*" that displaced the earlier idealism of the Prophet's ﷺ time.[2]

In the realm of thought and culture, however, Arab and Iranian Muslims inaugurated a magnificent breakthrough in the Islamic world. But it is an unfortunate paradox that this period of enlightenment lasting two centuries was hardly appreciated by the orthodox religious establishment of the larger Islamic world. Great thinkers, scientists, poets, mystics, mathematicians, historians, and geographers shone like stars on the till then barren cultural firmament of Damascus and Baghdad, but intellectual giants like Kindi (d. CE 873), Farabi (d. CE 950), Ibn Sina (d. CE 1037), Ibn Tufail (d. CE 1185), Al-Beruni (d. CE 1048), Ibn Rushd (d. CE 1198), *et al.* were hardly honored by their own contemporaries. Indeed, they lived in fear of being persecuted if not declared as heretics because of their creative and dynamic approach to the Qur'an and the dogmas of Islam. In their own eyes they were good Muslims but they were compelled to be secretive and circumspect in speech and in writing lest they attract the wrath of the orthodox religious leaders. On the other hand, the great Muslim theologians and jurists, such as Abu Hanifa (d. CE 767), Malik (d. CE 795), Shafai (d. CE 820), Hambal (d. CE 855), and Jafar Sadiq (d. CE 765), were greatly respected and celebrated. But even these religious leaders were, at times, persecuted by some Caliphs who had other ideas. In short, Islamic society never enjoyed the blessings of real freedom of inquiry and conscience and never mastered the democratic art of agreeing to differ. Indeed, if we in the modern era have come to admire the genius and magnificent contribution of Ibn Khaldun to Sociology and the Philosophy of history, this is due to the objective research and humanist empathy of a large number of modern Western intellectuals.[3]

Regard and Reverence for the Prophet ﷺ

Millions and millions of Muslim believers will surely and rightly continue to venerate Prophet Muhammad ﷺ as the perfect exemplar for humanity. An ever swelling number of non-Muslims of eminence now also acknowledge the administrative, moral, and spiritual genius of Prophet Muhammad ﷺ as one of the super architects and shapers of human destiny on the world scale. But the crucial question is what should be the concrete form, in the modern age, of a true Muslim's veneration for Prophet Muhammad ﷺ.

In answer to the above crucial question, I submit that true reverence and fidelity to Prophet Muhammad ﷺ consists in trying to make his basic values and objectives, rather than the details of the Prophet's ﷺ conduct, the pivot of our own lives and activities. The promotion of Prophet Muhammad's ﷺ basic values (even if this task today requires modifying his instructions given in particular situations) is the real meaning of following his example (*sunnah*) in an ever-changing world. This is, precisely, what Caliph Umar had done. The following considerations should help perplexed Muslim believers to realize this liberating truth.

First, development or growth takes place in different fields of human activity despite interruptions, retrogressions, and reverses. This applies not only to factual knowledge, but also to human ideals, values, and institutions. Thus have arisen fresh interpretations of the good life. Universal human rights, rule by consent, peaceful transfer of power, tolerance of dissent, gender equality, and equality of opportunity are some of the ideals that are the fresh characteristics of the modern age. Static norms of perfection cannot but arrest the natural movement of ideas and ideals. No particular stage of development can be said to be perfect.

It may be thought that, for the committed Muslim, at least, the Qur'an is beyond the shadow of imperfection. But the crucial point is that the Qur'an has to be understood by human beings whose conceptual framework is bound to changes with the passage of time. This framework will always remain subject to various imperfections or limitations. Thus, even if we concede the Qur'an, as the Word of God, to be perfect, its human understanding will always remain a matter of perfection aspired to rather than perfection achieved. Ceaseless growth toward perfection rather than perfection as such is all that man can hope for.

Second, a clear distinction should be made between basic values and instrumental rules. The Muslim segment of the human family will not advance forward, but move in ruts alone, if Muslims do not sift the instrumental prescriptions of the Prophet ﷺ from his basic goals and objectives. The making of this distinction between basic objectives and the means for realizing them should not be confused with the rather facile view that the end justifies the means.

Third, a clear distinction will also have to be made between matters of personal taste and matters of morality and spirituality. Real and honest commitment to the values of the Prophet ﷺ does not mean that the individual gives up his inclinations and preferences in matters of taste.

Fourth, the reported sayings and doings of Prophet Muhammad ﷺ are not sufficiently authentic despite the arduous efforts by dedicated and gifted Muslim researchers to separate the chaff from the grain. Though it is true that several Qur'anic texts are inexplicable or will remain vague unless read in the light of reported sayings or doings of the Prophet, ﷺ there is no justification for bracketing the Qur'an and the *hadith* as equally authentic or binding. Respect for the latter does not mean unquestioning acceptance.

Keeping the above four considerations in mind should help us to realize that the real meaning of fidelity to Prophet Muhammad ﷺ is not the literal imitation of his conduct but the honest and intelligent endeavor to translate the basic values of the Qur'an and hence of the Prophet ﷺ into practice in an ever-changing human situation.

The Theory of Conceptual Evolution

The need of the hour for Muslims is to pay sufficient heed to what may be called the phenomenon of "conceptual evolution"—the growth of ideas and ideals as a part of the general spiritual, moral, and intellectual growth in the atmosphere of free and honest search for truth. Muslims do not apply the idea of growth to the ideas and ideals of Islam. The overwhelming majority of Muslims frown at the prospect of conceptual pluralism within the tradition, apart from the already accepted four schools of jurisprudence, among the Sunnis, and Jafriya School, among the Shia Muslims. Even the Shiite version of Islam, despite its long history of thousand years or more is permitted with a grudge rather than graceful acceptance due to old and deeply entrenched political and cultural factors. However, the march of the democratic ethos in the modern technological age irresistibly demands a mature and joyful acceptance of the inevitability of plural interpretations of all religious faiths, including Islam.

Muslims will have to learn to overcome their inner feeling of insecurity and the fear of disintegration of the Islamic tradition at the prospect of conceptual growth. Muslims must become willing upholders of the idea of tolerance of dissent and freedom of conscience, and boldly repudiate the traditional concept of apostasy (*irtedad*), which (according to the great jurists) invites the death penalty. Muslim intellectuals and religious leaders must also get together to review and redefine the essential function and jurisdiction of religion (including their own) in a multireligious world society, fast turning into one global city. Thus alone will authentic faith become possible and Islamic ideals come really alive in the modern age.

The Qur'an and Prophet Muhammad ﷺ are the pivot of Islamic piety. But this should not lead to spiritual or cultural insularity in the mistaken belief that other traditions, both religious and secular, have nothing to offer Muslims. In fact, many Islamic values and ideals, which born Muslims assimilate from their milieu and naturally take as exclusively Islamic are, in fact, common to all religions. The same misunderstanding prevails in other religious quarters.

Each religion is an organic blend of a metaphysical view regarding the origin and destiny of man in the Universe and a pattern of holistic response to the mystery of existence. This holistic response enables the believer to face the trials and tribulations of life with fortitude and courage. Every religion succeeds pretty well in this regard, but none succeeds in penetrating into the inscrutable mystery of Being, which continues to escape the metaphysical views or conceptual schemes different religions project to explain the origin and destiny of the Universe.

These different world perspectives or conceptual pictures can be accepted and mentally enjoyed but not proved or disproved like scientific or logical truth-claims. The different perspectives or conceptual pictures may be said to be different "languages of the spirit" just as there are different natural languages all serving the same purpose. Every individual picks up the language of the spirit, along with the natural language spoken in his milieu. He must speak his own language of the spirit correctly to the best of his ability.

An agnostic or atheist who cannot find God or a spiritual basis of the Universe even after honest and patient reflection also opts for a particular language of the spirit (though he may not realize this) and also for a particular value system. His honest existential response to the mystery of existence must also be respected, even though the religious believer may passionately wish the atheist's inner convictions had been different or that they may now change. In no case should human freedom and the dignity of the individual be diminished. And, finally, the authentic commitment to our own faith should not stop us from gladly picking up the pearls of the spirit embedded in other religious and cultural streams of the human family.

Religion and Human Life

Religion, in some sense or the other, has always been an integral part of the human story from the very beginning, and this will remain so till the story ends, whenever and whatever the end might be. What is new and peculiar to the modern age, however, is that different religions have become much better acquainted with each other's beliefs and values than ever before (though much more remains to be done in this regard). Several excellent studies now exist that describe, with accuracy and sympathy, the basic beliefs and values of different religions, without taking sides or trying to prove the exclusive truth of any particular creed or sect. These studies are not polemical but reconciliatory or "irenic." The works of Huston Smith are, to my mind, an outstanding example of this approach to the study of world religions. These studies make it pretty evident that all religions project a basic metaphysical view of humankind as if it was the final truth about the ultimate Reality. The view includes a basic value system, which, in the course of time, blossoms into a set of social customs, laws, and a penal code.[4]

Different societies over the course of time gradually arrive at diverse world views, basic values, social customs, art forms, spoken and written languages, methods of production, distribution, trade, social gradation, and power structures to maintain stability and defend the society against external aggression. Though societies greatly differ in the above matters, all have a common core of faith—that the limitless variety in nature, the cycles of night and day and of the seasons, the mystery of life, birth, and death are not accidental happenings but all controlled by one Supreme Creator or Power that is, however, beyond human "conceptualization." The symbol of light and the practice of deep silence, meditation and prayer (directly to the Supreme Being or with the help of some sacred medium) are universal core features of all developed religions. Theologies and concrete moral and legal codes gradually grow around this spiritual core with the passage of time.

Religions differ only in how they "conceptualize" the nature and workings of the Supreme Power, the identity of the charismatic founders of the tradition concerned, sacred sites, and incidents of their life story, the sacramental rites, and the sacred symbols of the tradition. Considerable as these differences can be, they do not cancel the essential similarity of a common core belief—every finite existent or event is dependent and fleeting, but there is only one eternal and Supreme Self-Existent Being that is the Source of all that exists or happens.[5]

One may say that different organized religions are different cultural fruits that have evolved in social space time on the stem of one basic and perennial idea or proto faith—the world is not a chaos but a cosmos controlled by a Supreme Power (by whatever name He may be called) and that humankind's highest good and felicity lies in total submission or surrender to the Supreme Being, beyond our understanding. This common proto faith underlies all the different organized religious traditions. Every child acquires it along with the rest of the beliefs and cultural symbols of the in-group to express and articulate his or her "sense of the sacred," just as one acquires the "ordinary" language, gestures, morals, social attitudes, musical and artistic sensibility, and dress code of the group concerned.

To my mind, these differences do not contradict the core faith in one Supreme Being or diminish the status and dignity of individuals professing different faiths so long as the individual is truthful in thought, word and deed, in terms of one's tradition, provided the tradition does not violate a few universally accepted "categorical imperatives" concerning cannibalism, murder, rape, fraud, hypocrisy, stealing, falsehood, and the like. Several Qur'anic texts support this line of spiritual pluralism.[6]

It is also a matter of common experience that the simple goodness of the heart, truthfulness, honesty, and compassion are found in individuals irrespective of what religion they may profess. The mere profession of any theological creed (be it Islam or otherwise) makes no difference to the inner life and spiritual state of the individual unless he actually develops integrity of character and a "good heart." Some are born with a "good heart" just as some are born with lovely eyes or a good memory or some gift such as musical or poetical sensibility, or the capacity of sharp analytical reasoning. In general, spiritual development or excellence takes place when the impact of some truly pious or saintly person "awakens" an ordinary human being (troubled by perplexity and groping in the dark) and the person finds an "inner peace and wellness" welling from his depths, and making him an integrated and humane person at peace with the entire world. He passes through a sort of "boundary experience" in the language of the profound German thinker of the 20th century, Karl Jaspers, and this helps trigger the birth of an "authentic human being."[7]

What enables the mentor to "awaken" a person from the "slumber of the spirit"—a pervasive condition of self-alienation, perplexity and negativity—and brings him to the state of abiding peace and spiritual integration is, in the final analysis, the mentor's own elevated spiritual level rather than his intellectual prowess or professed religious or theological creed. This inner transformation of the spirit requires no declaration of joining any religious body, and it also raises no expectations of receiving special treatment from God, guru or life in general. The "awakened soul" tries to understand one's duties and to discharge them without any fear of punishment or expectation of reward. He may, or he may not like to accept the mentor's own professed world view or religious affiliation, if any.[8]

In the normal course of spiritual rebirth the "awakened soul" accepts the moral or ethical code as defined by the tradition of his milieu. However, it may and usually does happen that some elements in the tradition create some inner dissonance and his inner being no longer echoes back an authentic approval of such elements. Obedience to such elements in the (venerated) moral heritage creates an existential conflict between a total commitment to the tradition and one's autonomous authentic conscience. In such a situation the spiritual learner may be tempted to take to "apologetical" or "defensive reasoning" in regard to those elements. However, case histories show that the really "awakened souls" do not fall into this trap or the trap of reactive nihilism. They re-integrate their inner being in other ways, say, (*a*) honest admission of a spiritual antinomy but willing deference to the "collective wisdom" of the mother tradition or of the Ultimate Authority (whatever this be), and they learn to live in inner peace with this existential perplexity; (*b*) genuine commitment to the tradition as a whole minus the objectionable elements concerned; (*c*) affirming complete spiritual autonomy combined with stress on "good will," as such, without any concern for creed, dogma, or "transcendental" matters at all.

To my mind, all the above responses are valid, though none can be justified as the only valid or true response. Every individual should find his or her own existential truth as the gateway to the "peace that passeth understanding." What really counts is truthfulness, rather than attainment of "the" truth, which lies with the Creator alone. Humans can only strive to arrive but they never fully arrive. However, we can arrive into the haven of humility, and we can respect all who seek the truth, and we can travel together in mutual companionship on the long and unending road to God's truth. Indeed, this respect should be extended even to those who, for whatever reason, have grown totally alienated from God but do care for the good in general. This is the modern concept of tolerance at its best.[9]

There are some verses of the Qur'an, (3: 28, 118; 5: 51, quoted in note 6 of chapter 1, *Perennial Islam*) among others that exhort the Muslim believer not to trust and befriend the "rejectors" or the enemies of God and the Prophet, ﷺ and to kill them "wherever they are found." Some critics of Islam have concluded, after coming across such verses, that the God of Islam and Judaism is the god of wrath and hatred, while the God of Christians is the god of love and compassion. Such a hasty inference is a clear oversimplification of complex matters.

The Qur'an is not a systematic book but an extended homily, and its texts must be understood in the proper situational context rather than as general statements. The fact is that the general message and underlying "thrust" of the Qur'an is that of human brotherhood and tolerance of plurality. The Qur'an contains repeated reminders to humankind not to quarrel with others since only God knows the whole truth and that He will inform and judge all creation on the Day of Judgment. The few Qur'anic texts that, avowedly, prohibit Muslim believers from befriending or trusting the disbelievers were, manifestly, wartime regulations meant to apply to the Prophet's ﷺ contemporary Arab opponents who were desperately planning to kill the Prophet ﷺ and destroy the nascent movement.[10]

Likewise, the Qur'anic texts that describe the sufferings and tortures of hell and the pleasures and rewards of heaven are meant to motivate simple and unlettered folk whose limited understanding could hardly go beyond the physical level of reward and punishment. For others the Qur'an speaks in a different idiom— the highest reward for the faithful being the spiritual vision of the Creator, and their worst suffering the fear of losing nearness to or the pleasure of God. Indeed, the Sufi interpretation of the Qur'anic vision and piety is a remarkable contribution to the collective wisdom of the human family, along with the wisdom of ancient China, India, and Greece.[11]

What Is Perennial Islam?

Every religious tradition does have some theological beliefs or "dogmas" that cannot be proved rationally but are essential ingredients of faith. The Islamic dogma is that the Qur'an is the "Word of God" just as the official Christian dogma is that Jesus is the "Son of God." However, the moment one tries to determine the exact meaning of any dogma (including the Islamic dogma) all efforts breakdown. Let me explain how and why this happens.

The expanded Islamic belief is that (a) God communicated the Divine Word (fully formed Arabic sentences or verses) to the angel Gabriel who revealed them to Prophet Muhammad ﷺ as and when God willed; (b) God empowered the Prophet ﷺ to remember exactly the revealed text; (c) the Prophet ﷺ dictated the text to some reliable scribe/scribes who wrote down what they heard from the Prophet ﷺ on any available surface such as palm leaves, vellum, pieces of bark or of cloth; (d) these separate transcriptions were later collected and arranged under 114 "surahs" or chapters in the order that is still extant; (e) no portion of the text has been lost, corrupted, or changed after the original revelation. This expanded belief is silent on the question whether the order of the chapters and the sequence of the verses within each chapter were also revealed to the Prophet ﷺ, or whether he merely authorized it, at his discretion. It is also a matter of dispute between the different Islamic sects or schools of thought as to when the very first full collection of all the 114 surahs came into physical existence, but it definitely existed in the time of the third Caliph, Uthman, some twenty years after the passing away of the Prophet ﷺ.[12]

A close scrutiny of the five articles of the above Islamic belief about the Qur'an shows a radical difference between the first article and the remaining four. The first article refers to extra-human subjects or beings and their acts of which humans have no ordinary knowledge or clear ideas at all. The rest of the four articles, however, we can understand just as we understand ordinary statements concerning persons or things. This is the crucial difference between believing a dogma and believing an ordinary truthclaim. A dogma, not only cannot be proved, it cannot be clearly understood or explained as we can understand and explain ordinary beliefs about ordinary matters. This crucial difference between belief and dogma is because the words we use in ordinary perceptual or conceptual discourse are all backed by experience, actual or possible, but when we use the same set of words in talk about God, angels, the Devil, heaven or hell, the words, which have a clear meaning to begin with, become opaque and the source of insoluble perplexity. We, then, begin to grope and stumble in "connotative darkness." This is why the language of theology is condemned to be analogical or metaphorical, and all perceptive theologians and religious thinkers accept this rider on all theological truthclaims.[13]

The above semantic difference between a dogma and an ordinary belief, thus, clearly implies that religious disputes involving or touching upon any religious dogma (no matter what the religion) are absolutely futile and pointless. We can argue, for instance, that Jesus was the fount of compassion and altruistic love, but we just cannot prove that he was the "Son of God." Likewise, we can argue that the power and beauty of the Arabic Qur'an remains unmatched to date, but we just cannot prove that the Qur'an is the "Word of God." Exactly identical remarks hold good of the dogmas of all other religious traditions. If this be accepted, the basic concept of "argumentative religious conversion" or peaceful rational persuasion of the entire world to the one and only true religion/ creed turns into a virtual illusion born out of ignorance of semantics and the ground realities of the human situation. What, then, should the ardent Christian or Muslim believer (burning with the duty to "save" humankind) do to be fully convinced that one is a "true" believer fully dedicated to serving God?[14]

In all humility, I say let such souls give up arguing and proving that Muhammad ﷺ is the last messenger of God or that the Qur'an is "the Word of God," and take to implementing, in his/her own life, the basic spiritual and moral values of the Qur'an, as exemplified in the sublime life and character of the historical Muhammad ﷺ. Likewise, let Christian believers not stress converting others to the Church's Ontology of Christ, but to practice the love and compassion the historical Jesus preached and practiced in his life. It seems the Church has almost come to this position thanks to their most enlightened and creative religious leaders who are well-exposed to the complexities of the human situation in the modern world. The same remarks apply to Buddhism, Hinduism, and other religious traditions. The basic message of Buddha, not Buddhist ontology, the basic message of the Gita, not Vedic cosmology or *Hindutva*, the basic message of Guru Nanak, not Sikh orthodoxy, is what humanity needs. And when one reaches to the heart of all these messages, one finds they are essentially the same expressed in different languages and in different human scenarios.

What, then, lies behind all the hatred and strife in the name of religion? It is the human ego and the will to power, which makes us cling to the illusion that one's own language, conceptual imagery, and sacramental rites are the only and exclusive paths to truth and salvation. In the final analysis, the paths are many, but the goal is the same. One should follow the path whose call stirs one to the depths of his or her being, no matter what name or label it carries. What is supremely important is that one actively strives to reach the shore rather than just drift at the mercy of the waves. It is here that one realizes the importance of remaining attached to one's cultural roots whatever they might be. Hindu spirituality, at its best (as exemplified in the Gita, and in the life and doings of the saints and sages of modern Hinduism, such as Ramakrishna [d. CE 1886], Tagore [d. CE 1941], Maharishi Raman [d. CE 1950], Gandhiji [d. CE 1948], Bhagwan Das [d. CE 1958], Pandit Sundarlal [d. CE 1980], Yogananda [d. CE 1952], Maharishi Mahesh Yogi [d. CE 2008], and many others) always welcomed spiritual pluralism.[15]

The great Sufi saints and poets of the Islamic world, Jalaluddin Rumi (d. CE 1273), Fariduddin Attar (d. CE 1230), Shaikh Sadi (d. CE 1292), Nizamuddin Auliya (d. CE 1325), Baba Farid Chishti (d. CE 1266), Mian Mir (d. CE 1635), Kabir (d. CE 1518), Sarmad (d. CE 1659), and many others have done the same. And this path of spiritual pluralism, be it noted, is not any departure from, but the very implementation, of the spiritual and moral values of the Qur'an, though Islamic orthodoxy may have pursued the belief in exclusive salvation for Muslims. It seems, the belief in exclusive salvation is an easy short cut to spiritual conceit or self-importance.[16]

Modern science and technology have turned the wide world into an Olympic village having intercom facilities in every camp. The issue today is not, which is the biggest and the best camp, but who performs best. Religious polemics is useless and pointless when it comes to matters of faith. The Christian creed of the Divinity of Jesus, the Islamic creed of the Divinity of the Qur'an, the Hindu creed of the Divinity of the *Atma*, and the special *anthro theistic* status of Rama and Krishna, are all matters of faith, not demonstrable truths. The human family today, therefore, must heed the life giving and liberating message of the inter-faith movement whose call comes simultaneously from both secular and spiritual platforms in the Western world. I have no doubt that the goal of this remarkable movement is genuine peaceful co-existence of all faiths, and that it has no secret agenda. Long live the spirit of interfaith, which is, precisely, the message of peren-nial Islam, according to my understanding of the Qur'an.[17]

The quintessence of Islam is belief or faith in one Supreme Creator of all that exists, and the guidance provided by a long line of Divinely inspired messengers who appeared in history at all times and places, especially the guidance contained in the Qur'an, which was "revealed" to Prophet Muhammad ﷺ of Arabia, who is the "Seal of the prophets" and through whom the Creator completed the process of Divine guidance (*wahy*) as embodied in the corpus of the Arabic Qur'an. As already explained, the Qur'an need not and should not be viewed as a systematic book or document. The Qur'anic corpus consists of approximately 6,200 lin-guistic units of very varying lengths, and the overwhelmingly major portion of these linguistic expressions or sentences glorify the Creator, affirm what is good and what is evil (in very general terms), and exhort, encourage, console, warn, and give inner strength and stability to humankind to live the good life under the shadow of the inscrutable purpose and wisdom of Divine creation. Only a very small portion of the Qur'anic contents are prescriptive or mandatory in the concrete sense of being specific rules of conduct or categorical commands. All Muslims must, therefore, defer to such injunctions or imperatives in a manner that combines loyalty to basic values with freedom to modify instrumental rules in an ever-changing human situation.[18]

It is, indeed, a pity and a matter of the utmost and urgent concern that Muslim society all over the world still remains perplexed and bewildered by the diverse challenges of the modern age. The deadlock and stagnation of Muslim society cannot be overcome by Islamic apologetics, or the strategy of making ad hoc adjustments to situational demands, or the relatively more integrated schemes of reforming *Shariah* radiating from the subcontinent of erstwhile India, Egypt, Arabia, or Iran. The scheme of the *"Islamization of Knowledge"* is a well-intentioned but failed attempt to correct the one-sided "scientism" and conceit of some Western thinkers.[19]

The message of Messianic hope that sustains some quarters of the Muslim community, and the waging of the "holy war" (*jihad*) by some other quarters against the "Godless West" are even less calculated to overcome the spiritual predicament and stagnation of the Muslim world. The basic remedy lies in the democratic acceptance of the idea of conceptual growth in the tradition of perennial Islam. This should include free inquiry, spiritual pluralism, modern representative democracy, and tolerance in its core thought and value system. The traditional ethos of mechanical and absolute conformity to "the Book and the Example" must develop into the ethos of "creative fidelity" to the "Word of God" and the character of His messenger. Will this happen and when? Well, I hope and trust this century will prove to be the turning point in the history of the human family.

Iranian Muslims, for all their great dynamism and courage, are still at the threshold of the idea of the principled separation of religion from politics, while the Arab world is mired in great internal problems and the Palestine issue. Turkey, which was the first secular Muslim state, is facing strong winds of reversal as a consequence of the earlier authoritarian zeal of the great founder of modern Turkey. Indian Muslims are still reeling under the blow of shattered dreams due to the "mirage" of Pakistan. The people of Pakistan too are paying a heavy price for what (in great humility) I might well call "the sad abortion of liberal secularism" in the India of 1947.[20]

In view of the tremendous facilities of higher education and opportunities of interfaith dialogue, Western European and American Muslims, to my mind, are perhaps best poised to initiate and promote fresh thinking on the theme of perennial Islam.

13

2

The Qur'an as a Revealed Book: Some Issues

Introductory Remarks

ACCORDING TO ISLAMIC BELIEF, all that exists has come into being and is sustained by one Supreme Being or Power Whose nature and attributes are beyond human comprehension, except for the inner conviction that the Supreme Being is not a mere idea but the ultimate Source of all that exists and of all values. The Creator, in His infinite wisdom and compassion, creates innumerable forms of creation and endows them with the capacity to praise and serve the Creator in their own respective ways. The Creator has also created the diverse races, ethnic groups, and languages of humankind. God also blesses some humans in every race and region with the special gift of prophecy and entrusts them with the mission of warning, and guiding their respective people according to Divine will and wisdom. The Qur'an clearly states that God "sends" or "ordains" prophets or messengers in all regions, but it names only a few prophets of Semitic origin such as Abraham, Moses, and Jesus, *et al.* among the thousands of Divine messengers. According to Islamic belief, Prophet Muhammad ﷺ was the *"Seal of the Prophets"* and the culminating crown of the long line of prophets or messengers of God.

The basic Islamic creed is summed up by the well-known formula, *"There is no god but God and Muhammad is His Messenger."* The formula does not mention that the Qur'an is the "Word of God," but this belief is an integral part of the faith. Indeed, the belief that the Qur'an is the "Word of God," not the words of the Prophet ﷺ, is the differentia of Islamic Monotheism. In what follows, I shall deal with three aspects of the faith that the Qur'an is a revealed scripture: (*a*) the Nature and Process of Revelation, (*b*) the Structure of the Qur'an, and (*c*) the Collection of the Qur'an.

14

The Nature and Process of Revelation

According to the Islamic faith, the first ever Divine revelation to Prophet Muhammad ﷺ took place in the cave of Hira, near Mecca, when he was forty. Prior to this momentous event, he had shown remarkable qualities of head and heart and extraordinary integrity of character. He used to spend long hours praying and meditating in the solitude and silence of the cave of Hira. Then, quite suddenly and unexpectedly, the first revelatory episode occurred in CE 610, one night in the closing week of the Arabic month of Ramadan. Revelatory episodes continued at irregular intervals during the last twenty-three of his life span of sixty-three years. In every episode the Prophet ﷺ "heard" fully formed Arabic verses or sentences, and he had no control over the timing and content of the revealed text. This is how the Qur'anic *surah*, 97:1–5 describes the night of the first revelation.

> *We have indeed revealed this (Message) in the Night of Power: And what will explain to thee what the night of power is? The Night of Power is better than a thousand months. Therein come down the angels and the Spirit by Allah's permission, on every errand: Peace!...This until the rise of Morn!**

What "exactly happened in the cave" during the first "revelatory episode" is, I submit, not fully or accurately known, to date, by any human being. Several accounts have been in circulation from early times, but they are extremely vague, sketchy, and varied. The obvious reason for this is that the event of "revelation" was not a normal instance of linguistic communication between a "communicator" and a "communicatee", but something supernatural or paranormal, and no observer or witness was present apart from the Prophet ﷺ himself. Even if one accepts (as I myself do) the absolute veracity and sincerity of the Prophet ﷺ himself, one has no access to what the Prophet ﷺ himself thought or believed to have happened in the cave on that momentous occasion in human history. Whether one be a Muslim believer or not, one's access to the knowledge of the truth of what exactly had happened in the cave is limited to reports made by some contemporaries of the Prophet ﷺ on the strength of what they claim the Prophet ﷺ had told them. But the question remains what exactly the Prophet ﷺ said. This is a question of history or the biography of the Prophet ﷺ.

The earliest biographer of the Prophet ﷺ is Ibn Ishaq (d. CE 768) who wrote the work more than hundred years after the passing away of the Prophet ﷺ, in CE 632. This work is not extant in the original form, but it exists in the version of the original as edited by fellow Arab writer, Ibn Hisham (d. CE 833). Prior to these

---

* Translations of Qur'anic text are from Abdullah Yusuf Ali's *The Morning of the Holy Qur'an*.

written records, some Arab writers had composed chronicles of the wars, battles, and expeditions that had occurred in the time of the Prophet ﷺ. These are extant, but they do not deal with the crucial issue of the "event of the cave." Al-Tabari (d. CE 922), the great historian and Qur'anic scholar, dealt with this issue in his monumental work *History of the Prophets and the Kings*, but sectarian prejudices entertained by the Sunni mainstream group came in the way of appreciating his genius. Ibn Khaldun (d. CE 1406) whom Rosenthal, arguably, compares with Aristotle himself, also remained rather unappreciated by his own contemporaries. The only authentic source of our information concerning the "event of the cave" comes from *hadith* literature, which purports to report the sayings and doings of the Prophet ﷺ. But here again, much controversy exists in reports emanating from the majority Sunni and dissident Shia sources within the house of Islam. In actual practice one opts to accept the set of putative authentic reports emanating from one side or the other. This is the typical ethnocentric attitude, and the vast majority of Muslim believers, be they Sunni or Shia, adopt this approach as a fish takes to water. However, if one aspires to know the whole truth and nothing but the truth of "what really happened in the cave," one will get stuck in the sands of perplexity. The only infallible source of assurance for a Muslim believer is the Qur'an, as such, but the Qur'anic revelation does not at all enlighten the believer in regard to the nature or mechanics of the mode of revelation. The Qur'an does describe or refer to the mysterious event of Divine revelation to a human mortal and the contents of revelation, obviously, inspire, guide, and edify the believer, but he or she is left absolutely clueless as to the dynamics or mechanics of the revelatory process, as such. The few Qur'anic references to the angel Gabriel or the Holy Spirit or to the different ways in which the Creator blesses and pours His grace upon His chosen messengers do not give any clear picture or idea of the mystery of Divine revelation to His human messengers.[1]

The variant reports in regard to what exactly happened in the cave are as follows: The Prophet ﷺ "saw" on the horizon some mysterious figure addressing him; the Prophet ﷺ heard some mysterious voice commanding him to recite; the Prophet ﷺ saw on the horizon some Arabic verses written on some mysterious surface; the Prophet ﷺ experienced (in a vision) that he was being very tightly embraced by some mysterious "presence" or agent who asked him to read or recite in the name of the Lord. This totally unexpected and strange experience unnerved and baffled the Prophet ﷺ and he could not grasp or understand what had happened and was happening. The "Holy Spirit" assured him that all was well and again asked him to recite what he was told. The Prophet ﷺ, thereafter, accurately recited the first "revealed" Arabic verses. Believers as well as all students of the Qur'an are almost unanimous that the following first five verses of *surah Alaq/ Iqra* constitute the first Qur'anic revelation.

96:1–5:

Proclaim! (or read!) In the name of thy Lord and Cherisher, Who created—Created man out of a (mere) clot of congealed blood: Proclaim! And thy Lord is Most Bountiful—He Who taught (the use of) the pen,—Taught man that which he knew not.

Soon afterward, the Prophet ﷺ left for his home in a state of profound awe and excitement, still unsure of what had occurred. He was perspiring and trembling and in a state of shock and apprehended he had lost his sanity or mental balance. On reaching home, his wife, Bibi Khadijah, wrapped him in a blanket and comforted him. Thereafter the Prophet ﷺ related his strange experience to her. She promptly concluded that, far from having lost his sanity or been overpowered by some evil demon, he had been blessed by the Creator and that he should rejoice at what had happened. Shortly afterward, she proceeded to meet her first cousin, Waraqah, who was a pious Christian "*Hanif*" by religion, and a trusted friend, and well-wisher. On hearing the reported experience of the Prophet, Waraqah confirmed her intuitive hunch or belief that Muhammad ﷺ had been blessed by God.[2]

Bibi Khadijah was now fully convinced that her husband was, indeed, a recipient of Divine revelation and God's messenger to the Arabs. She thus became the very first person to accept Muhammad ﷺ as the Prophet of God. Shortly afterward, the Prophet's ﷺ paternal cousin, Ali, aged about ten, and very close to and a great admirer of his senior brother, also declared his faith in the Prophet's ﷺ mission. The third person to accept the Prophet's mission was Zayd whom the Prophet ﷺ, later on, adopted as his son. Abu Bakr was the fourth (and the first adult male, not related to the Prophet ﷺ) to join this spiritual fellowship. Abu Bakr profoundly venerated his close friend, Muhammad ﷺ, for his extraordinary truthfulness and integrity of character. This was the beginning of a little spiritual stream that was later on to swell into a broad and mighty current.

Most accounts of the Prophet's ﷺ first and early experiences of revelation say that there was a brief period (whose duration is variously estimated) in which the revelatory process did not occur, and this caused considerable anxiety and suffering to the Prophet ﷺ. It is said that this was the context of the revelation of *surah* 93:1–11. The *surah* runs as follows:

By the Glorious Morning Light, And by the Night when it is still, Thy Guardian-Lord hath not forsaken thee, nor is He displeased. And verily the Hereafter will be better for thee than the present. And soon will thy Guardian-Lord give thee (that wherewith) thou shalt be well-pleased.

Did He not find thee an orphan and give thee shelter (and care)? And He found thee wandering, and He gave thee guidance. And He found thee in need, and made thee independent. Therefore, treat not the orphan with harshness, Nor repulse the petitioner (unheard); But the bounty of the Lord-rehearse and proclaim!

The Prophet ﷺ had to overcome tremendous hurdles and obstacles in the way, which even necessitated the Prophet's ﷺ migration, in CE 622, from his native Mecca to Medina. Meanwhile, his two great human well-wishers and sources of strength, apart from his inner conviction in his Divine mission, as such, passed away one after the other. The first was his senior paternal uncle, Abu Talib, whose minor son, Ali had already accepted Islam. The next was his faithful wife and soul mate, the very first fellow human to accept his Divine call. However, the, relatively, unsuccessful thirteen year long struggle by the Prophet ﷺ in Mecca was followed by a string of striking successes during his last ten years at Medina. This culminated in his eventual triumphant peaceful return to Mecca. A year later he passed away in his adopted Medina in CE 632.[3]

The truth of the above very broad narrative cannot be denied, though this does not prove that Muhammad ﷺ was God's messenger (in the Islamic sense) or that the Qur'an is the "Word of God." The Prophet ﷺ persistently claimed he was a Divinely ordained messenger, and the Qur'an repeatedly affirmed that the Prophet ﷺ was, indeed, the recipient of Divine revelations. However, the proud tribal leaders of Mecca and the vast majority of the populace persisted in denial and called him a liar, or as one deluded, mentally unsound, sorcerer, poet, or whatnot. The situation today remains basically the same. It shall ever remain so until doomsday. The reason is simply that the belief that the Qur'an is the "Word of God" is a "faith axiom," not a belief in the domain of empirical history, that could, possibly, be verified in accordance with the generally agreed or well-established criteria of historical verifiability. This fact, however, merely throws into relief the differentia of all religious faith, in general, from the beliefs in the domain of mathematics, natural science, and history. In view of this, the effort to probe into the mystery of revelation, though natural and desirable, is commendable, only up to a point. Carried beyond that point, theoretical curiosity becomes futile, rather an obstacle in the complete and integrated pursuit of truth when there may be *"more things in heaven and earth than are dreamt of in philosophy."* How can one understand matters without having any experience thereof?

One discussant may be inclined to accept one theory or conceptual model, while the second some other theory and the third yet another. For instance, one may hold that the Holy Spirit (Gabriel), under God's command, flashed the revelatory content before the mental eye of the Prophet ﷺ. Another discussant may think that the Prophet ﷺ heard (mentally or physically) the revealed text and then retained it in his memory. Yet another discussant may be inclined to the view that the Arabic text welled forth from the Prophet's ﷺ heart under God's command. The conceptualization of an avowedly mysterious process may take endless forms, when there is no clear method to settle, which projection is the true one. In all humility, I dare to suggest that the mechanics of revelation remained a mystery to the closest companions of the Prophet, ﷺ and even to the Prophet ﷺ himself.

In short, the "how" of the revelatory process was and still is a mystery. But the "what" of the process was and remains exquisite Arabic sentences/ verses that got effortlessly imprinted in the Prophet's ﷺ consciousness and were retained in his memory. At his very first convenience, he dictated the revealed Arabic text to some reliable scribe who wrote it down for permanent record on palm leaves, pieces of bark, or leather as paper and vellum (most probably) were then not easily available in Arab society.[4]

The Structure of the Qur'an

Muslims generally call the Qur'an "the Book of Allah" or "the Speech of Allah." The latter expression is, by far, more apt because the term "book" raises, in the hearer, expectations that are not fulfilled. A book is expected to have an inner structure reflected in chapters, divided into sections, subsections, and, finally, a good or perfect book must have a logical or systematic arrangement of themes and subthemes. This, to my mind, cannot be said of the Qur'an. The reason is that the 114 "surahs", or chapters, are distinct and independent units of communication rather than chapters of a treatise. This point is crucially important since many Muslims (lay believers as well as eminent scholars and theologians) insist that the Qur'an, in its present standard form, is, indeed, a highly systematic and logically interconnected book. This traditional belief, however, does not take into account several hard facts about the Qur'anic corpus in its present form, viz, the widely scattered verses dealing with the same theme, extensive repetitions of the same theme, prima facie contradictions in the text (if the words are understood in the plain literal sense) and yet other contradictions (when the text is read, shorn of the full context of the revelation), the paucity of many details crucially important for fully understanding or implementing Qur'anic injunctions, and finally, the mingling of Meccan and Medinian verses in the same *surah*.[5]

The Qur'an, quite clearly, is not divided into chapters, sections, and subsections like a normally well-composed book or lengthy composition. Moreover, numerous verses perform several functions of language (such as description, interpretation, evaluation, exhortation, and prescription, etc.) in quick succession or simultaneously. As a result, it is not very easy to arrive at clear-cut, non-controversial interpretations of the text even for Arabic-speaking people, or those who are well-familiar with Arabic.

Some learned Muslim commentators and scholars have taken pains to show that there is a logical connection between the sequences of the different Qur'anic *surahs*, and the verse sequence in each *surah*. But to my mind, the present arrangement or order of the verses confuses the ordinary reader as to what the Qur'an ordains concerning different matters unless he seeks help from a detailed index of subjects, and unless he takes pains to understand Qur'anic stylistics and semantics, in general, in addition to understanding the specific situational context of the revelation concerned. Saying this does not imply any devaluation of the Qur'an. Nor does it imply that the traditional arrangement of the Qur'an needs to be altered in any way. I only wish to point out the primary error and futility involved in treating the Qur'an as a book, in the literal sense, and the secondary error of those who (vainly) attempt to prove that the Qur'an is a systematic book.[6]

The Collection of the Qur'an

Another set of difficulties concern the collection and sequence of the *surahs*, their numbering, and their standard prefix of Allah's name. According to one school of Sunni Islam, the Prophet ﷺ himself had prepared the proto edition of the Qur'anic corpus in its present traditional form and handed it over to either his close companion, Abu Bakr, or to Bibi Hafsa, (the daughter of Umar and one of the wives of the Prophet ﷺ). Another version states that, during the Caliphate of Abu Bakr, Umar first mooted the urgent need for collecting the fragments of the Qur'an and Abu Bakr, after some initial hesitation, agreed to the proposal and ordered that the work should start. Another version is that the third Caliph, Uthman, undertook this work some twenty years after the passing away of the Prophet ﷺ. Yet another version (Shia) is that the Prophet ﷺ had prepared a proto edition of the Qur'an and entrusted it to his daughter, Bibi Fatima, who passed it on to her husband, the fourth Caliph, Ali. None of these views is completely free from some difficulty or the other.

The difficulty in accepting the first two versions is that, although some sort of paper or papyrus was in use as a writing surface in Egypt, Central Asia, and China, access to paper was very scarce in Arabia in the time of the Prophet ﷺ though the use of paper had spread by the time of the third Caliph, Uthman. It is significant that, even if the proto edition of the Qur'anic corpus in its present form was, in fact, prepared by the Prophet ﷺ himself or jointly by the first and the second Caliphs, no such copy is extant today. However, to the best of my knowledge, the edition produced by the third Caliph was, supposedly, preserved (in some form) in the museum library of the Ottomon Sultans in Turkey. By the time of Caliph Uthman, Syria, Iraq, Palestine, Iran, Egypt, and some parts of Central Asia had been incorporated into the Islamic commonwealth and the use of vellum or paper had definitely spread in Arab society. In any case, very early copies of Uthman's edition are definitely extant. This edition became the standard and rapidly spread in the entire Islamic world. The text, however, did not carry any vowels or diacritical marks, which obviously, were unnecessary for Arabic-speaking Muslims. The vowels were inserted much later and are not present even today in printed copies of the Qur'an used in Arabia proper and, perhaps, in other Arabic-speaking countries. The division into thirty equal parts (now found in all standard traditional editions of the Qur'an) was also a later device.[7]

The main difficulty, however, is not why the original proto Qur'an in book form has not been preserved, but something entirely different. This difficulty is as follows: Did Caliph Uthman himself select the present established order, or did he merely follow some previous scheme? If so, who was the author of this proto scheme or arrangement? If it was the Prophet ﷺ himself, was the arrangement, as such, Divinely revealed or was it at the Prophet's ﷺ own discretion? (This question also applies to the titles of the different *surahs*). The plain fact is that different Muslims sects and subsects have different views on such matters. To my mind, however, different answers to these questions do not affect the core essence of the Islamic faith. This core essence, to my mind, is as follows:

1. The Prophet ﷺ did not author or compose the Qur'anic text that he dictated to his scribes from time to time, shortly after the revelatory episode was over, but that the Prophet ﷺ "received" (in some paranormal way) the text of the Arabic Qur'an through the mediation of some paranormal being or agency designated as the "Holy Spirit" or the angel Gabriel in the Islamic tradition.
2. The entire Qur'anic text has been preserved, free from error or alteration in the Qur'anic corpus, as such, though the present textual arrangement of the Qur'an differs from the chronological sequence of revelation.

The above twofold belief remains unscathed in spite of different interpretations of the faith that the Qur'an is the "Word of God," or different views regarding the collection or sequence of the verses (*ayats*) and *surahs*. The different concrete formulations of faith are the result of the differences in the conceptual framework and life situation of different believers. The different views regarding the collection of the Qur'anic verses are the result of incomplete knowledge of the history of the times of the Prophet ﷺ and his successors. To my mind, there can be honest doubt or difference of opinion as to how much of the total corpus of the Qur'an was reduced to writing in the lifetime of the Prophet ﷺ and what was the order or sequence of the verses in respect of their revelation or their placement in different *surah*s. This difficulty is due to the fact that the use of paper as a writing surface was either not available to the Prophet ﷺ, or, if available, was rare. This situation changed by the time of the Caliphate of Umar. It is significant that the orthodox Islamic tradition itself says that Qur'anic texts were written, in the times of the Prophet ﷺ, on pieces of parchment, cloth, wood, metal, and palm leaves, etc., and a substantial section of Muslim believers holds that the third Caliph, Uthman, was the first to collect the scattered texts in one volume.[8]

Controversies about the collection and order of *surah*s or verses do not touch the core of the Islamic faith, as I see it. The nuclear core of the faith is that the Qur'anic verses were revealed to the Prophet ﷺ and were not authored or composed by him as a writer composes a book. Fully formed Arabic sentences or verses were heard by him or flashed before him while he was wide awake and they issued forth from his lips without any volition or effort and simultaneously got fixed in his memory before he dictated the text to some scribe.

It is true that the episodes of revelation were accompanied by physical stress and strain for the Prophet ﷺ. Nevertheless, every episode fortified and encouraged him in his faith in his Divine mission. The above core belief remains unaffected despite controversies or doubts about the arrangement of the Qur'anic verses in its present form that has lasted for more than 1,400 years. No other scripture could perhaps rightly claim this high degree of textual authenticity of the original version. At the same time the well-informed and intellectually honest Muslim believer must willingly concede that the Islamic faith that the Qur'an is the "Word of God" and that the entire revealed contents have been accurately preserved in the Qur'anic corpus as it exists to date is, after all, a matter of faith, and not a claim that can be proved or established.

The above limitation, however, applies to all dogmas, as such, of all religions or value systems, and not merely to the Islamic faith. Faith does not require any proof if it be authentic and rooted in inner certitude. This "inner certitude" is existential, not logical, scientific, or historical certainty. The believer treasures this certainty as his or her life anchor and source of everlasting bliss and peace, far beyond the power and range of some other types of judgments (in the sphere of morality, art, taste, and sensory pleasures) that also cannot be proved or established in the scientific or logical sense.[9]

3

The Semantics of the Qur'an: Some Basic Aspects

Introductory Remarks

SEMANTICS IS THE STUDY, AMONG OTHER THINGS, of the relationship between words and the objects or states of affairs to which they refer, the different types of meaning and function of words or human speech, how and why disagreements arise, and how they can be settled. Semantics makes it evident that the words, as such, of any natural language system do not have any inherent and fixed meaning. The actual conventional use of words, expressions and sentences, over long periods results in a particular language or communication system. There can be no language without a substantial group, which consents and habitually uses some sounds for the same purpose. Once some conventions become operative, a process of inner growth or conditioning of the individual and the group is set into motion and this process then impacts the further objective of social development of the group speaking the common language. This usage is subject to change in an ever-changing environment. No language system can fully capture the concrete uniqueness or specificity of any particular human experience or situation since words are, necessarily, abstract, while experiences or situations are, necessarily, individual and concrete, though sufficiently similar to make the same words or expressions "fit" individual cases.[1]

The crucial question at this point is: Given the Islamic belief or faith that the Qur'an is a "revealed" linguistic communication and not an anthology of Prophet Muhammad's ﷺ speech-acts over a long period of twenty-three years (like his reported sayings), shall the above and similar basic semantic principles apply to the proper understanding of the Qur'an? Even if one believes in the Divine revelation of the Qur'an (as I do), is it a "must" for the Muslim believer to hold that the Arabic tongue, fundamentally, differs from all other human languages and that its vocabulary, syntax, and grammar have *not* evolved in the course of history like other languages? My clear answer is that this view or approach is *not* an integral part of the Islamic faith, even though it may be the conscious or unconscious belief of millions of Muslim believers, theologians, and interpreters of the Qur'an.[2]

My concern in this chapter, therefore, is not with metaphysical or theological issues. Whatever the ontological status of the Qur'an might be, it is plain that it is a linguistic communication system, and no communication system can function effectively unless its conventional rules, the primary purpose of the communicator, and the context of any particular unit of communication are properly understood. It is also plain that the vocabulary, grammar, and rules of syntax of the Arabic language much predate the birth of the Prophet ﷺ. Even if one holds that the genesis of the Qur'an was a Divine miracle, its vocabulary and grammar were ordinary linguistic phenomena, just like any other language. The language of the Qur'an was Arabic as spoken and written in the Hijaz region of the Arabia of CE 7th century. Indeed, the Qur'an itself says that God guides and teaches people in their own language. I shall now state some basic semantic points one must bear in mind whenever one recites, hears, or studies the contents of the Qur'an.

1. The Qur'anic texts perform a wide variety of semantic functions—they project a cosmic vision of the creation, sustenance, and destruction of all existence, the final Day of Judgment, allude to the inscrutable mystery of existence, give very brief historical narratives, morally exhort to righteous action, issue some imperatives and injunctions, give insight into human nature, provide wisdom through fable, parable, and metaphor, motivate believers to righteous action through promising reward, punishment, or spiritual felicity (as the case may be), provide consolation, counsel patience and trust in Divine Providence, and so on. Qur'anic chapters or verses, however, do not separate these functions, which are all rolled into one long verse or section or unit of communication. At times, these functions overlap, and there is lot of repetition of the same theme, as happens in an epistle, speech, or homily. However, this does not imply any defect in the Qur'an, as such, if we look at it not as a systematic book, but as an extraordinary extended epistle to an audience more or less conditioned by the ideas, values, and symbols provided by the Jewish and Christian traditions.[3]

2. Arabic words, like words of all other languages, have multiple meanings or uses in different contexts and also overlapping shades of meaning in similar contexts. No single word has an inherent atomic meaning. Perhaps, Arabic words have the largest spectrum of meaning and use. The spectrum itself changes (grows or shrinks) with the passage of time.

Consider the Qur'anic prohibition of "*riba*" (Q 3: 130). Almost all premodern Islamic sects or schools of law mechanically equated "*riba*" with the Hebrew word "*ribbat*" (as used in the medieval period), and with the English word "interest" (as used in modern times). But does this translation reflect the actual functional role of usury in ancient times or of interest in the medieval? Comparative philology and the history of ideas inform us that the word "*riba*" (whose literal meaning is "increase" or "growth") dates from Babylonian times and that in that remote age the borrower had to return three or four times the borrowed amount within a fixed time, failing which he had to serve a term of bonded labor extending from three to seven years. Now when the Qur'an prohibited "*riba*," this was the practice that it prohibited. But what happened was that, though the economic institution or practice, as such, underwent a sea change over the centuries due to a combination of social, political, and technological factors, the word remained the same. The interpreters were unable to see the difference between the living operational meaning or function of the word in their own times and the original meaning of the word. The question arises whether the modern economic practice or concept of "interest" can rightly be equated with "*riba*" in the ancient Hebrew sense.[4]

3. The Qur'an describes the phenomena of nature—change of seasons, succession of night and day, expanse of the earth, sky and ocean, the sun, moon and stars, the birth, growth, and death of plants, animals, and humans, the stages of biological conception and prenatal growth—all as examples of created things or beings obeying, without fail, the commands of one Supreme Creator and Sustainer of all that exists. Likewise, the Qur'an also describes the phenomena of psychological effects of pride, and rejection of the Creator's numerous signs and blessings as if God seals the heart and covers the eyes of the unbelievers. It is impossible to accept such texts in the literal sense of the Arabic expressions used in the Qur'an.[5]

4. The descriptive/narrative verses are allusive and skeletal rather than explanatory or comprehensive. It is, therefore, very difficult to understand many themes of the Qur'an without a background knowledge or acquaintance with pre-Qur'anic scriptures or historical happenings and events under reference. If one goes by the literal sense of any single verse or set of Qur'anic verses, without carefully reading other verses that directly or indirectly bear on the subject matter at hand, one is in danger of going far astray from the truth of the matter. In such cases confusion and perplexity are almost inevitable.

5. The evaluative and exhortative verses are direct, concise, and marked by great persuasive power. The interpretative and ontogenetic verses are models of superb literary beauty and power, and it is these verses that captivate and inspire the faithful as well as numerous enlightened thinkers, poets, mystics, and others. Poetry provides an extremely insightful and instructive example of how the reader's conceptual framework or "inner world" leads to plural levels of interpretation, and existential impact of the same text. That many interpretative Qur'anic verses are amenable to plural meanings is, to my mind, a positive gain rather than any negative feature. However, the individual and society will gain only when

freedom of conscience and full tolerance (in the modern humanist sense) have been accepted as unassailable foundational values.

6. The prescriptive verses of the Qur'an have a direct and simple style. They are Divine commands to do such and such or not to do such and such, and this is, precisely, the rationale for the expression "Ten Commandments of the Bible." However, there is a crucial distinction between commands that deal with basic values or foundational norms of society, on the one hand, and on the other, commands that deal with instrumental rules for protecting and promoting the basic values, as such. To my mind, Islamic or Qur'anic piety, ideally speaking, requires that we first thoroughly clarify and understand the full implications of this crucial distinction. When some very pious and spiritually developed Muslims (whom I deeply venerate) place the greatest stress on "nonreflective literal obedience" to Qur'anic prescriptions on the ground that they are included in the infallible "Word of God" (without giving even a moment's thought to the vital distinction mentioned above). This approach, inevitably, generates a problem or, rather, a pseudo problem for the Muslim mind. This vital matter is fully discussed in Chapter 4.

7. The reader must accept and appreciate that the Qur'an has a style of its own, and that the Qur'an uses different styles of communication. At times the Qur'an speaks in a very direct, simple, and clear style; at times in a very elliptical manner, which can easily confuse the reader if he were to interpret Arabic words in the literal sense; at times the Qur'an speaks in metaphors; at times in rather ambiguous/perplexing terms; at times in prima facie contradictory terms; at times in highly suggestive and "malleable" terms; at times in the style of parable and anecdote; at times in the style of descriptive biography or history; and so on.

In several texts the Qur'an uses ordinary Arabic words or phrases with respect to God in a manner, which quite obviously, does not make any sense if we go by the literal meaning of the words or expressions. For instance, God "seeks a loan," "speaks on oath," "curses" disbelievers, "misleads" persons, "seals the hearts and blocks the ears of disbelievers," and so on. Such verses, quite understandably, create intellectual doubts and difficulties for both Muslims as well as others. These difficulties, however, dissolve if we are aware of Qur'anic semantics. The point is that we must know when it is right and proper to interpret the text in the literal sense and when it is wrong to do so. This discretion is very important, and we must have sufficient knowledge and insight to assess when to understand the text in the literal sense and when not to do so. The literal meaning of many verses can seriously mislead and perplex the reader unless he is well aware of the stylistics and semantics of the Qur'an.[6]

8. In many cases the Qur'an itself makes it plain that the text is meant to be a parable or a similitude or metaphor, but in many places the reader is left guessing.

Thus the insistence in some Islamic quarters that we must stick to the plain and simple literal meaning of all Qur'anic verses, to my mind, is a dangerous (even if it be passionately sincere) oversimplification. Several descriptions of heaven, hell, the sky, or mountains are not literal truths but rather poetic or figurative accounts to exhort, warn, console, and promote the individual's spiritual growth. However, we must also rigorously avoid the opposite error of indulging in speculative and fanciful interpretations of plain Arabic texts as a justification for one's own pet theories or beliefs.[7]

9. Like all prescriptive discourse, Qur'anic prescriptions or commands also presuppose a given situation or states of affairs, and the command is meant either to preserve or to change the situation in some manner or other. Now if the human agent is not properly aware of the antecedent situation and the basic intention or intended objective of the authority or law giver, the agent's action will hardly be the best means of serving or promoting the "*telos*" of the Supreme Law Giver.

10. The Qur'an at times refers to future happenings and events as if they have already happened or have been accomplished. This is a peculiar Qur'anic style of expression. It does not involve any actual historical error or confusion. On the other hand, several Qur'anic texts refer to remarkable and then unknown natural phenomena.[8]

It is essential that Muslim believers clearly understand both the function and style of expression of Qur'anic texts. If this preparatory task is not thoroughly done, the believer will grope in the dark no matter how passionately and sincerely he may desire to follow the "Word of God" without any "ifs and buts." Unquestioning adherence to Qur'anic injunctions and implicit acceptance of several Qur'anic verses in the absolutely literal sense leads, in several cases, to confusion, perplexity, and even internal contradiction.[9]

In short, the literal understanding of Qur'anic texts without taking into account the basic rules of semantics and of Qur'anic stylistics is like moving on a road without following the rule of the road or traveling in the dark without the lights on. After the above brief remarks related to the semantics and stylistics of the Qur'an, I shall describe, at some length and with examples: (*a*) the major functions of Qur'anic verses and (*b*) their recurring "styles of expression."

Different Functions of Qur'anic Verses

1. Description/Narration
2. Moral or Ethical Evaluation
3. Exhortation
4. Prescription

5. General Interpretation of the Cosmic Creation and Human Situation

6. Spiritual Ontogenesis—the inner growth and the experience of felicity, peace, and "grace" through spiritual activities such as meditation, adoration, prayer, and reciting or singing of "holy" words.

Description/Narration

The descriptive/narrative verses describe or refer to things, persons, events, and their interconnections. Pure description or narration, as such, is hardly ever found in the Qur'an whose primary purpose is not to give information but to impart wisdom, to educate the emotions and foster pure morality and spirituality in the individual and society. The pure descriptive function, therefore, imperceptibly turns into the interpretative, evaluative, exhortative, or prescriptive function or whatever. Indeed, the preponderant portion of the Qur'anic corpus performs multiple functions of a language system. Nevertheless, we must make a clear distinction between the different semantic functions themselves. The reason is that if one knows the underlying purpose or "*telos*" of any communication, one can better promote or realize the purpose as such. Moreover, understanding the different types of discourse and the different functions of language reduces disagreements and enhances the spirit of mutual accommodation of plural interpretations of those Qur'anic verses, which by definition, deal with "transcendental" matters such as creation of the cosmos and humankind, Day of Judgment, revelation, angels, and so on. Let me illustrate this point with the help of some Qur'anic verses.

3:96
The first House (of worship) appointed for men was that at Bakka: Full of blessing and of guidance for all kinds of beings:[10]

4:157
That they said (in boast), "We killed Christ Jesus the son of Mary, the Messenger of Allah"—but they killed him not, nor crucified him, but so it was made to appear to them, and those who differ therein are full of doubts, with no (certain) knowledge, but only conjecture to follow, for of a surety they killed him not—[11]

2:67–71
And remember Moses said to his people: "Allah commands that ye sacrifice a heifer." They said: "Makest thou a laughing stock of us?" He said: "Allah save me from being an ignorant (fool)!" They said: "Beseech on our behalf Thy Lord to make plain to us what (heifer) it is!" He said:

"He says: The heifer should be neither too old nor too young, but of mid-dling age. Now do what ye are commanded!" They said: "Beseech on our behalf Thy Lord to make plain to us her color." He said: "He says: A fawn colored heifer, pure and rich in tone, the admiration of beholders!" They said: "Beseech on our behalf Thy Lord to make plain to us what she is: To us are all heifers alike: We wish indeed for guidance, if Allah wills." He said: "He says: A heifer not trained to till the soil or water the fields; sound and without blemish." They said: "Now hast thou brought the truth." Then they offered her in sacrifice, but not with good will.[12]

61:5

And remember, Moses said to his people: "O my people! Why do ye vex and insult me, though ye know that I am the messenger of Allah (sent) to you?" Then when they went wrong, Allah let their hearts go wrong. For Allah guides not those who are rebellious transgressors.[13]

2:113

The Jews say: "The Christians have naught (to stand) upon"; and the Christians say: "The Jews have naught (to stand) upon." Yet they (profess to) study the (same) Book. Like unto their word is what those say who know not; but Allah will judge between them in their quarrel on the Day of Judgment.

46:15

We have enjoined on man kindness to his parents: In pain did his mother bear him, and in pain did she give him birth. The carrying of the (child) to his weaning is (a period of) thirty months. At length, when he reaches the age of full strength and attains forty years, he says, "O my Lord! Grant me that I may be grateful for Thy favor, which Thou has bestowed upon me, and upon both my parents, and that I may work righteousness such as Thou mayest approve; and be gracious to me in my issue. Truly have I turned to Thee and truly do I bow (to Thee) in Islam.

Now the first verse (3:96) is a pure descriptive verse that has a clear meaning on the assumption that "Bakka" is equivalent to "Mecca." The second verse (4:157) is not merely descriptive, but also expresses Divine disapproval of the opponents of Jesus. Out of the five verses of the third excerpt (2:67–71) the first four are purely descriptive, but the last verse expresses Divine disapproval of the negative attitude of the Jewish community. The fourth verse (61:5) is partly descriptive and partly explains how God punishes the doers of evil through psychological laws. Likewise, the fifth verse (2:113) describes how Jews and Christians were actually behaving in this world, and what God would do on the Day of Judgment. The first part of the verse concerns an ordinary matter, while the second a "transcendental" matter. Similar remarks apply to other verses.

Moral or Ethical Evaluation

The evaluative verses of the Qur'an express Divine approval/disapproval of human conduct or character. The evaluation is, at times, direct, at other times, indirect. At times the Divine judgment is followed by exhortation or even a categorical command. Sometimes the command is supplemented by warning of dire punishment or announcement of rewards, here in this very life or in the hereafter. At times all these features or functions of language overlap. However, the conceptual clarification of the different semantic functions of the Qur'anic text does lead to a more accurate and fruitful understanding of the "Word of God" for all readers, Muslim or otherwise. Let us consider some Qur'anic verses:

2:263
Kind words and the covering of faults are better than charity followed by injury. Allah is free of all wants, and He is Most Forbearing.

3:113–115
Not all of them are alike: Of the People of the Book are a portion that stand (for the right): They rehearse the Signs of Allah all night long, and they prostrate themselves in adoration. They believe in Allah and the Last Day; they enjoin what is right, and forbid what is wrong; and they hasten (in emulation) in (all) good works: They are in the ranks of the righteous. Of the good that they do, nothing will be rejected of them; for Allah knoweth well those that do right.[14]

4:10
Those who unjustly eat up the property of orphans, eat up a Fire into their own bodies: They will soon be enduring a Blazing Fire!

9:112
Those that turn (to Allah) in repentance; that serve Him, and praise Him; that wander in devotion to the cause of Allah; that bow down and prostrate themselves in prayer; that enjoin good and forbid evil; and observe the limit set by Allah;—(These do rejoice). So proclaim the glad tidings to the Believers.

25:43

Seest thou such a one as taketh for his god his own passion (or impulse)?
Couldst thou be a disposer of affairs for him?[15]

61:3

Grievously odious is it in the sight of Allah that ye say that which ye
do not.[16]

Exhortation to Righteous Action

Exhortation is the act of prompting a person or persons actually to perform what they ought to perform out of respect for the moral law, rather than any desire for personal gain or fear of punishment. Here are some exhortative verses from the Qur'an:

2:271

If ye disclose (acts of) charity, even so it is well, but if ye conceal them,
and make them reach those (really) in need, that is best for you: It
will remove from you some of your (stains of) evil. And Allah is well-
acquainted with what ye do.

3:64

Say: "O People of the Book! Come to common terms as between us and
you: That we worship none but Allah; that we associate no partners
with him; that we erect not, from among ourselves, Lords and patrons
other than Allah." If then they turn back, say ye: "Bear witness that we
(at least) are Muslims (bowing to Allah's Will).

3:103

And hold fast, all together, by the rope, which Allah (stretches out for
you), and be not divided among yourselves; and remember with grati-
tude Allah's favor on you; for ye were enemies and He joined your
hearts in love, so that by His Grace, ye became brethren; and ye were
on the brink of the pit of Fire, and He saved you from it. Thus doth
Allah make His Signs clear to you: That ye may be guided.

3:146

How many of the prophets fought (in Allah's way), and with them
(fought) large bands of godly men? But they never lost heart if they met
with disaster in Allah's way, nor did they weaken (in will) nor give in.
And Allah loves those who are firm and steadfast.

3:200
O ye who believe! Persevere in patience and constancy; vie in such per-severance; strengthen each other; and fear Allah; that ye may prosper.

7:26
O ye Children of Adam! We have bestowed raiment upon you to cover your shame, as well as to be an adornment to you. But the raiment of righteousness,—that is the best. Such are among the Signs of Allah, that they may receive admonition![17]

7:205
And do thou (O reader!) Bring thy Lord to remembrance in thy (very) soul, with humility and in reverence, without loudness in words, in the mornings and evenings; and be not thou of those who are unheedful.

Prescription

The prescriptive verses of the Qur'an are Divine commands to do what is ethically right and must be done and what is ethically wrong and must not be done. The latter category includes prohibited actions. The text of the Qur'an does not state any hard and fast demarcation or distinction between basic intrinsic values, on the one hand, and instrumental rules on the other. However, analytical reasoning and ethical reflection on the human situation makes us see very clearly the distinction between intrinsic values and instrumental rules and their respective roles in maintaining and enhancing the "good life."

Many, rather most, of the Qur'anic prescriptive texts refer to basic intrinsic values, a small number to instrumental rules for realizing the said basic values, while in some prescriptive texts there is an overlap. Here are some prescriptive verses of the Qur'an:

2:149
From whencesoever thou startest forth, turn thy face in the direction of the sacred Mosque; that is indeed the truth from the Lord. And Allah is not unmindful of what ye do.

2:183
O ye who believe! Fasting is prescribed to you as it was prescribed to those before you, that ye may (learn) self-restraint,—

3:130
O ye who believe! Devour not usury, doubled and multiplied; but fear Allah; that ye may (really) prosper.

4:2

To orphans restore their property (when they reach their age), nor sub-stitute (your) worthless things for (their) good ones; and devour not their substance (by mixing it up) with your own. For this is indeed a great sin.

4:84

Then fight in Allah's cause—Thou art held responsible only for thyself —and rouse the believers. It may be that Allah will restrain the fury of the Unbelievers; for Allah is the strongest in might and in punishment.

4:92

Never should a believer kill a believer; but (if it so happens) by mistake, (compensation is due): If one (so) kills a believer, it is ordained that he should free a believing slave, and pay compensation to the deceased's family, unless they remit it freely. If the deceased belonged to a peo-ple at war with you, and he was a believer, the freeing of a believing slave (is enough). If he belonged to a people with whom ye have treaty of mutual alliance, compensation should be paid to his family, and a believing slave be freed. For those who find this beyond their means, (is prescribed) a fast for two months running: by way of repentance to Allah: for Allah hath all knowledge and all wisdom.[18]

4:103

When ye pass (congregational) prayers, celebrate Allah's praises, standing, sitting down, or lying down on your sides; but when ye are free from danger, set up Regular Prayers: For such prayers are enjoined on believers at stated times.

4:135

O ye who believe! Stand out firmly for justice, as witnesses to Allah, even as against yourselves, or your parents, or your kin, and whether it be (against) rich or poor: for Allah can best protect both. Follow not the lusts (of your hearts), lest ye swerve, and if ye distort (justice) or decline to do justice, verily Allah is well-acquainted with all that ye do.[19]

5:87

O ye who believe! Make not unlawful the good things, which Allah hath made lawful for you, but commit no excess: for Allah loveth not those given to excess.[20]

5:101

O ye who believe! Ask not questions about things, which if made plain to you, may cause you trouble. But if ye ask about things when the Qur'an is being revealed, they will be made plain to you, Allah will forgive those: for Allah is Oft Forgiving, Most Forbearing.[21]

General Interpretation

The general interpretative verses of the Qur'an refer to the basic world view or existential perspective on the cosmos and human destiny and status in the general scheme of things. Such interpretative verses touch upon Monotheism, creation of the cosmos, revelation, angels, life after death, the phenomena of nature and society, good and evil, etc. Qur'anic texts on these subjects, however, are not systematic analyses or detailed expositions of these matters, but very elegantly simple, yet extremely powerful, deeply convincing observations. Here are some verses from the Qur'an:

6:38

There is not an animal (that lives) on the earth, nor a being that flies on its wings, but (forms part of) communities like you. Nothing have we omitted from the Book, and they (all) shall be gathered to their Lord in the end.[22]

6:59

With Him are the keys of the unseen, the treasures that none knoweth but He. He knoweth whatever there is on the earth and in the sea. Not a leaf doth fall but with His knowledge: there is not a grain in the darkness (or depths) of the earth, nor anything fresh or dry (green or withered), but is (inscribed) in a record clear (to those who can read).[23]

3:83

Do they seek for other than the Religion of Allah?—while all creatures in the heavens and on earth have, willing or unwilling, bowed to His Will (accepted Islam), and to Him shall they all be brought back.[24]

11:7

He it is Who created the heavens and the earth in six Days—and His Throne was over the waters—that He might try you, which of you is best in conduct. But if thou wert to say to them, "Ye shall indeed be raised up after death," the Unbelievers would be sure to say, "This is nothing but obvious sorcery!"

21:16

Not for (idle) sport did We create the heavens and the earth and all that is between!

24:41

Seest thou not that it is Allah Whose praises all beings in the heavens and on earth do celebrate, and the birds (of the air) with wings outspread? Each one knows its own (mode of) prayer and praise. And Allah knows well all that they do.[25]

35:13

He merges Night into Day, and he merges Day into Night, and he has subjected the sun and the moon (to his Law): each one runs its course for a term appointed. Such is Allah your Lord: to Him belongs all Dominion. And those whom ye invoke besides Him have not the least power.

45:3–5

Verily in the heavens and the earth, are Signs for those who believe. And in the creation of yourselves and the fact that animals are scattered (through the earth), are Signs for those of assured Faith. And in the alternation of Night and Day, and the fact that Allah sends down Sustenance from the sky, and revives therewith the earth after its death, and in the change of the winds, are Signs for those that are wise.[26]

2:269

He granteth wisdom to whom He pleaseth; and he to whom wisdom is granted receiveth indeed a benefit overflowing; but none will grasp the Message but men of understanding.[27]

Spiritual Ontogenesis

While every verse of the Qur'an deeply moves and inspires the Muslim believer, several verses stand out as the peaks of spiritual nourishment and illumination for all who understand and appreciate the strange power and charm of the Arabic tongue. Such verses touch upon several themes, such as the adoration of the Creator, the vastness, wonder, and beauty of creation, the harmony and regularity of nature as well as its terrifying and destructive power, the beneficence of the Lord and so on. Some verses deal with invocative and evocative prayers to the Creator. However, here as elsewhere ontogenetic verses mingle with the other types. Here are some examples:

35

3:8

"Our Lord!" (they say), "Let not our hearts deviate now after Thou hast guided us, but grant us mercy from Thine own Presence; for Thou art the Grantor of bounties without measure.

3:191

Men who celebrate the praises of Allah, standing, sitting, and lying down on their sides, and contemplate the (wonders of) creation in the heavens and the earth, (with the thought): "Our Lord! not for naught hast Thou created (all) this! Glory to Thee! Give us salvation from the penalty of the Fire.[28]

17:44

The seven heavens and the earth, and all beings therein, declare His glory: there is not a thing but celebrates His praise; And yet ye understand not how they declare His glory! Verily He is Oft Forbearing, Most Forgiving![29]

3:193

"Our Lord! we have heard the call of one calling (us) to Faith, 'Believe ye in the Lord,' and we have believed. Our Lord! Forgive us our sins, blot out from us our iniquities, and take to Thyself our souls in the company of the righteous.

2:286

On no soul doth Allah Place a burden greater than it can bear. It gets every good that it earns, and it suffers every ill that it earns. (Pray:) "Our Lord! Condemn us not if we forget or fall into error; our Lord! Lay not on us a burden like that which Thou didst lay on those before us; Our Lord! Lay not on us a burden greater than we have strength to bear. Blot out our sins, and grant us forgiveness. Have mercy on us. Thou art our Protector; Help us against those who stand against faith."[30]

2:255

Allah! There is no god but He—the Living, the Self-subsisting, Eternal. No slumber can seize Him nor sleep. His are all things in the heavens and on earth. Who is there can intercede in His presence except as He permitteth? He knoweth what (appeareth to His creatures as) before or after or behind them. Nor shall they compass aught of His knowledge except as He willeth. His Throne doth extend over the heavens and the earth, and He feeleth no fatigue in guarding and preserving them for He is the Most High, the Supreme (in glory).[31]

Different Styles of Expression of Qur'anic Verses

Following are the different styles of expression of Qur'anic verses:

1. *Direct/Plain style*
2. *Parabolic/Metaphorical Style*
3. *Elliptical Style for Describing Natural Phenomena*
4. *Elliptical Style for Describing Psychological/Cultural Phenomena*
5. *Suggestive Style*
6. *Rhetorical Style*

While every portion of the Qur'anic text is the "Word of God," the "Word" has certainly been expressed not in one style, but in many different styles, indeed. Generally speaking, the descriptive and prescriptive verses have a direct or plain style characterized by minimum words and maximum impact. Parables, fables, and metaphors have been used to exhort humankind to live the good life and practice virtue. The "Word of God," however, uses "elliptical expressions" for describing the phenomena of nature and also of human psychology. "Transcendental" matters —the nature of Reality, the attributes of the Creator, the mode and mechanics of the revelatory process or revelation, cosmic creation, the role of "angels" and Satan, Day of Judgment and heaven and hell—have been referred to and dealt with in the "suggestive" style, which partakes of both metaphors and conceptual opaqueness for the simple reason that humankind has no experience of such matters. The rhetorical style is used, perhaps, to lay stress upon some point or create literary beauty. Here are some examples of the different styles of the Qur'anic texts:

Direct and Plain Style

2:252, 253
These are the Signs of Allah: We rehearse them to thee in truth: verily thou art one of the messengers. Those messengers We endowed with gifts, some above others: To one of them Allah spoke; others He raised to degrees (of honor); to Jesus the son of Mary We gave clear (Signs), and strengthened him with the Holy Spirit. If Allah had so willed, succeeding generations would not have fought among each other, after clear (Signs) had come to them, but they (chose) to wrangle, some believing

and others rejecting. If Allah had so willed, they would not have fought each other; but Allah Fulfilleth His plan.[32]

12:109
Nor did We send before thee (as messengers) any but men, whom we did inspire—(men) living in human habitations. Do they not travel through the earth, and see what was the end of those before them? But the home of the hereafter is best, for those who do right. Will ye not then understand?

46:15
We have enjoined on man kindness to his parents: In pain did his mother bear him, and in pain did she give him birth. The carrying of the (child) to his weaning is (a period of) thirty months. At length, when he reaches the age of full strength and attains forty years, he says, "O my Lord! Grant me that I may be grateful for Thy favor, which Thou has bestowed upon me, and upon both my parents, and that I may work righteousness such as Thou mayest approve; and be gracious to me in my issue. Truly have I turned to Thee and truly do I bow (to Thee) in Islam."

5:48
To thee We sent the Scripture in truth, confirming the scripture that came before it, and guarding it in safety: so judge between them by what Allah hath revealed, and follow not their vain desires, diverging from the Truth that hath come to thee. To each among you have we prescribed a law and an open way. If Allah had so willed, He would have made you a single people, but (His plan is) to test you in what He hath given you: so strive as in a race in all virtues. The goal of you all is to Allah; it is He that will show you the truth of the matters in which ye dispute;

10:16
Say: "If Allah had so willed, I should not have rehearsed it to you, nor would He have made it known to you. A whole lifetime before this have I tarried amongst you: will ye not then understand?"

24:39, 40
But the Unbelievers—their deeds are like a mirage in sandy deserts, which the man parched with thirst mistakes for water; until when he comes up to it, he finds it to be nothing: But he finds Allah (ever) with him, and Allah will pay him his account: and Allah is swift in taking account. Or (the Unbeliever's state) is like the depths of darkness in a

vast deep ocean, overwhelmed with billow topped by billow, topped by (dark) clouds: depths of darkness, one above another: if a man stretches out his hands, he can hardly see it! For any to whom Allah giveth not light, there is no light!

25:32

Those who reject Faith say: "Why is not the Qur'an revealed to him all at once? Thus (is it revealed), that We may strengthen thy heart thereby, and We have rehearsed it to thee in slow, well-arranged stages, gradually.

Parabolic/Metaphorical Style

13:17

He sends down water from the skies, and the channels flow, each according to its measure: But the torrent bears away to foam that mounts up to the surface. Even so, from that (ore) which they heat in the fire, to make ornaments or utensils therewith, there is a scum likewise. Thus doth Allah (by parables) show forth Truth and Vanity. For the scum disappears like forth cast out; while that which is for the good of mankind remains on the earth. Thus doth Allah set forth parables.

14:24–26

Seest thou not how Allah sets forth a parable?—A goodly word like a goodly tree, whose root is firmly fixed, and its branches (reach) to the heavens—It brings forth its fruit at all times, by the leave of its Lord. So Allah sets forth parables for men, in order that they may receive admonition. And the parable of an evil Word is that of an evil tree: It is torn up by the root from the surface of the earth: it has no stability.

39:29

Allah puts forth a Parable a man belonging to many partners at variance with each other, and a man belonging entirely to one master: are those two equal in comparison? Praise be to Allah! But most of them have no knowledge.[33]

24:35

Allah is the Light of the heavens and the earth. The Parable of His Light is as if there were a Niche and within it a Lamp: the Lamp enclosed in Glass: the glass as it were a brilliant star: Lit from a blessed Tree, an

Olive, neither of the East nor of the West, whose oil is well nigh luminous, though fire scarce touched it: Light upon Light! Allah doth guide whom He will to His Light: Allah doth set forth Parables for men: and Allah doth know all things.[34]

59:21
Had We sent down this Qur'an on a mountain, verily, thou wouldst have seen it humble itself and cleave asunder for fear of Allah. Such are the similitudes, which We propound to men, that they may reflect.[35]

Elliptical Style Dealing with Natural Phenomena

7:54
Your Guardian-Lord is Allah, Who created the heavens and the earth in six days, and is firmly established on the throne (of authority): He draweth the night as a veil o'er the day, each seeking the other in rapid succession: He created the sun, the moon, and the stars, (all) governed by laws under His command. Is it not His to create and to govern? Blessed be Allah, the Cherisher and Sustainer of the worlds!

24:41
Seest thou not that it is Allah Whose praises all beings in the heavens and on earth do celebrate, and the birds (of the air) with wings outspread? Each one knows its own (mode of) prayer and praise. And Allah knows well all that they do.[36]

25:53
It is He Who has let free the two bodies of flowing water: one palatable and sweet, and the other salt and bitter; yet has He made a barrier between them, a partition that is forbidden to be passed.

30:21
And among His Signs is this, that He created for you mates from among yourselves, that ye may dwell in tranquility with them, and He has put love and mercy between your (hearts): verily in that are Signs for those who reflect.[37]

35:41
It is Allah Who sustains the heavens and the earth, lest they cease (to function): and if they should fail, there is none—not one—can sustain them thereafter: Verily He is Most Forbearing, Oft-Forgiving.

36:38–40

And the sun runs his course for a period determined for him: that is the decree of (Him), the Exalted in Might, the All-Knowing. And the Moon—We have measured for her mansions (to traverse) till she returns like the old (and withered) lower part of a date-stalk. It is not permitted to the Sun to catch up the Moon, nor can the Night outstrip the Day: Each (just) swims along in (its own) orbit (according to Law.)[38]

39:6

He created you (all) from a single Person: then created, of like nature, his mate; and he sent down for you eight head of cattle in pairs: He makes you, in the wombs of your mothers, in stages, one after another, in three veils of darkness. Such is Allah, your Lord and Cherisher: to Him belongs (all) dominion. There is no god but He: then how are ye turned away (from your true Center)?[39]

67:19

Do they not observe the birds above them, spreading their wings and folding them in? None can uphold them except (Allah) Most Gracious: truly it is He that watches over all things.

Elliptical Style for Describing Social/Cultural Phenomena

2:251

By Allah's will they routed them; and David slew Goliath; and Allah gave him power and wisdom and taught him whatever (else) He willed. And did not Allah check one set of people by means of another, the earth would indeed be full of mischief: but Allah is full of bounty to all the worlds.[40]

30:58–59

Verily We have propounded for men, in this Qur'an every kind of Parable: But if thou bring to them any Sign, the Unbelievers are sure to say, "Ye do nothing but talk vanities." Thus does Allah seal up the hearts of those who understand not.

6:123

Thus have We placed leaders in every town, its wicked men, to plot (and burrow) therein: but they only plot against their own souls, and they perceive it not.

7:179

Many are the Jinns and men we have made for Hell: They have hearts wherewith they understand not, eyes wherewith they see not, and ears wherewith they hear not. They are like cattle,—nay more misguided: for they are heedless (of warning).

10:99

If it had been thy Lord's Will, they would all have believed—all who are on earth! Wilt thou then compel mankind, against their will, to believe!

17:45, 46

When thou dost recite the Qur'an, We put, between thee and those who believe not in the Hereafter, a veil invisible: And We put coverings over their hearts (and minds) lest they should understand the Qur'an, and deafness into their ears: when thou dost commemorate thy Lord and Him alone in the Qur'an, they turn on their backs, fleeing (from the Truth.)[41]

18:57

And who doth more wrong than one who is reminded of the Signs of his Lord, but turns away from them, forgetting the (deeds) which his hands have sent forth? Verily We have set veils over their hearts lest they should understand this, and over their ears, deafness, if thou callest them to guidance, even then will they never accept guidance.

2:26

Allah disdains not to use the similitude of things, lowest as well as highest. Those who believe know that it is truth from their Lord; but those who reject Faith say: "What means Allah by this similitude?" By it He causes many to stray, and many He leads into the right path; but He causes not to stray, except those who forsake (the path)—[42]

2:7

Allah hath set a seal on their hearts and on their hearing, and on their eyes is a veil; great is the penalty they (incur).

33:72

We did indeed offer the Trust to the Heavens and the Earth and the Mountains; but they refused to undertake it, being afraid thereof: but man undertook it;—He was indeed unjust and foolish;—

45:23

Then seest thou such a one as takes as his god his own vain desire? Allah has, knowing (him as such), left him astray, and sealed his hearing and his heart (and understanding), and put a cover on his sight. Who, then, will guide him after Allah (has withdrawn Guidance)? Will ye not then receive admonition?[43]

Suggestive Style

5:38,39

As to the thief, male or female, cut off his or her hands: a punishment by way of example, from Allah, for their crime: and Allah is Exalted in power. But if the thief repents after his crime, and amends his conduct, Allah turneth to him in forgiveness; for Allah is Oft Forgiving, Most Merciful.[44]

2:65

And well ye knew those amongst you who transgressed in the matter of the Sabbath: We said to them: "Be ye apes, despised and rejected."

41:53

Soon will We show them our Signs in the (furthest) regions (of the earth), and in their own souls, until it becomes manifest to them that this is the Truth. Is it not enough that thy Lord doth witness all things?

51:20, 21

On the earth are signs for those of assured Faith, As also in your own selves: Will ye not then see?[45]

53:1–18

By the Star when it goes down—Your Companion is neither astray nor being misled. Nor does he say (aught) of (his own) Desire. It is no less than inspiration sent down to him: He was taught by one Mighty in Power, Endued with Wisdom: for he appeared (in stately form); While he was in the highest part of the horizon: Then he approached and came closer, And was at a distance of but two bow lengths or (even) nearer; So did (Allah) convey the inspiration to His Servant—(conveyed) what He (meant) to convey. The (Prophet's) (mind and) heart in no way falsified that which he saw. Will ye then dispute with him concerning what he saw? For indeed he saw him at a second descent, Near the Lote tree beyond which none may pass: Near it is the Garden of Abode. Behold, the Lote-tree was shrouded (in mystery unspeakable!) (His) sight never swerved, nor did it go wrong! For truly did he see, of the Signs of his Lord, the Greatest![46]

13:11
For each (such person) there are (angels) in succession, before and behind him: They guard him by command of Allah. Allah does not change a people's lot unless they change what is in their hearts. But when (once) Allah willeth a people's punishment, there can be no turning it back, nor will they find, besides Him, any to protect.

23:62
On no soul do We place a burden greater than it can bear: before Us is a record which clearly shows the truth: they will never be wronged.

70:4
The angels and the spirit ascend unto Him in a Day the measure whereof is (as) fifty thousand years:[47]

Rhetorical Style

2:245
Who is he that will loan to Allah a beautiful loan, which Allah will double unto his credit and multiply many times? It is Allah that giveth (you) want or plenty, and to Him shall be your return.

16:56
And they (even) assign, to things they do not know, a portion out of that which We have bestowed for their sustenance! By Allah, ye shall certainly be called to account for your false inventions.

68:1
Nun. By the Pen and the (Record), which (men) write,—

93:1–3
By the Glorious Morning Light, And by the Night when it is still,—Thy Guardian Lord hath not forsaken thee, nor is He displeased.

56:75, 76
Furthermore I call to witness the setting of the Stars,—And that is indeed a mighty adjuration if ye but knew,—

12:111
There is, in their stories, instruction for men endued with understanding. It is not a tale invented, but a confirmation of what went before it—a detailed exposition of all things, and a Guide and a Mercy to any such as believe.

Mystique of the Qur'an

The expression, "Mystique of the Qur'an," as used here, refers to some perplexities, obscurities, ambiguities, or intellectual difficulties that usually arise in perceptive and honest students of the Qur'an. Speaking for myself, I feel rather uneasy when some Islamic apologists try to explain away these difficulties or objections with the help of rather devious or defensive reasoning. However, I am quite satisfied that the usually felt difficulties do not touch the heart of the Islamic faith, as I understand it—faith in the Supreme Creator, the Day of Judgment, the absolute veracity and integrity of Prophet Muhammad ﷺ who declared that the contents of the Qur'an were "revealed" to him and were not composed or authored by his own efforts. Let me now mention the difficulties I have in mind.

1. All *surahs* of the Qur'an begin with the invocation of Allah's name, with one exception, namely, *surah* 9. This seems an anomaly.
2. Out of the total number of 114 *surahs*, 29 *surahs* have for their first verse one or more letters of the Arabic alphabet (*Muqattat*) that prima facie do not have any meaning or function. The presence of these letters has generated a lot of controversy and debate, and this also goes contrary to the Qur'anic claim that it provides guidance in plain language and makes clear all things.
3. God refers to Himself in the Qur'anic texts generally as "We," but in a few places as "I." This produces a jarring note in the symphony of Divine revelation. At least one verse contains both the singular "I" and the plural "We" in close proximity.
4. Some verses or sentences are extremely long and involved while others consist of only two words.
5. Several narrative verses relating to Biblical themes or events are so "thin" that it is hardly possible to determine their meaning or import. This appears to clash with the Qur'anic claim that it explains things in plain language and gives clear guidance.

45

6. Some other verses are also extremely vague and allusive and completely mystify the reader.

7. Qur'anic texts dealing with the same topic are widely scattered. Accurate and comprehensive information on any topic requires collating the scattered texts and ascertaining the date and context of their revelation. This is not an easy task. Here are some examples of the Mystique:

27:82

And when the Word is fulfilled against them (the unjust), we shall produce from the earth a Beast to (face) them: He will speak to them, for that mankind did not believe with assurance in Our Signs.[48]

37:6–10

We have indeed decked the lower heaven with beauty (in) the stars; (For beauty) and for guard against all obstinate rebellious evil spirits, (So) they should not strain their ears in the direction of the Exalted Assembly but be cast away from every side, Repulsed, for they are under a perpetual penalty, Except such as snatch away something by stealth, and they are pursued by a flaming fire, of piercing brightness.[49]

15:16–18

It is We Who have set out the zodiacal signs in the heavens, and made them fair seeming to (all) beholders; And (moreover) We have guarded them from every evil spirit accursed: But any that gains a hearing by stealth, is pursued by a flaming fire, bright (to see).

37:60–68

Verily this is the supreme achievement! For the like of this let all strive, who wish to strive. Is that the better entertainment or the Tree of Zaqqum? For We have truly made it (as) a trial for the wrongdoers. For it is a tree that springs out of the bottom of Hell Fire: The shoots of its fruit stalks are like the heads of devils: Truly they will eat thereof and fill their bellies therewith. Then on top of that they will be given a mixture made of boiling water. Then shall their return be to the (Blazing) Fire.

54:1, 2

The Hour (of Judgment) is nigh, and the moon is cleft asunder. But if they see a Sign, they turn away, and say, "This is (but) transient magic."[50]

69:16, 17
And the sky will be rent asunder, for it will that Day be flimsy, And the angels will be on its sides, and eight will, that Day, bear the Throne of thy Lord above them.[51]

70:1–4
A questioner asked about a Penalty to befall the Unbelievers, the which there is none to ward off—(A Penalty) from Allah, Lord of the Ways of Ascent. The angels and the spirit ascend unto him in a Day the measure whereof is (as) fifty thousand years…[52]

Conclusion

Some eminent Muslim thinkers and Qur'an scholars of the creative era of Islam did valuable work in the field of Qur'anic Semantics. However, due to several reasons the Muslim body politic has not benefited from their intellectual acumen. Muslims, generally speaking, have gravitated much more enthusiastically to either the theologian, or the jurist, or the collector of the reported sayings and doings of the Prophet 🌸, or to the (allegedly) miracle performing Sufi. In fact, Muslims on the whole (even among the educated and professional classes) have been quite content to read or recite the Qur'an in Arabic (to earn "spiritual merit" and felicity in Paradise) without much caring to understand and acting upon the "Word of God." To me this is a tragic irony since the Qur'an repeatedly exhorts and invites believers to think and reflect as an act of religious piety, as such. In fact the Qur'an itself commends a "semantic approach" to the "Word of God" per se. Says the Qur'an,

3:7

He it is Who has sent down to thee the Book: In it are verses basic or fundamental (of established meaning); they are the foundation of the Book: others are allegorical. But those in whose hearts is perversity follow the part thereof that is allegorical, seeking discord, and searching for its hidden meanings, but no one knows its hidden meanings except Allah. And those who are firmly grounded in knowledge say: "We believe in the Book; the whole of it is from our Lord:" and none will grasp the Message except men of understanding.[53]

The dominant traditional Sunni version of Islam, on the whole, has abjured independent critical research and thinking on Islam and the Qur'an, especially after Ghazali's monumental integration of Sunni Theology and Sufi Islam. Ibn Khaldun's genius and his magnificent contribution to sociology went unsung and unhonored in the Islamic world, which fell into a great abyss of intellectual torpor or "dogmatic slumber" from which it has not yet risen.

The traditional closed Sunni approach mentioned above unconsciously equates human interpretations of Qur'anic verses with Divine revelation, per se. This approach also unconsciously presumes that only some privileged persons have exclusive access to God's own interpretation or what God Himself meant when He revealed the concerned verses to His messenger. Such people reduce belief in the infallibility of the "Word of God" to the belief in the infallibility of some humans, whosoever they may be. This approach to Qur'anic exegesis is highly misleading. The Qur'an is not a compendium of approximately 6,200 specific categorical truthclaims that have one and only one clear-cut or fixed meaning already fully spelt out by some infallible interpreter or interpreters. I look upon the Qur'an as an infinite source of continuing inner growth and moral exhortation and a powerful call to the finite soul from the mysterious depths of the ineffable mystery of Being or Ultimate Reality conceived as the Supreme Creator and Sustainer of the worlds (*Rabbul Alameen*).

The primary function of the Qur'an, to my mind, is to extend and deepen the individual's awareness of the human and cosmic situation through inner illumination and to exhort and fortify him in his never ending quest for value. Those who would like to treat the Qur'an as a readymade, rigid legal code appear to miss the wood for the trees, as it were. They feel compelled to follow static instructions without the inner concern to develop progressively more effective means of promoting the basic values of the Qur'an, that are beautifully reflected in the character of the Prophet ﷺ. This task is much more demanding and difficult in an ever-changing Universe than merely following readymade Qur'anic injunctions or the Prophet's ﷺ own instructions without any careful and honest reflective analysis of the present human situation.

In the final analysis, it is impossible to reduce the rich Qur'anic style and the varied functions of its contents to any single category or formula. The Qur'an is neither poetry, nor a legal code, nor a piece of theological casuistry, nor an anthology of knowledge or wisdom. All these human pursuits require ceaseless free inquiry and the dedicated will and moral courage to go where the evidence or the argument leads. I, in all humility, look upon the Qur'anic text as the permanent linguistic residue of the infusion of the highest degree and level of Divine grace and blessing in the consciousness of Prophet Muhammad ﷺ. Creative poets, artists, musicians, and thinkers also get this gift, but at a lower level.

The Qur'an itself says that God "appoints" or "sends" messengers and warners to guide the human family at different times and places. To attempt any conceptualization of the "how" of this Divine "selection" or "appointment" or the mechanics of this Divine "blessing," in the absence of any direct experience thereof, seems futile. In all humility I ask: Does it really matter if one accepts this rare phenomenon as a mystery? Does it matter if the light of Divine inspiration comes through different linguistic channels? Does it matter if one, quite honestly and sincerely, be unable to see anything special or compelling about the phenomenon under discussion—the Prophet's ﷺ untutored, effortless and spontaneous recitation of Arabic verses of the highest simplicity, beauty, and power? To my mind, what really matters is the individual's authentic response to the phenomenon or the mystery. In addition, what really matters is the individual's inner commitment to righteous action despite the pull and power of desire or impulse.

Reciting and reflecting on the Qur'an is, for the Muslim believer, like the obligatory disciplinary prayers, the means of the deepest communion of the individual soul with the Divine dimension of the cosmos. Both these forms of communion are meant continually to purify and "groom" the individual soul for reaching the plane of a stable and permanent "good will," to use the famous expression coined by the great German thinker of the 18th century, Immanuel Kant. To live at the plane of the "good will" is (functionally) similar to loving God and acting purely out of love for God, rather than for the sake of entering Paradise or escaping Hell. However, the ideal of surrendering to God (*islam*) and Kant's ideal of the "good will" and "action out of a pure sense of duty" both require continual prayerful meditation, honest self analysis and total commitment to intellectual honesty and practical self consistency to determine what exactly would be "righteous action" in any given situation.[54]

Mere conformity to the instrumental rules without intelligently searching for what exactly right action means in the ever-changing human situation/society will yield only marginal benefits. The principled acceptance of the semantic distinction between prescriptive Qur'anic verses referring to basic values and those referring to instrumental rules prepares the ground for the believer's own free commitment to basic values without any loss of spiritual autonomy. This transforms obedience to the "Word of God" into the enjoyment of inner freedom.

The Prophet's ﷺ character beautifully exemplifies these basic values, which can never be exhausted by the instrumental rules of the *Shariah*. The character of the historical Muhammad ﷺ, however, is a perennial source of inspiration to humankind in its ceaseless (but ever incomplete) aspiration for attaining perfection and truth. And the authentic and prayerful reflection on the Qur'an touches the deepest chord of the authentic human conscience, which is itself the Divine spark in humanity after the individual learns to deconstruct his or her natural ethnocentricity. This is, indeed, the miracle of the Qur'an.[55]

4

The Vision of the Qur'an: Selected Texts

Introductory Remarks

THE MUSLIM BELIEVER, as well as the general reader, who approaches the Qur'an with an open mind finds many references to what may be called a world view or a general picture of the origin and destination of humankind. This general conceptual picture, however, is not a readymade and rounded camera image that could be seen in one act of perception or conception. The reason is that the Qur'an is not a systematic treatise divided into interconnected chapters. The Arabic contents of the Qur'an were "revealed" over a long period in different contexts. The general conceptual picture of the Universe that the Qur'an presents has to be patiently constructed in the light of the Qur'anic texts.

Every individual who constructs such a conceptual picture of the human situation out of "revealed" texts, therefore, inevitably injects (to some extent or other) one's own existential inputs and responses to the mystery of the cosmos. No individual's statement of the Qur'anic vision can claim exclusive truth, and no question arises of proving or verifying it like a scientific truthclaim. However, one can and should refer to the original Arabic texts as the original datum for constructing his or her "Vision of the Qur'an." I submit every individual should enjoy the freedom of inquiry, and society should ensure complete tolerance of plural interpretations of one's cherished scripture.

The expression "Piety of the Qur'an" refers to the basic spiritual and moral values the Qur'an enshrines/prescribes. These values underpin the specific prescriptions and injunctions of the Qur'an. I look upon these latter as "instrumental rules of conduct" meant to promote the said basic values. The basic value terms found in the Qur'an, such as love, devotion to duty, truthfulness, compassion, justice, striving for justice, kindness, forgiveness, generosity, gratitude, tolerance, empathy, contentment, loyalty, chastity, and so on, have themselves to be interpreted before they can be used as "instrumental rules of conduct" in concrete human contexts or situations. The core content of the above values remains constant, but if humankind is denied the freedom to review and revise the instrumental rules of conduct in an ever-changing human situation, the values lose their grip and power of inner conviction, and individuals and societies begin to use value terms devoid of all commitment. Stagnation, double standards, hypocrisy and empty ritual displace integrity, consistency, and committed action, and society, eventually, turns into a decaying organism. Several Qur'anic texts describe this social phenomenon in its elliptical style as Divine punishment to the wrongdoers and rejectors of the "Signs of Allah." In other words, basic values also must be allowed to grow and develop and there must be loving tolerance of dissent and plurality in the sphere of pure morality as in the sphere of pure reason.

Core of the Qur'anic Vision

1. All that exists is the creation of one self-existent eternal Supreme and Sovereign Creator. All nature is thus completely dependent for its existence and mode of functioning and attributes to the Creator's command (amr) and the Creator can annihilate it as and when He wills. The entire creation is for God and returns to God. The Qur'an does not seek to argue this foundational truth, but just calls upon and exhorts humankind to observe nature in all its overpowering variety and reflect on its regularity, power, and beauty. These features are the "signs of God"—the One Supreme Creator, Sustainer, and Lord of all that exists.

The discrete finite things that exist and behave, as they actually do, their respective qualities and interconnections are not self made and eternal, but are so due to God's command (amr). He creates, preserves, guides, rewards, punishes, annihilates, recreates as He pleases and He is ever compassionate and just. Everything depends upon and turns to Him, but He depends on none. His knowledge and vision comprehends all that exists, but no one can comprehend Him or His knowledge, except what He permits. He commands humankind to strive for knowledge (ilm), and acquiring knowledge of external nature as well as man's inner nature is, indeed, a form of worship or surrender to God's commands that all creation carries out without fail, with the sole exception of such humans who fall into wrongdoing. Knowledge, thus, is not sufficient for complete human growth and felicity unless it be supplemented by righteous action in accordance with the Divine will. This the Creator makes known or "reveals" to His chosen messengers from among humankind itself. God's messengers have appeared from time to time in every part of the globe, communicated the same Divine message or vision of the good life (din) to their people who spoke different languages and followed their own way of life. Prophet Muhammad ⁕, however, is *"the Seal of the*

51

Prophets" and the Qur'anic revelation confirms and completes the one common Divine Call or Message to humankind.

2. The concrete way in which the Creator and Lord of all creation reveals His Divine will as to what is good and what is the appropriate or right behavior for the numerous kinds and species of His created beings depends upon the level or grade of the creature. It is obvious that different creatures behave in different ways, and this is exactly according to the Divine Will and command of the Supreme Creator. It is He who commands the fire to burn and consume what it touches, and water to flow and turn the earth green, or to quench thirst; it is He who commands the air to support the birds in the air and the ships on the oceans, the embryo to grow in the mother's womb, the lion to kill the lamb for his food, fruits to be formed on trees, and pearls in the depths of the ocean, the sun and the moon and the stars shine or move as commanded by the Lord. And all this is done through a form or mode of Divine Guidance (*wahy*) according to the level and needs of the creatures concerned. Birds chirp in different ways and bees make and store honey because they are guided or "inspired" through "*wahy*" suited for their level of existence. For humankind the highest possible level of Divine "inspiration" is God's verbal revelation to a few spiritually gifted souls—the messengers of God. These messengers, purified and directly guided by the Creator, overcome all self pride, self interest, personal ambition for wealth or power, fear, anger, hatred, and all other base human drives or passions though they retain their essential humanity, humility, and fallibility. They never claim any supernatural or exalted status, but only yearn that humankind should surrender to the one Supreme Creator and Lord of all creation. This is the literal meaning of Islam. According to the Qur'an, all prophets previous to Muhammad ﷺ and the true followers of those prophets were Muslims. Even after the advent of Prophet Muhammad ﷺ, the Qur'an clearly says that those among Jews, Christians, Magians, and Sabians, and others who worship one Supreme Being and act righteously and do not try to harm Prophet Muhammad ﷺ and the Muslim community have nothing to fear and shall be given their due reward.

3. Surrender to God does not mean mere verbal surrender but righteous action in accord with the Divine will and command. Moreover, even if the believer surrenders and acts according to the law but his motive is fear or love of reward, this is not Islam in the highest or best sense of the term. In the highest form of Islamic piety, according to Qur'anic texts (much highlighted by the great Sufi saints), the motive of right action is not fear but love for God, in other words, the unconditional commitment to basic values. In the Sufi ethos the fear of God means not the fear of being punished by an angry or wrathful God, but the fear of Divine displeasure or losing the much coveted nearness to the Sovereign Loving Creator.[1]

4. The Qur'an holds that the pain and suffering one finds in the world are the result of the evil deeds of human agents who have been given the power of free choice. When, however, the good and virtuous suffer, their suffering is not a punishment but a trial, and they should patiently wait for the return of a better future. Not being a systematic work of theology or philosophy, the Qur'an does not first raise and then resolve the "problem of evil and suffering." The Qur'an merely exhorts humankind to be patient in adversity, take positive and proper action, and to trust in God's power and mercy. In the final analysis, the frequent occurrence of, prima facie, unmerited suffering, particularly, the suffering caused by natural calamities of different kinds, remains inexplicable if one were to accept them as Divine punishments, in the literal sense, for the sins of human agents.[2]

5. Qur'anic texts refer to the prehuman, angelic creation, the initial high status and subsequent rebellion and fall from Divine grace of the archangel, Iblis (or *Shaitan*), the exalted status and role of Gabriel in the Divine revelation of the Qur'an, the still higher status of humankind as "*Ashraf ul Makhluqat*," and finally the apex status of Prophet Muhammad ﷺ in the long line of God's messengers from the earliest times to date. Muslims cannot but accept the Qur'anic texts as true. But, to my mind, the exact sense in which they are true is beyond human comprehension as in the case of beliefs or statements concerning the nature and attributes of God. The reason why all statements that refer to trans-empirical or supernatural subjects is that we have no experience of and no clear method of checking the truth or falsity of the truthclaim concerned, even if we antecedently accept that the person who makes the claim is genuinely truthful. We just use analogies from ordinary human experiences or situations to understand supernatural beings or events. The capacity for conceptual analysis and deductive reasoning cannot fill the gap in our clear understanding of metaphysical or theological statements or beliefs.[3]

6. Humans can have no understanding of the Divine wisdom or purpose of creation, though the Creator has endowed them with organs and the capacity of deductive reasoning (*aql*), which enables them to acquire knowledge (*ilm*) within certain limits fixed by God. This knowledge gives them control over the rest of creation. The Qur'an exhorts and also warns humankind to act with full responsibility and to beware of crossing the limits fixed by the Creator. The Qur'an repeatedly warns that earthly life and pleasures are temporary while life after death (*akhira*) is permanent. Indeed, the Qur'anic verses describing the processes of the final annihilation of the cosmos have an overpowering cathartic effect upon millions of readers, be they Muslim or others.[4]

7. The Qur'an clearly says that there is no compulsion in religion. The Prophet ﷺ was the first to follow this basic principle. However, he was passionately eager that his dear uncle, Abu Talib, his true benefactor and fearless defender against

the Prophet's ﷺ deadly Meccan foes, should see the light of Islam. In fact, the Prophet ﷺ both prayed to God and fervently pleaded with his loved one, but all in vain. He was also consumed with the desire that the whole Arab world should become a close knit Muslim brotherhood at the earliest. The Qur'anic wisdom spoke differently and counseled patience and the acceptance of spiritual pluralism. The Qur'an says that God could have created all humanity as born believers but He has a plan of His own and He will unfold it and judge all people on the Day of Judgement. The Prophet ﷺ is asked not to worry or lose hope in God's mercy and absolute power. However, the Qur'an strongly affirms the duty of all Muslims resolutely and vigorously to defend themselves if they be attacked by the enemy.[5]

I now proceed to give an extended selection of Qur'anic texts in support of my formulation of the Qur'anic vision. I have arranged the Qur'anic texts under five subheadings and have used throughout my work Abdullah Yusuf Ali's monumental English translation of the Qur'an, except where indicated in this work.

Selected Qur'anic Texts

The Creator, Purpose of Divine Creation, Signs of Allah, and the Destiny of Man and the Cosmos

2:255

Allah! There is no God but He —the Living, the Self-subsisting, the Eternal. No slumber can seize Him, nor sleep, His are all things in the heavens and on earth. Who is there that can intercede in his presence except as He permitteth? He knoweth what (appeareth to His creatures as) before or after or behind them. Nor shall they compass aught of His knowledge except as He willeth. His Throne doth extend over the heavens and the earth, and He feeleth no fatigue in guarding and preserving them for He is the most High, the Supreme (in glory).[6]

24:35–46

Allah is the Light of the heavens and the earth. The parable of His Light is as if there were a niche and within it a Lamp: the Lamp enclosed in Glass; the glass as it were a brilliant star; lit from a blessed Tree, an Olive, neither of the East nor of the West, whose oil is well-nigh Luminous, though fire scarce touched it: Light upon Light! Allah doth guide whom He will to His Light: Allah doth set forth parables for men: and Allah doth know all things.

(Lit is such a light) in houses, which Allah has permitted to be raised to honor; for the celebration in them of His name: in them is He glorified in the mornings and the evenings, (again and again)—

By men whom neither traffic nor merchandise can divert from remembrance of Allah, nor from regular prayer, nor from the practice of regular charity: their (only) fear is for the Day when hearts and eyes will be transformed (in a world wholly new)—

That Allah may reward them according to the best of their deeds, and add even more out of His grace: for Allah doth provide for those whom He will, without measure.

But the Unbelievers—their deeds are like a mirage in sandy deserts, which the man parched with thirst mistakes for water; until when he comes up to it, he finds it to be nothing: But he finds Allah (ever with him), and Allah will pay him his account: and Allah is swift in taking account.

Or (the Unbeliever's state) is like the depths of darkness in a vast deep ocean, overwhelmed with billow topped by billow, topped by (dark clouds); depths of darkness, one above another: if a man stretches out his hand he can hardly see it! For any to whom Allah giveth not light there is no light!

Seest thou not that it is Allah Whose praise all beings in the heavens and on earth do celebrate, and the birds (of the air) with wings outspread? Each one knows its own (mode of) prayer and praise. And Allah knows well all that they do.

Yea, to Allah belongs the dominion of the heavens and the earth: and to Allah is the final goal (of all).

Seest thou not that Allah makes the clouds move gently, then joins them together, then makes them into a heap?—then wilt thou see rain issue forth from their midst. And He sends down from the sky mountain masses (of clouds) wherein is hail: He strikes therewith whom He pleases and He turns it away from whom He pleases. The vivid flash of His lightning well-nigh blinds the sight.

It is Allah Who alternates the Night and the Day: Verily in these things is an instructive example for those who have vision!

And Allah has created every animal from water: of them there are some that creep on their bellies; some that walk on two legs; and some that walk on four. Allah creates what He wills; for verily Allah has power over all things.

We have indeed sent down Signs that make things manifest: and Allah guides whom He wills to a Way that is straight.

112:1–4
Say: He is Allah, the One and Only; Allah, the Eternal, Absolute; He begetteth not, nor is He begotten; And there is none like unto Him.

6:59
With Him are the keys of the unseen, the treasures that none knoweth but He. He knoweth whatever there is on the earth and in the seas. Not a leaf doth fall but with His knowledge: there is not a grain in the darkness (or depths) of the earth, nor anything fresh or dry (green or withered) but is (inscribed) in a record clear (to those who can read).

6:103
No vision can grasp Him, but His grasp is over all vision: He is above all comprehension, yet is acquainted with all things.

28:88
And call not, besides Allah, on another god. There is no god but He. Everything (that exists) will perish except His own Face. To Him belongs the Command, and to Him will ye (all) be brought back.

30:20–27
Among His Signs in this, that He created you from dust; and then—behold, ye are men scattered (far and wide)! And among His Signs is this, that He created for you mates from among yourselves, that ye may dwell in tranquility with them, and He has put love and mercy between your (hearts): verily in that are Signs for those who reflect.

And among His Signs is the creation of the heavens and the earth, and the variations in your languages and your colors: verily in that are

Signs for those who know. And among His Signs is the sleep that ye take by night and by day, and the quest that ye (make for livelihood) out of His Bounty: verily in that are signs for those who hearken. And among His Signs, He shows you the lightning, by way both of fear and of hope, and He sends down rain from the sky and with it gives life to the earth after it is dead: verily in that are Signs for those who are wise. And among His Signs is this, that heaven and earth stand by His Command: then when He calls you, by a single call, from the earth, behold, ye (straightway) come forth. To Him belongs every being that is in the heavens and on earth: all are devoutly obedient to Him. It is He Who begins (the process of) creation; then repeats it; and for Him it is most easy. To Him belongs the loftiest similitude (we can think of) in the heavens and the earth: for He is Exalted in Might, full of wisdom.

36:36–40
Glory to Allah, Who created in pairs all things that the earth produces, as well as their own (human) kind and (other) things of which they have no knowledge. And a Sign for them is the Night: We withdraw therefrom the Day, and behold they are plunged in darkness; And the Sun runs his course for a period determined for him: that is the decree of (Him), the Exalted in Might, the All Knowing. And the Moon,— We have measured for her mansions (to traverse) till she returns like the old (and withered) lower part of a date-stalk. It is not permitted to the Sun to catch up the Moon, nor can the Night outstrip the Day: Each (just) swims along in (its own) orbit (according to Law).[7]

35:13
He merges Night into Day, and He merges Day into Night, and He has subjected the sun and the moon (to his Law): each one runs its course for a term appointed. Such is Allah your Lord: to Him belongs all Dominion. And those whom ye invoke besides Him have not the least power.

67:19
Do they not observe the birds above them, spreading their wings and folding them in? None can uphold them except (Allah) Most Gracious: Truly it is He that watches over all things.

54:49, 50
Verily, all things have We created in proportion and measure. And Our Command is but a single (act)—like the twinkling of an eye.[8]

56:63–74

See ye the seed that ye sow in the ground? Is it ye that cause it to grow, or are We the Cause? Were it Our Will, We could crumble it to dry powder, and ye would be left in wonderment, (Saying), "We are indeed left with debts (for nothing): "Indeed are we shut out (of the fruits of our labor)" See ye the water, which ye drink? Do ye bring it down (in rain) from the cloud or do We? Were it Our Will, We could make it salt (and unpalatable): then why do ye not give thanks? See ye the Fire which ye kindle? Is it ye who grow the tree, which feeds the fire, or do We grow it? We have made it a memorial (of Our handiwork), and an article of comfort and convenience for the denizens of deserts. Then celebrate with praises the name of thy Lord, the Supreme!

56:83–89

Then why do ye not (intervene) when (the soul of the dying man) reaches the throat,—And ye the while (sit) looking on,—But We are nearer to him than ye, and yet see not—If you are exempt from (future) account—Call back the soul, if ye are true (in the claim of independence)? Thus, then, if he be of those nearest to Allah, (there is for him) Rest and Satisfaction, and a Garden of Delights.

21:16–17

Not for (idle) sport did We create the heavens and the earth and all that is between! If it had been Our wish to take (just) a pastime, We should surely have taken it from the things nearest to Us, if We would do (such a thing)!

21:30

Do not the Unbelievers see that the heavens and the earth were joined together (as one unit of creation), before we clove them asunder? We made from water every living thing. Will they not then believe?

21:47

We shall set up scales of justice for the Day of Judgment, so that not a soul will be dealt with unjustly in the least, and if there be (no more than) the weight of a mustard seed, We will bring it (to account): and enough are We to take account.

21:104

The Day that We roll up the heavens like a scroll rolled up for books (completed),—even as We produced the first creation, so shall We produce a new one: a promise We have undertaken: truly shall We fulfill it.

22:5, 6

O mankind! if ye have a doubt about the Resurrection, (consider) that We created you out of dust, then out of sperm, then out of a leech like clot, then out of a morsel of flesh, partly formed and partly unformed, in order that We may manifest (our power) to you; and We cause whom We will to rest in the wombs for an appointed term, then do We bring you out as babes, then (foster you) that ye may reach your age of full strength; and some of you are called to die, and some are sent back to the feeblest old age, so that they know nothing after having known (much), and (further), thou seest the earth barren and lifeless, but when We pour down rain on it, it is stirred (to life), it swells, and it puts forth every kind of beautiful growth (in pairs).

This is so, because Allah is the Reality: it is He Who gives life to the dead, and it is He Who has power over all things.[9]

22:18

Seest thou not that to Allah bow down in worship all things that are in the heavens and on earth,—the sun, the moon, the stars; the hills, the trees, the animals; and a great number among mankind? But a great number are (also) such as are fit for Punishment: and such as Allah shall disgrace —None can raise to honor: for Allah carries out all that He wills.

3:85

If anyone desires a religion other than Islam (submission to Allah), never will it be accepted of him; and in the Hereafter he will be in the ranks of those who have lost (all spiritual good).

5:44

It was We who revealed the law (to Moses): therein was guidance and light. By its standard have been judged the Jews, by the prophets who bowed (as in Islam) to Allah's will, by the rabbis and the doctors of law: for to them was entrusted the protection of Allah's book, and they were witnesses thereto: therefore fear not men, but fear Me, and sell not my signs for a miserable price. If any do fail to judge by (the light of) what Allah hath revealed, they are (no better than) Unbelievers.

7:143

When Moses came to the place appointed by Us, and his Lord addressed him, He said: "O my Lord! Show (Thyself) to me, that I may look upon thee." Allah said: "By no means canst thou see Me (direct); But look upon the mount; if it abide in its place, then shalt thou see Me." When his Lord manifested His glory on the Mount, He made it as dust. And Moses fell down in a swoon. When he recovered his senses he said: "Glory be to Thee! To Thee I turn in repentance, and I am the first to believe."[10]

38:71–83

Behold, thy Lord said to the angels: "I am about to create man from clay: "When I have fashioned him (in due proportion) and breathed into him of My spirit, fall ye down in obeisance unto him." So the angels prostrated themselves, all of them together: Not so Iblis: he was haughty, and became one of those who reject Faith. (Allah) said: "O Iblis! What prevents thee from prostrating thyself to one whom I have created with my hands? Art thou haughty? Or art thou one of the high (and mighty) ones?"

(Iblis) said: "I am better than he: thou created me from fire, and him thou created from clay." (Allah) said: "Then get thee out from here: for thou art rejected, accursed. "And My curse shall be on thee till the Day of Judgment." (Iblis) said: "O my Lord! Give me then respite till the Day the (dead) are raised." (Allah) said: "Respite then is granted thee—Till the Day of the Time Appointed." (Iblis) said: "Then, by Thy power, I will put them all in the wrong—"Except Thy Servants amongst them, sincere and purified (by Thy Grace)."[11]

33:72, 73

We did indeed offer the Trust to the Heavens and the Earth and the Mountains; but they refused to undertake it, being afraid thereof: but man undertook it;—He was indeed unjust and foolish;—(With the result) that Allah has to punish the Hypocrites, men and women, and the Unbelievers, men and women, and Allah turns in Mercy to the Believers, men and women: for Allah is Oft-Forgiving, Most Merciful.[12]

44:38, 39
We created not the heavens, the earth, and all between them, merely in (idle) sport: We created them not except for just ends: but most of them do not understand.

2:45, 46
Nay, seek (Allah's) help with patient perseverance and prayer: It is indeed hard, except to those who bring a lowly spirit—Who bear in mind the certainty that they are to meet their Lord, and that they are to return to Him.

2:214
Or do ye think that ye shall enter the Garden (of bliss) without such (trials) as came to those who passed away before you? They encountered suffering and adversity, and were so shaken in spirit that even the Messenger and those of faith who were with him cried: "When (will come) the help of Allah?" Ah! Verily, the help of Allah is (always) near!

5:68
Say: "O People of the Book! Ye have no ground to stand upon unless ye stand fast by the Law, the Gospel, and all the revelation that has come to you from your Lord." It is the revelation that cometh to thee from thy Lord, that increaseth in most of them their obstinate rebellion and blasphemy. But sorrow thou not over (these) people without Faith.

5:69
Those who believe (in the Qur'an), those who follow the Jewish (scriptures), and the Sabians and the Christians,—any who believe in Allah and the Last Day, and work righteousness,—on them shall be no fear, nor shall they grieve.

3:83
Do they seek for other than the Religion of Allah?—While all creatures in the heavens and on earth have, willing or unwilling, bowed to His Will (accepted Islam), and to Him shall they all be brought back.

2:111–113
And they say: "None shall enter Paradise unless he be a Jew or a Christian." Those are their (vain) desires. Say: "Produce your proof if ye are truthful." Nay, whoever submits His whole self to Allah and is a doer of

good,—He will get his reward with his Lord; on such shall be no fear, nor shall they grieve. The Jews say: "The Christians have naught (to stand) upon; and the Christians say: "The Jews have naught (to stand) upon." Yet they (profess to) study the (same) Book. Like unto their word is what those say who know not; but Allah will judge between them in their quarrel on the Day of Judgment.[13]

44:38, 39
We created not the heavens, the earth, and all between them, merely in (idle) sport: We created them not except for just ends: but most of them do not understand.[14]

45:3, 4, 5
Verily in the heavens and the earth, are Signs for those who believe. And in the creation of yourselves and the fact that animals are scattered (through the earth), are Signs for those of assured Faith. And in the alternation of Night and Day, and the fact that Allah sends down Sustenance from the sky, and revives therewith the earth after its death, and in the change of the winds—are Signs for those that are wise.

45:13
And He has subjected to you, as from Him, all that is in the heavens and on earth: Behold, in that are Signs indeed for those who reflect.

45:22
Allah created the heavens and the earth for just ends, and in order that each soul may find the recompense of what it has earned, and none of them be wronged.

45:23
Then seest thou such a one as takes as his god his own vain desire? Allah has, knowing (him as such), left him astray, and sealed his hearing and his heart (and understanding), and put a cover on his sight. Who, then, will guide him after Allah (has withdrawn Guidance)? Will ye not then receive admonition?[15]

39:6
He created you (all) from a single person: then created, of like nature, his mate; and he sent down for you eight head of cattle in pairs: He makes you, in the wombs of your mothers, in stages, one after another,

in three veils of darkness. Such is Allah, your Lord and Cherisher: to Him belongs (all) dominion. There is no god but He: then how are ye turned away (from your true Center)?[16]

16:65–70
And Allah sends down rain from the skies, and gives therewith life to the earth after its death: verily in this is a Sign for those who listen. And verily in cattle (too) will ye find an instructive sign. From what is within their bodies between excretions and blood, We produce, for your drink, milk, pure and agreeable to those who drink it. And from the fruit of the date-palm and the vine, ye get out wholesome drink and food: behold, in this also is a Sign for those who are wise. And thy Lord taught the Bee to build its cells in hills, on trees, and in (men's) habitations; then to eat of all the produce (of the earth), and find with skill the spacious paths of its Lord: there issues from within their bodies a drink of varying colors, wherein is healing for men: verily in this is a Sign for those who give thought. It is Allah who creates you and takes your souls at death; and of you there are some who are sent back to a feeble age, so that they know nothing after having known (much): for Allah is All-Knowing, All Powerful.[17]

95:4, 5
We have indeed created man in the best of molds, Then do We abase him (to be) the lowest of the low.

6:38
There is not an animal (that lives) on the earth, nor a being that flies on its wings, but (forms part of) communities like you. Nothing have We omitted from the Book, and they (all) shall be gathered to their Lord in the end.[18]

16:79
Do they not look at the birds, held poised in the midst of (the air and) the sky? Nothing holds them up but (the power of) Allah. Verily in this are signs for those who believe.

20.50
He said: Our Lord is He Who gave to each (created thing) its form and nature, and further, gave (it) guidance.

31:28

And your creation or your resurrection is in no wise but as an individual soul: for Allah is He Who hears and sees (all things.)[19]

27:88

Thou seest the mountains and thinkest them firmly fixed: but they shall pass away as the clouds pass away: (such is) the artistry of Allah, who disposes of all things in perfect order: for he is well-acquainted with all that ye do.

17:44

The seven heavens and the earth, and all beings therein, declare His glory: there is not a thing but celebrates His praise; and yet ye understand not how they declare His glory! Verily He is Oft-Forbearing, Most Forgiving!

24:41

Seest thou not that it is Allah Whose praise all beings in the heavens and on earth do celebrate, and the birds (of the air) with wings outspread? Each one knows its own (mode of) prayer and praise. And Allah knows well all that they do.[20]

31:20

Do ye not see that Allah has subjected to your (use) all things in the heavens and on earth, and has made his bounties flow to you in exceeding measure, (both) seen and unseen? Yet there are among men those who dispute about Allah, without knowledge and without guidance, and without a Book to enlighten them!

99:1–5

When the earth is shaken to her (utmost) convulsion, And the earth throws up her burdens (from within), And man cries (distressed): 'What is the matter with her?'—On that Day will she declare her tidings: For that thy Lord will have given her inspiration.

10:45

One day He will gather them together: (It will be) as if they had tarried but an hour of a day: they will recognize each other: assuredly those will be lost who denied the meeting with Allah and refused to receive true guidance.[21]

11:7

He it is Who created the heavens and the earth in six Days—and His Throne was over the waters— that He might try you, which of you is best in conduct. But if thou wert to say to them, "Ye shall indeed be raised up after death," the Unbelievers would be sure to say, "This is nothing but obvious sorcery!"

68:44, 45

Then leave Me alone with such as reject this Message: by degrees shall We punish them from directions they perceive not. A (long) respite will I grant them: truly powerful is My Plan.[22]

God as the Sovereign Lord and Sustainer of Creation

22:40

(They are) those who have been expelled from their homes in defiance of right,—(for no cause) except that they say, "our Lord is Allah." Did not Allah check one set of people by means of another, there would surely have been pulled down monasteries, churches, synagogues, and mosques, in which the name of Allah is commemorated in abundant measure. Allah will certainly aid those who aid his (cause);— for verily Allah is full of Strength, Exalted in Might, (able to enforce His Will).

22:47

Yet they ask thee to hasten on the Punishment! But Allah will not fail in His Promise. Verily a Day in the sight of thy Lord is like a thousand years of your reckoning.

19:83, 84

Seest thou not that We have set the Evil Ones on against the unbelievers, to incite them with fury? So make no haste against them, for We but count out to them a (limited) number (of days.)[23]

20:111, 112

(All) faces shall be humbled before (Him)—the Living, the Self-Subsisting, Eternal: hopeless indeed will be the man that carries iniquity (on his back). But he who works deeds of righteousness, and has faith, will have no fear of harm nor of any curtailment (of what is his due).

35:44, 45
Do they not travel through the earth, and see what was the End of those before them,—though they were superior to them in strength? Nor is Allah to be frustrated by anything whatever in the heavens or on earth: for He is All-Knowing. All-Powerful. If Allah were to punish men according to what they deserve. He would not leave on the back of the (earth) a single living creature: but He gives them respite for a stated Term: when their Term expires, verily Allah has in His sight all His Servants.

2:251
By Allah's will they routed them; and David slew Goliath; and Allah gave him power and wisdom and taught him whatever (else) He willed. And did not Allah check one set of people by means of another, the earth would indeed be full of mischief: But Allah is full of bounty to all the worlds.

6:123
Thus have We placed leaders in every town, its wicked men, to plot (and burrow) therein: but they only plot against their own souls, and they perceive it not.

8:53
"Because Allah will never change the grace, which He hath bestowed on a people until they change what is in their (own) souls: and verily Allah is He Who heareth and knoweth (all things)."

10:44
Verily Allah will not deal unjustly with man in aught: It is man that wrongs his own soul.

Divine Revelation to Prophets

3:7
He it is Who has sent down to thee the Book: In it are verses basic or fundamental (of established meaning); they are the foundation of the Book: others are allegorical. But those in whose hearts is perversity follow the part thereof that is allegorical, seeking discord, and searching for its hidden meanings, but no one knows its hidden meanings except Allah. And those who are firmly grounded in knowledge say:

"We believe in the Book; the whole of it is from our Lord:" and none will grasp the Message except men of understanding.

81:19–29
Verily this is the word of a most honorable Messenger, Endued with Power, with rank before the Lord of the Throne, With authority there, (and) faithful to his trust. And (O people!) your companion is not one possessed; And without doubt he saw him in the clear horizon. Neither doth he withhold grudgingly a knowledge of the Unseen. Nor is it the word of an evil spirit accursed. When whither go ye? Verily this is no less than a Message to (all) the Worlds: (with profit) to whoever among you wills to go straight: But ye shall not will except as Allah wills,— the Cherisher of the Worlds.[24]

25:29–32
"He did lead me astray from the Message (of Allah) after it had come to me! Ah! the Evil One is but a traitor to man!" ... Then the Messenger will say: "O my Lord! Truly my people took this Qur'an for just foolish nonsense." Thus have We made for every prophet an enemy among the sinners: but enough is thy Lord to guide and to help. Those who reject Faith say: "Why is not the Qur'an revealed to him all at once? Thus (is it revealed), that We may strengthen thy heart thereby, and We have rehearsed it to thee in slow, well-arranged stages, gradually.

12:111
There is, in their stories, instruction for men endued with understanding. It is not a tale invented, but a confirmation of what went before it,—a detailed exposition of all things, and a guide and a mercy to any such as believe.

80:11–16
By no means (should it be so)! For it is indeed a Message of instruction: Therefore let whoso will, keep it in remembrance. (It is) in Books held (greatly) in honor, Exalted (in dignity), kept pure and holy, (written) by the hands of scribes-Honorable and Pious and Just.

56:77–80
That this is indeed a Qur'an Most Honorable, in a Book well-guarded, Which none shall touch but those who are clean: A Revelation from the Lord of the Worlds.

98:2, 3
A messenger from Allah, rehearsing scriptures kept pure and holy:
Wherein are laws (or decrees) right and straight.[25]

20:114
High above all is Allah, the King, the Truth! Be not in haste with the
Qur'an before its revelation to thee is completed, but say, "O my Lord!
Advance me in knowledge."

75:16–18
Move not thy tongue concerning the (Qur'an) to make haste therewith.
It is for Us to collect it and to promulgate it: But when We have prom-
ulgated it, follow thou its recital (as promulgated)...[26]

53:1–18
By the Star when it goes down—Your Companion is neither astray nor
being misled. Nor does he say (aught) of (his own) Desire. It is no less than
inspiration sent down to him: He was taught by one Mighty in Power,
Endued with Wisdom: for he appeared (in stately form); While he was in
the highest part of the horizon: Then he approached and came closer, And
was at a distance of but two bow lengths or (even) nearer; So did (Allah)
convey the inspiration to His Servant—(conveyed) what He (meant) to
convey. The (Prophet's) (mind and) heart in no way falsified that which he
saw. Will ye then dispute with him concerning what he saw? For indeed he
saw him at a second descent, Near the Lote tree beyond which none may
pass: Near it is the Garden of Abode. Behold, the Lote tree was shrouded
(in mystery unspeakable!) (His) sight never swerved, nor did it go wrong!
For truly did he see, of the Signs of his Lord, the Greatest![27]

53:19–23
Have ye seen Lat. and Uzza, And another, the third (goddess), Manat?
What! For you the male sex, and for Him, the female? Behold, such
would be indeed a division most unfair! These are nothing but names,
which ye have devised, ye and your fathers,—for which Allah has sent
down no authority (whatever). They follow nothing but conjecture and
what their own souls desire!—Even though there has already come to
them Guidance from their Lord!

22:52–54
Never did We send a messenger or a prophet before thee but, when he
framed a desire, Satan threw some (vanity) into his desire: but Allah

will cancel anything (vain) that Satan throws in, and Allah will confirm
(and establish) His Signs: for Allah is full of Knowledge and Wisdom:
That He may make the suggestions thrown in by Satan, but a trial for
those in whose hearts is a disease and who are hardened of heart: verily
the wrong-doers are in a schism far (from the Truth): And that those
on whom knowledge has been bestowed may learn that the (Qur'an) is
the Truth from thy Lord, and that they may believe therein, and their
hearts may be made humbly (open) to it: for verily Allah is the Guide of
those who believe, to the Straight Way.[28]

The Unity of Humankind and a Common "Deen"

The basic thrust of all the following approximately forty Qur'anic texts taken from
different *surahs* is that God created humankind as one family and sent Divinely
guided messengers to guide different people to the path of truth and goodness.
Why, then, does the family get fractured into warring groups? This crucial question can be answered at many levels and from different points of view. We shall
find an integrated and balanced answer only when we do not reduce the complexity of the phenomenon under discussion to a single factor or dimension and
exclude other equally or even more important factors.

Religious minded persons generally explain the problem of human conflict
and hatred in terms of the human weakness to succumb to the machinations of
Satan who functions as the arch enemy to humans. There is no reason to disagree
with the basic thrust of this religious or theological answer. But this answer, by
itself, does not prove to be very helpful in containing or defeating the tricks of the
arch enemy. This theological answer needs to be supplemented by sociological
analysis of the human situation. Sociological analysis does not contradict religious
faith, but shows the practical way of removing the situational factors that create
opportunities for Satan's tricks in the first place. The prayer mat, rosary, and the
sermon are all very good, but they will not deliver unless social justice is added
to the therapeutic prescription for curing the ills of the human family. The propagation of religious faith or the virtues of democracy must be supplemented by
vigorous programs of "righteous action" based on social justice, without opposing
the cultural and religious pluralism that naturally obtains in the human family.

2:213

Mankind was one single nation, and Allah sent Messengers with glad
tidings and warnings; and with them He sent the Book in truth, to judge
between people in matters wherein they differed; but the People of the
Book, after the clear Signs came to them, did not differ among them-
selves, except through selfish contumacy. Allah by His Grace Guided

the believers to the Truth, concerning that wherein they differed. For Allah guided whom He will to a path that is straight.

21:92–94
Verily, this brotherhood of yours is a single brotherhood, and I am your Lord and Cherisher: therefore serve Me (and no other). But (later generations) cut off their affair (of unity), one from another: (yet) will they all return to Us. Whoever works any act of righteousness and has faith—His endeavor will not be rejected: We shall record it in his favor.

10:99–101
If it had been thy Lord's will, they would all have believed,—all who are on earth! Wilt thou then compel mankind, against their will, to believe! No soul can believe, except by the will of Allah, and He will place doubt (or obscurity) on those who will not understand. Say: "Behold all that is in the heavens and on earth"; but neither Signs nor Warners profit those who believe not.

22:67
To every People have We appointed rites and ceremonies, which they must follow: let them not then dispute with thee on the matter, but do thou invite (them) to thy Lord: for thou art assuredly on the Right Way.

2:62
Those who believe (in the Qur'an), and those who follow the Jewish (scriptures), and the Christians and the Sabians,—any who believe in Allah and the Last Day, and work righteousness, shall have their reward with their Lord; on them shall be no fear, nor shall they grieve.

5:48
To thee We sent the Scripture in truth, confirming the scripture that came before it, and guarding it in safety: so judge between them by what Allah hath revealed, and follow not their vain desires, diverging from the Truth that hath come to thee. To each among you have we prescribed a law and an open way. If Allah had so willed, He would have made you a single people, but (His plan is) to test you in what He hath given you: so strive as in a race in all virtues. The goal of you all is to Allah; it is He that will show you the truth of the matters in which ye dispute;

5:69
Those who believe (in the Qur'an), those who follow the Jewish (scriptures), and the Sabians and the Christians,—any who believe in Allah and the Last Day, and work righteousness,— on them shall be no fear, nor shall they grieve.[29]

22:78
And strive in His cause as ye ought to strive, (with sincerity and under discipline). He has chosen you, and has imposed no difficulties on you in religion; it is the cult of your father Abraham. It is He Who has named you Muslims, both before and in this (Revelation); that the Messenger may be a witness for you, and ye be witnesses for mankind! So establish regular Prayer, give regular Charity, and hold fast to Allah! He is your Protector—the Best to protect and the Best to help!

3:84
Say: "We believe in Allah, and in what has been revealed to us and what was revealed to Abraham, Ismail, Isaac, Jacob, and the Tribes, and in (the Books) given to Moses, Jesus, and the prophets, from their Lord: We make no distinction between one and another among them, and to Allah do we bow our will (in Islam)."

4:157, 158
That they said (in boast), "We killed Christ Jesus the son of Mary, the Messenger of Allah";—but they killed him not, nor crucified him, but so it was made to appear to them, and those who differ therein are full of doubts, with no (certain) knowledge, but only conjecture to follow, for of a surety they killed him not: Nay, Allah raised him up unto Himself; and Allah is Exalted in Power, Wise;—

4:164
Of some messengers We have already told thee the story; of others We have not—and to Moses Allah spoke direct;—

45:14
Tell those who believe, to forgive those who do not look forward to the Days of Allah: It is for Him to recompense (for good or ill) each people according to what they have earned.

45:24

And they say: "What is there but our life in this world? We shall die and we live, and nothing but time can destroy us." But of that they have no knowledge: they merely conjecture:

2:136

Say ye: "We believe in Allah, and the revelation given to us, and to Abraham, Ismail, Isaac, Jacob, and the Tribes, and that given to Moses and Jesus, and that given to (all) prophets from their Lord: We make no difference between one and another of them: And we bow to Allah (in Islam)."

2:253

Those messengers We endowed with gifts, some above others: To one of them Allah spoke; others He raised to degrees (of honor); to Jesus the son of Mary We gave clear (Signs), and strengthened him with the Holy Spirit. If Allah had so willed, succeeding generations would not have fought among each other, after clear (Signs) had come to them, but they (chose) to wrangle, some believing and others rejecting. If Allah had so willed, they would not have fought each other; but Allah fulfilleth His plan.

28:52–56

Those to whom We sent the Book before this—they do believe in this (revelation): And when it is recited to them, they say: "We believe therein, for it is the Truth from our Lord: indeed we have been Muslims (bowing to Allah's Will) from before this. Twice will they be given their reward, for that they have persevered, that they avert Evil with Good, and that they spend (in charity) out of what We have given them. And when they hear vain talk, they turn away there from and say: "To us our deeds, and to you yours; peace be to you: we seek not the ignorant." It is true thou wilt not be able to guide every one, whom thou lovest; but Allah guides those whom He will and He knows best those who receive guidance.

3:64

Say: "O People of the Book! Come to common terms as between us and you: That we worship none but Allah; that we associate no partners with him; that we erect not, from among ourselves, lords and patrons other than Allah." If then they turn back, say ye: "Bear witness that we (at least) are Muslims (bowing to Allah's Will).

4:124

If any do deeds of righteousness—be they male or female—and have faith, they will enter Heaven, and not the least injustice will be done to them.

3:102

O ye who believe! Fear Allah as He should be feared, and die not except in a state of Islam.

3:110

Ye are the best of peoples, evolved for mankind, enjoining what is right, forbidding what is wrong, and believing in Allah. If only the People of the Book had faith, it were best for them: among them are some who have faith, but most of them are perverted transgressors.

3:113–117

Not all of them are alike: Of the People of the Book are a portion that stand (for the right): They rehearse the Signs of Allah all night long, and they prostrate themselves in adoration. They believe in Allah and the Last Day; they enjoin what is right, and forbid what is wrong; and they hasten (in emulation) in (all) good works: They are in the ranks of the righteous. Of the good that they do, nothing will be rejected of them; for Allah knoweth well those that do right. Those who reject Faith—neither their possessions nor their (numerous) progeny will avail them aught against Allah: They will be companions of the Fire, dwelling therein (for ever). What they spend in the life of this (material) world may be likened to a wind, which brings a nipping frost: It strikes and destroys the harvest of men who have wronged their own souls: it is not Allah that hath wronged them, but they wrong themselves.

5:82, 83

Strongest among men in enmity to the believers wilt thou find the Jews and Pagans; and nearest among them in love to the believers wilt thou find those who say, "We are Christians": because amongst these are men devoted to learning and men who have renounced the world, and they are not arrogant. And when they listen to the revelation received by the Messenger, thou wilt see their eyes overflowing with tears, for they recognize the truth: they pray: "Our Lord! We believe; write us down among the witnesses.[30]

2:285

The Messenger believeth in what hath been revealed to him from his Lord, as do the men of faith. Each one (of them) believeth in Allah, His angels, His books, and His messengers. "We make no distinction (they say) between one and another of His messengers." And they say: "We hear, and we obey: (We seek) Thy forgiveness, our Lord, and to Thee is the end of all journeys."

The Qur'an on Prophet Muhammad ﷺ

The Qur'anic texts in this section reveal the pure Qur'anic view of the status, character, and role of the Prophet ﷺ in history. It will be seen that the Qur'an depicts the Prophet ﷺ of Islam in very human terms, indeed, completely devoid of all supernatural powers or claims of his infallibility. The Qur'anic account highlights the fully human gifts and limitations of the Prophet ﷺ and his susceptibility to the normal joys and sorrows of life, its dangers and risks, and the errors or mistakes of commission and omission to which all humans are liable. The picture of Prophet Muhammad ﷺ in popular imagination of Muslim believers and Islamic devotional literature is entirely different, as we all know. To my mind, the Qur'anic picture of the Prophet ﷺ is the glory of Islam as the natural or rational religion for our times, entirely devoid of miracles, myths, and a minimum of mystique.

21:107

We sent thee not, but as a mercy for all creatures.[31]

33:40

Muhammad is not the father of any of your men, but (he is) the Messenger of Allah, and the Seal of the Prophets: and Allah has full knowledge of all things.[32]

28:86–88

And thou hadst not expected that the Book would be sent to thee except as a Mercy from thy Lord: Therefore lend not thou support in any way to those who reject (Allah's Message). And let nothing keep thee back from the Signs of Allah after they have been revealed to thee: and invite (men) to thy Lord, and be not of the company of those who join gods with Allah. And call not, besides Allah, on another god. There is no god but He. Everything (that exists) will perish except His own Face. To Him belongs the Command, and to Him will ye (all) be brought back.

67:25, 26
They ask: When will this promise be (fulfilled)? If ye are telling the truth. Say: "As to the knowledge of the time, it is with Allah alone: I am (sent) only to warn plainly in public."[33]

46:9
Say: "I am no bringer of new-fangled doctrine among the messengers, nor do I know what will be done with me or with you. I follow but that which is revealed to me by inspiration; I am but a Warner open and clear."

7:188
Say: "I have no power over any good or harm to myself except as Allah willeth. If I had knowledge of the unseen, I should have multiplied all good, and no evil should have touched me: I am but a Warner, and a bringer of glad tidings to those who have faith."

6:50
Say: "I tell you not that with me are the treasures of Allah, nor do I know what is hidden, nor do I tell you I am an angel. I but follow what is revealed to me." Say: "Can the blind be held equal to the seeing?" Will ye then consider not?

40:77
So persevere in patience; for the Promise of Allah is true: and whether We show thee (in this life) some part of what We promise them—or We take thy soul (to Our Mercy) (before that),—(in any case) it is to Us that they shall (all) return.

13:40
Whether We shall show thee (within thy lifetime) part of what we promised them or take to ourselves thy soul (before it is all accomplished)—thy duty is to make (the Message) reach them: it is our part to call them to account.

3:144
Muhammad is no more than a messenger: many were the messengers that passed away before him. If he died or were slain, will ye then turn back on your heels? If any did turn back on his heels, not the least harm will he do to Allah; but Allah (on the other hand) will swiftly reward those who (serve Him) with gratitude.

10:15

But when Our Clear Signs are rehearsed unto them, those who rest not their hope on their meeting with Us, Say: "Bring us a reading other than this, or change this," Say: "It is not for me, of my own accord, to change it: I follow naught but what is revealed unto me: if I were to disobey my Lord, I should myself fear the penalty of a Great Day (to come)."

3:159

It is part of the Mercy of Allah that thou dost deal gently with them. Wert thou severe or harsh—hearted, they would have broken away from about Thee: so pass over (their faults), and ask for (Allah's) forgiveness for them; and consult them in affairs (of moment). Then, when thou hast taken a decision put thy trust in Allah. For Allah loves those who put their trust (in Him).

16:37

If thou art anxious for their guidance, yet Allah guideth not such as He leaves to stray, and there is none to help them.

12:103

Yet no faith will the greater part of mankind have, however, ardently thou dost desire it.[34]

88:21, 22

Therefore do thou give admonition, for thou art one to admonish. Thou art not one to manage (men's) affairs.

80:1–10

(The Prophet) frowned and turned away, Because there came to him the blind man (interrupting). But what could tell thee but that perchance he might grow (in spiritual understanding)?—Or that he might receive admonition, and the teaching might profit him? As to one who regards himself as self-sufficient, to him dost thou attend; though it is no blame to thee if he grow not (in spiritual understanding). But as to him who came to thee striving earnestly, and with fear (in his heart), Of him wast thou unmindful.

8:67–69

It is not fitting for a prophet that he should have prisoners of war until he hath thoroughly subdued the land. Ye look for the temporal goods of *this world; but Allah looketh to the Hereafter: And Allah is exalted in might, Wise.*

Had it not been for a previous ordainment from Allah, a severe penalty would have reached you for the (ransom) that ye took.

But (now) enjoy what ye took in war, lawful and good: but fear Allah: for Allah is Oft-Forgiving, Most Merciful.

17:73–75
And their purpose was to tempt thee away from that which We had revealed unto thee, to substitute in our name something quite different; (in that case), behold! They would certainly have made thee (their) friend!

And had We not given thee strength, thou wouldst nearly have inclined to them a little.

In that case We should have made thee taste an equal portion (of punishment) in this life, and an equal portion in death: and moreover thou wouldst have found none to help thee against Us!

18:110
Say: "I am but a man like yourselves, (but) the inspiration has come to me, that your Allah is one Allah: whoever expects to meet his Lord, let him work righteousness, and, in the worship of his Lord, admit no one as partner.

69:43–47
(This is) a Message sent down from the Lord of the Worlds. And if the messenger were to invent any sayings in Our name, We should certainly seize him by his right hand, And We should certainly then cut off the artery of his heart: Nor could any of you withhold him (from Our wrath).

5

The Piety of the Qur'an: Selected Texts

Introductory Remarks

THIS CHAPTER SEEKS TO DESCRIBE the basic spiritual and moral values that are enshrined in the Qur'an and underpin its prescriptions or injunctions, which, to my mind, are instrumental rules for promoting the said basic values. The basic values mentioned in the Qur'an are not peculiar or confined to Islam, but are more or less universal. However, it is as natural for a Muslim to term them Islamic/Qur'anic values as for a Christian to term them Christian values, or for a Hindu or Sikh to term them values of the Bhagwad Gita or values of the Granth Sahab, as the case may be.

It is also noteworthy that no value term has any fixed meaning or connotation inherent to it in the sense in which a common term for a physical object or entity has a more or less determinate connotation. Indeed, every value term has a large and wide spectrum of meaning and use relative to the basic thought and value system of a living autonomous culture. This means that value terms can be defined and their number can be fixed in different ways in different societies without involving any substantial difference to their overall value systems and the "quality of life" of their individual members. Thus, different religions or different segments within the same religion may use different terms to denote the same value. In any case what is of supreme importance is not how elegant or complete is the value system of any religion or society, but how much it is actually practiced by the members of any society.

Numerous Qur'anic verses command the faithful *"to believe in the Creator and act righteously."* In fact, the expression *"those who believe and act righteously"* is one of the most frequently used Qur'anic expressions, while only a very small number of verses can be called concrete injunctions, as such, that spell out "righteous action" in different life situations.

The reason why the concrete injunctions are so few in number is, to my mind, none other than the fact that instrumental rules to a very large extent are "situation specific," while basic spiritual and moral values are permanent though even they have to be redefined and re-understood afresh because of the never ceasing movement of life.

The historical Islamic tradition itself makes a distinction between "*deen*" and "*Shariah*" and also between "*farz*" and "*sunnah*." I submit that Muslim believers living in the modern age must pursue this line of thought to its logical conclusion. This means that while caring for and respecting the instrumental rules of the traditional *Shariah*, the focus of the Muslim believer must be on the spirit of Qur'anic piety and he or she should be very clear that "righteous action" means authentic commitment to basic Qur'anic values rather than rigid adherence to instrumental rules. It is imperative to realize that structural and technological changes in human society may well erode the therapeutic effectiveness of any stagnant value system (be it religious or secular) that does not allow periodic objective evaluations of its instrumental rules under the conditions actually prevailing.[1]

Core of the Qur'anic Piety

1. Living in the Presence of God: The Qur'anic ethos encourages and exhorts the Muslim to use, enjoy, and celebrate the good things of life and be thankful to the Creator for His blessings, which are the "Signs of God"—the wealth, bounty, and beauty of nature, the delights of sight, sound, the bliss of sleep, and the joy of lawful sexual union, the legitimate use of and power over the mineral, vegetable, and animal worlds, the pursuit of knowledge and wisdom, the pursuit of wealth and affluence through trade and commerce free from exploitation of the weak, the seeking of the pleasure of the Creator through submission to Divine Commands. Piety only means that the celebration of such Divine blessings should not make the believer forget the Divine source of these blessing and alienate him from his Creator and the concern for the much greater and more lasting joy and felicity of life after death. Here again, the *summum bonum* is not the pleasures of Paradise (though they are mentioned in the Qur'an itself), but rather the mystical "vision of God."

2. Fear of God: The expression "fear of God" frequently occurs in the Qur'anic value system. A comprehensive conceptual analysis makes it quite clear that the fear of God is not the fear of an external wrathful Creator, but the fear of the humble and diffident human soul of losing its mystical nearness and spiritual closeness to the Supreme Source of all creation through committing some lapse or error of judgment. The fear relates to the loss of Divine grace rather than to retribution or the terrors of hell. Fear, in this sense, is, thus, the ceaseless concern

not to deviate from "righteous action"; it is the mystical love of ever living in nearness to the Supreme Creator and Sustainer and the horror of alienation from the Source of one's own self and of all that exists.

3. Adoration of the Creator and Remembrance of Divine Blessings: This act reinforces the human love for God and lifts the weary and despairing traveler from the "vale of tears" to the "ocean of delight" and the "peace that passeth understanding."

4. Love of Truth: This means the unconditional concern to be truthful in all one's thoughts, words and deeds. It is the "mother of all virtues" (*umm al-fazael*). Being truthful does not mean actually "possessing" the truth or knowing all that is true; it means sincerity or total honesty in expressing what one authentically believes to be the case. If one can grasp the full "operational meaning" and practical significance of ever being truthful, all other spiritual values or human virtues would start sprouting in the depths of the human soul. The reason is that these virtues are, in the final analysis, the fruits growing upon the stem of truthfulness.

5. Universal Empathy and Concern for Equity: Empathy is an individual's ability to understand with accuracy how others perceive, feel, and respond to a situation or event of common concern. Equity is the concern to optimize the welfare of all concerned in any disputed matter when different parties have interests that conflict or clash with each other. Equity cannot be practiced if the individual's empathy is not all-inclusive. However, excessive empathy for all is in danger of degenerating into sentimental appeasement or populism if the individual is deficient in equity. Social justice requires a blend of the two and this is what the Qur'an affirms.

6. Universal Kindness and Forgiveness: Kindness is the spontaneous willing disposition to help and nurture others out of pure human feeling without any hope or expectation of return or reward from them. Forgiveness is the inner release or letting go of the hurt and pain caused to us by other's wrongdoing or hostility.

7. Generosity and Succor to the Weak: This is caring for the weak through willingly sharing with them one's possessions, wealth, and resources purely out of sympathy and loving concern for their welfare. The more it costs the giver in terms of self deprivation, the greater becomes the degree and the value of generosity.

8. Reverence for Parents: One's parents are the human source of one's coming into existence and survival. The debt of gratitude children owe to their parents is, indeed, irreparable. Reverence for and service to the parents, especially in their old age, is gratitude and loyalty at the highest level.

9. Mutual Respect and Fidelity to the Spouse: If parents be the human creators and sustainers of their progeny, spouses are the mutual caretakers of

psycho-physical health, comfort, companionship, the joy of total communion, solace, and inspiration. Deception, hypocrisy, or breach of faith, in any sense, is suicide of the spirit.

10. Patience and Contentment: Patience is not passivity but the preserving of equanimity at the ups and downs of life. Patience does not imply or involve the giving up or dilution of striving but faith and trust in Divine Providence. Contentment is willing acceptance of the limits of one's endowments without turning jealous of others better endowed or placed in life than us.

11. Self-Control: Any unchecked passion, drive, or impulse, be it anger, revenge, hatred, fear, or sexual lust, harms both agent and victim and society as a whole. Even if the person carried away by passion escapes visible harm to himself, he suffers from the permanent mutilation of the spirit unless he redeems himself through genuine repentance and inner reformation.

12. Humility: This is awareness of the basic truth that the individual, no matter how great his gifts, achievements, wealth, power, and glory at any point of time, at the very next moment without his consent, nay, even without any notice or intimation, may be suddenly deprived of them all. Hubris! Thy name is Satan.

13. Quest for ego-transcendence: This complements and rounds off the value of humility. It is the conscious embracing of the death of the flame of earthly life and authentically rejoicing at the faith that every created object will perish except the "Countenance of the Lord." The quest for transcendence is the anticipated spiritual joy at the ego's return to the inscrutable Source of all creation some of whom might be blessed and rewarded with the "vision of God." However, only the Creator knows what will then happen.

14. Authentic Integrity: This is self-awareness combined with the acceptance of a single standard or criterion for evaluating or judging human agents including oneself. One may believe that one has attained this extremely high level, but this could well be his or her fond illusion. God, alone, knows the full truth. He is the knower of the seen and the unseen, and of the deepest secrets of the human heart.

Selected Texts from the Qur'an

1:1–7
Praise be to Allah, the Cherisher and Sustainer of the worlds; Merciful, Master of the Day of Judgment. Thee do we worship, and Thine aid we seek. Show us the straight way, The way of those on whom Thou hast bestowed Thy Grace, those whose (portion) is not wrath, and who go not astray.[2]

2:177

It is not righteousness that ye turn your faces toward East or West; but it is righteousness—to believe in Allah and the Last Day, and the Angels, and the Book, and the Messengers; to spend of your substance, out of love for Him, for your kin, for orphans, for the needy, for the wayfarer, for those who ask, and for the ransom of slaves; to be steadfast in prayer, and practice regular charity; to fulfill the contracts which ye have made; and to be firm and patient, in pain (or suffering) and adversity, and throughout all periods of panic. Such are the people of truth, the Allah-fearing.[3]

2:186

When My servants ask thee concerning Me, I am indeed close (to them): I listen to the prayer of every suppliant when he calleth on Me: let them also, with a will, listen to My call, and believe in Me: that they may walk in the right way.

3:92

By no means shall ye attain righteousness unless ye give (freely) of that which ye love; and whatever ye give, of a truth Allah knoweth it well.

3:191

Men who celebrate the praises of Allah, standing, sitting, and lying down on their sides, and contemplate the (wonders of) creation in the heavens and the earth (with the thought): "Our Lord! Not for naught hast Thou created (all) this! Glory to Thee! Give us salvation from the penalty of the Fire."[4]

4:59

O ye who believe! Obey Allah and obey the Messenger, and those charged with authority among you. If ye differ in anything among yourselves, refer it to Allah and his Messenger, if ye do believe in Allah and the Last day: that is best and most suitable for final determination.

33:56

Allah and His angels send blessings on the Prophet: O ye that believe! Send ye blessings on him, and salute him with all respect.

7:200, 201

If a suggestion from Satan assails thy (mind), seek refuge with Allah; for He heareth and knoweth (all things).

Those who fear Allah, when a thought from Satan assaults them, bring Allah to remembrance, when lo! They see (aright).

3:175
It is only the Evil One that suggests to you the fear of his votaries: be ye not afraid of them, but fear Me, if ye have Faith.

64:14
O ye who believe! Truly among your wives and your children are (some that are) enemies to yourselves: so beware of them! But if ye forgive and overlook, and cover up (their faults), verily Allah is Oft-Forgiving, Most Merciful.[5]

7:205
And do thou (O reader!) bring thy Lord to remembrance in thy (very) soul, with humility and reverence, without loudness in words in the mornings and evenings; and be not thou of those who are unheedful.

8:29
O ye who believe! If ye fear Allah He will grant you a criterion (to judge between right and wrong), remove from you (all) evil (that may afflict) you, and forgive you: for Allah is the Lord of grace unbounded.[6]

9:72
Allah hath promised to believers, men and women, Gardens under which rivers flow, to dwell therein, and beautiful mansions in Gardens of everlasting bliss. But the greatest bliss is the Good Pleasure of Allah: that is the supreme felicity.

9:109, 110
Which then is best?—he that layeth his foundation on piety to Allah and His Good Pleasure?—or he that layeth his foundation on an undermined sand-cliff ready to crumble to pieces? And it doth crumble to pieces with him, into the fire of hell. And Allah guideth not People that do wrong.

The foundation of those who so build is never free from suspicion and shakiness in their hearts, until their hearts are cut to pieces. And Allah is All-Knowing, Wise.

2:256

Let there be no compulsion in religion: Truth stands out clear from Error: whoever rejects Evil and believes in Allah hath grasped the most trustworthy handhold, that never breaks, and Allah heareth and knoweth all things.[7]

30:30–32

So set thy face steadily and truly to the Faith: (establish) Allah's handiwork according to the pattern on which He has made mankind: no change (let there be) in the work (wrought) by Allah: that is the standard Religion, but most among mankind understand not. Turn ye back in repentance to Him, and fear Him: establish regular prayers, and be not ye among those who join gods with Allah—Those who split up their Religion and become (mere) sects—each party rejoicing in that which is with itself![8]

31:14

And We have enjoined on man (to be good) to his parents: in travail upon travail did his mother bear him, and in years twain was his weaning: (hear the command), "Show gratitude to Me and to thy parents: To Me is (thy final) Goal."

3:134

Those who spend (freely), whether in prosperity, or in adversity; who restrain anger, and pardon (all) men—for Allah loves those who do good...[9]

109:4–6

And I will not worship that which ye have been wont to worship. Nor will ye worship that which I worship. To you be your way, and to me mine.[10]

22:36, 37

The sacrificial camels We have made for you as among the symbols from Allah: in them is (much) good for you: then pronounce the name of Allah over them as they line up (for sacrifice): when they are down on their sides (after slaughter), eat ye thereof, and feed such as (beg not but) live in contentment, and such as beg with due humility: thus have We made animals subject to you, that ye may be grateful. It is not their meat or their blood that reaches Allah: it is your piety that reaches Him: He has thus made them subject to you, that ye may glorify Allah for His guidance to you: and proclaim the Good News to all who do right.

2:285, 286

The Messenger believeth in what hath been revealed to him from his Lord, as do the men of faith. Each one (of them) believeth in Allah, His angels, His Books, and His Messengers. "We make no distinction (they say) between one and another of His Messengers." And they say: "We hear, and we obey: (we seek) Thy forgiveness, our Lord, and to Thee is the end of all journeys." On no soul doth Allah place a burden greater than it can bear. It gets every good that it earns, and it suffers every ill that it earns. (Pray) "Our Lord! Condemn us not if we forget or fall into error; our Lord! Lay not on us a burden like that which Thou didst lay on those before us; our Lord! Lay not on us a burden greater than we have strength to bear. Blot our sins, and grant us forgiveness. Have mercy on us. Thou art our Protector; help us against those who stand against Faith."[11]

113:1–5

Say: I seek refuge with the Lord of the Dawn, From the mischief of created things; From the mischief of Darkness as it overspreads; From the mischief of those that practice secret arts; And from the mischief of the envious one as he practices envy.

114:1–6

Say: I seek refuge with the Lord and Cherisher of Mankind, The King (or Ruler) of Mankind, The God (or Judge) of Mankind—From the mischief of the Whisperer (of Evil), who withdraws (after his whisper)— (The same) who whispers into the hearts of Mankind—Among Jinns and among Men.

2:193

And fight them on until there is no more tumult or oppression, and there prevail justice and faith in Allah; but if they cease, let there be no hostility except to those who practice oppression.[12]

2:262

Those who spend their substance in the cause of Allah, and follow not up their gifts with reminders of their generosity or with injury,—for *them their reward is with their Lord: on them shall be no fear, nor shall they grieve.*

2:263
Kind words and the covering of faults are better than charity followed by injury. Allah is free of all wants, and He is Most-Forbearing.

2:264
O ye who believe! Cancel not your charity by reminders of your generosity or by injury,—like those who spend their substance to be seen of men, but believe neither in Allah nor in the Last Day. They are in parable like a hard, barren rock, on which is a little soil: on it falls heavy rain, which leaves it (just) a bare stone. They will be able to do nothing with aught they have earned. And Allah guideth not those who reject faith.[13]

2:271
If ye disclose (acts of) charity, even so it is well, but if ye conceal them, and make them reach those (really) in need, that is best for you: It will remove from you some of your (stains of) evil. And Allah is well-acquainted with what ye do.

2:272
It is not required of thee (O Messenger), to set them on the right path, but Allah sets on the right path whom He pleaseth. Whatever of good ye give benefits your own souls, and ye shall only do so seeking the "Face" of Allah. Whatever good ye give, shall be rendered back to you, and ye shall not be dealt with unjustly.

49:11
O ye who believe! Let not some men among you laugh at others: It may be that the (latter) are better than the (former): Nor let some women laugh at others: It may be that the (latter) are better than the (former): Nor defame nor be sarcastic to each other, nor call each other by (offensive) nicknames: Ill-seeming is a name connoting wickedness, (to be used of one) after he has believed: And those who do not desist are (indeed) doing wrong.[14]

49:12
O ye who believe! Avoid suspicion as much (as possible): for suspicion in some cases is a sin: And spy not on each other behind their backs.

Would any of you like to eat the flesh of his dead brother? Nay, ye would abhor it...But fear Allah: For Allah is Oft-Returning, Most Merciful.[15]

4:69

All who obey Allah and the messenger are in the company of those on whom is the Grace of Allah,— of the prophets (who teach), the sincere (lovers of Truth), the witnesses (who testify), and the Righteous (who do good): Ah! What a beautiful fellowship![16]

33:21

Ye have indeed in the Messenger of Allah a beautiful pattern (of conduct) for any one whose hope is in Allah and the Final Day, and who engages much in the praise of Allah.[17]

7:26

O ye Children of Adam! We have bestowed raiment upon you to cover your shame, as well as to be an adornment to you. But the raiment of righteousness,—that is the best. Such are among the Signs of Allah, that they may receive admonition![18]

7:40

To those who reject Our signs and treat them with arrogance, no opening will there be of the gates of heaven, nor will they enter the garden, until the camel can pass through the eye of the needle: Such is Our reward for those in sin.[19]

3:185

Every soul shall have a taste of death: And only on the Day of Judgment shall you be paid your full recompense. Only he who is saved far from the Fire and admitted to the Garden will have attained the object (of Life): For the life of this world is but goods and chattels of deception.[20]

3:186

Ye shall certainly be tried and tested in your possessions and in your personal selves; and ye shall certainly Hear much that will grieve you, from those who received the Book before you and from those who worship many gods. But if ye persevere patiently, and guard against evil,— then that will be a determining factor in all affairs.[21]

61:2, 3

O ye who believe! Why say ye that which ye do not? Grievously odious is it in the sight of Allah that ye say that which ye do not.

28:50

But if they hearken not to thee, know that they only follow their own lusts: and who is more astray than one who follows his own lusts, devoid of guidance from Allah? For Allah guides not people given to wrongdoing.

35:18

Nor can a bearer of burdens bear another's burdens if one heavily laden should call another to (bear) his load. Not the least portion of it can be carried (by the other). Even though he be nearly related. Thou canst but admonish such as fear their Lord unseen and establish regular prayer. And whoever purifies himself does so for the benefit of his own soul; and the destination (of all) is to Allah.[22]

31:33

O mankind! Do your duty to your Lord, and fear (the coming of) a Day when no father can avail aught for his son, nor a son avail aught for his father. Verily, the promise of Allah is true: let not then this present life deceive you, nor let the chief Deceiver deceive you about Allah.

39:53

Say: "O my Servants who have transgressed against their souls! Despair not of the Mercy of Allah: for Allah forgives all sins: for He is Oft-Forgiving, Most Merciful."

4:79

Whatever good, (O man!) happens to thee, is from Allah; but whatever evil happens to thee, is from thy (own) soul. And We have sent thee as a messenger to (instruct) mankind. And enough is Allah for a witness.[23]

31:22

Whoever submits his whole self to Allah, and is a doer of good, has grasped indeed the most trustworthy hand hold: and with Allah rests the End and Decision of (all) affairs.

4:10

Those who unjustly eat up the property of orphans, eat up a Fire into their own bodies: They will soon be enduring a Blazing Fire![24]

83:1–3

Woe to those that deal in fraud,—Those who, when they have to receive by measure from men, exact full measure, But when they have to give by measure or weight to men, give less than due.[25]

22:11

There are among men some who serve Allah, as it were, on the verge: if good befalls them, they are, therewith, well-content; but if a trial comes to them, they turn on their faces: they lose both this world and the Hereafter: that is loss for all to see!

90:12–18

And what will explain to thee the path that is steep?—(It is) freeing the bondman; Or the giving of food in a day of privation to the orphan with claims of relationship, Or to the indigent (down) in the dust. Then will he be of those who believe, and enjoin patience, (constancy, and self-restraint), and enjoin deeds of kindness and compassion. Such are the Companions of the Right Hand.[26]

107:1–7

Seest thou one who denies the Judgment (to come)? Then such is the (man) who repulses the orphan (with harshness), And encourages not the feeding of the indigent. So woe to the worshippers Who are neglectful of their prayers, Those who (want but) to be seen (of men), But refuse (to supply) (even) neighborly needs.[27]

91:7–10

By the Soul, and the proportion and order given to it; And its enlightenment as to its wrong and its right;—Truly he succeeds that purifies it, And he fails that corrupts it![28]

26:221–227

Shall I inform you, (O people!), on whom it is that the evil ones descend? They descend on every lying, wicked person, (Into whose ears) they pour hearsay vanities, and most of them are liars. And the Poets,—It is those straying in Evil, who follow them: Seest thou not that they wander distracted in every valley?—And that they say what they practice not?—Except those who believe, work righteousness, engage much in the remembrance of Allah, and defend themselves only after they are unjustly attacked. And soon will the unjust assailants know what vicissitudes their affairs will take![29]

2:124
And remember that Abraham was tried by his Lord with certain commands, which he fulfilled: He said: "I will make thee an Imam to the Nations." He pleaded: "And also (Imams) from my offspring!" He answered: "But My Promise is not within the reach of evil doers."[30]

2:190–193
Fight in the cause of Allah those who fight you, but do not transgress limits; for Allah loveth not transgressors. And slay them wherever ye catch them, and turn them out from where they have turned you out; for tumult and oppression are worse than slaughter; but fight them not at the Sacred Mosque, unless they (first) fight you there; but if they fight you, slay them. Such is the reward of those who suppress faith. But if they cease, Allah is Oft-Forgiving, Most Merciful. And fight them on until there is no more tumult or oppression, and there prevail justice and faith in Allah; but if they cease, let there be no hostility except to those who practice oppression.[31]

6

The Injunctions
of the Qur'an

Introductory Remarks

THE TOTAL NUMBER OF QUR'ANIC VERSES is (approximately) 6,200 and out of these a rather small number are injunctions or specific prescriptions. These injunctions are scattered in several *surahs*, but mostly, they are found in *surahs* revealed at Medina in the last ten years of the Prophetic mission. These injunctions cover sacramental regulations (*ibadat*), and several aspects of social ethics (*moamilat*). The latter deal with rules of gender ethics, marriage and divorce, inheritance, food regulations, social and economic issues, and penalties for a few crimes or evil deeds. Some injunctions are far more specific or detailed than others. As explained in Chapter 3, a large portion of the Qur'anic verses perform mixed semantic functions. This makes it very difficult and also unnecessary to give an exact number of the different functional types of the verses. However, the number of verses that are "hard" injunctions is very small indeed. Thus, the Qur'an is a living source of moral inspiration and guidance for the Muslim believer rather than a "complete specific code of laws."

The breakup number of verses in different categories mentioned above is (approximately) as follows: sacramental regulations—16; rules of gender ethics—9; rules of marriage and divorce—18; rules of inheritance—4; food regulations—7; social and economic issues—21; penalties—5. The total of the above categories of verses comes to about eighty. The remaining number of the (approximately) 120 injunctive verses are so general that they practically fall in the category of evaluations and exhortations. The number of "hard" injunctive verses is, thus, infinitesimally small as compared to "soft" injunctions, which exhort more than they prescribe. However, the basic Qur'anic injunction that believers should follow "the example of the Prophet" ﷺ effectively serves to give practical and concrete content to the relatively generalized guidance found in the Qur'an. This is how the Islamic tradition soon led to the theory and practice of "bracketing the Book and the Example" as severally and jointly binding (in equal measure) upon the believers. This practice is, perhaps, the main factor that blurred or watered down the distinction between intrinsic values and instrumental rules in the great Islamic tradition. This position remains the deep and living faith of Islamic orthodoxy dispersed in every part of the globe.

The Distinction between Intrinsic Values and Instrumental Rules

A Qur'anic injunction (for a believer) is, by definition, a Divine command and is, therefore, mandatory. It is perfectly natural and logical (for a Muslim believer) to regard each and every Qur'anic injunction as mandatory. However, the distinction between intrinsic values and instrumental rules is also undeniable and becomes transparently clear after a little reflection. To my mind, this distinction holds good even in the case of the Qur'anic value system. The question arises, how would the believer know whether a particular Qur'anic injunction refers to intrinsic values or to instrumental rules? Well, reflective analysis of the Qur'anic text and its situational context, on the one hand, and the conceptual analysis of the spiritual or moral values concerned, on the other, suffice to clarify whether the Qur'anic injunction refers to a basic value or to an instrumental rule. Thus, Qur'anic verses, which command the believer to be truthful, to do one's duty, to be compassionate, to judge impartially, to weigh with the right measure, to respect all life, to be kind and loving, to be generous and forgiving, to be modest and sexually chaste, and so on and so forth, refer to intrinsic values and enunciate the foundational core of the permanent Qur'anic value system. On the other hand, verses, which prescribe or spell out details, refer to instrumental rules that (by the very nature of the case) are variables dependent upon specific conditions of human life in the broadest sense. Intrinsic values never lose their existential grip and power upon the human conscience, while instrumental rules may well-lose their optimum efficacy in the natural course or flux of history.[1]

Admittedly, the Qur'an repeatedly exhorts Muslims to obey the Prophet ﷺ and follow his example. But what does "following the example of the Prophet" ﷺ mean in operational terms? Does it mean "replicating in the literal sense" the daily practice and conduct of the Prophet ﷺ? The extremists among the more orthodox, as is well-known, were opposed to photography, cinema, the microphone, and earlier on even to translating and printing the Qur'an as "satanic" innovations. Though with the passage of time the traditionalists have relented on their original stand, they still resist any change or innovation in the social, economic, legal, and cultural matters on the ground that this implies deviating from the Prophet's ﷺ

example. These quarters, thus, also continue to oppose secular democracy, gender equality, family planning, women's higher education, and so on.[2]

The basic logic of the ultra conservative section was that the "Word of God" was final and its proper or real meaning had already been established by the Prophet ﷺ himself in the form of the *Shariah*. As long as the Prophet ﷺ lived, it was, in theory, possible that a new or fresh Qur'anic revelation could modify an earlier one because of some radical change in the objective ground realities the original revelation had sought to address. Indeed, this did happen a few times. But this possibility no longer remained after his passing away. The classical Islamic jurists did address themselves to this problem, and they carefully formulated a well-thought-out procedure for modifying or adapting the *Shariah* to the new situation. Logically sound as was their position, they failed to make a clear distinction between basic intrinsic values and instrumental rules, and also overlooked the crucial fact that, while some Qur'anic injunctions deal with basic values, others deal with instrumental rules.

To my mind the correct interpretation of "following the Prophet's example" ﷺ is that the Muslim believer be actively committed to the spirit of the basic values of the Qur'an exemplified in the actions of the Prophet ﷺ rather than in the instrumental rules framed by the Prophet ﷺ or even mentioned in the Qur'an in view of the prevailing conditions of life in 7th century Arab society. These instrumental rules are, unavoidably, "space-time bounded cultural constructs" that need ceaseless review and revision in the light of human experience if we want to protect and augment their capacity to serve the permanently valid spiritual values of the Qur'an exemplified in the actions of the Prophet ﷺ.

The practical corollary of accepting the above distinction between intrinsic values and instrumental rules may be summed up as follows: if due to changes in the human situation (due to various factors) it becomes quite clear that literal obedience to any instrumental rule has become counter-productive of the intrinsic value it was meant to preserve or promote, while suitably modifying the instrumental rule renders it a more effective promoter of the intrinsic or basic value, then "reflective obedience" to the Divine injunction is a higher form of obedience or piety than "literal obedience" to the original rule. Among the closest companions of the Prophet ﷺ, the second Caliph, Umar, actually practiced this approach.

Muslims must seriously ponder over the question why sizeable Muslim quarters have a rather blurred idea of the distinction between intrinsic values and instrumental rules. Perhaps, they reason that since every portion of the Qur'an is "the Word of God" it is unconditionally true and binding on the believer without any "ifs and buts." This approach to the Qur'an is quite natural and understandable. While it is true, it misses the whole truth, since it does not take into account the crucial distinction between intrinsic values and instrumental rules, as mentioned above. The traditional position results in a closed morality and legality, while ceaseless change is the life breath of social reality. Knowledge, wisdom, and morality all grow and develop in time just like rocks, plants, and other organisms. Perfection is a regulative ideal, never a fixed feature or fact. Some basic values remain constant in the flux of history, but their concrete forms cannot escape change. New nuances and dimensions, inevitably, emerge that enrich and deepen the full scope and connotation of the words or terms that refer to the basic "value constants." Making a clear and conscious distinction between intrinsic values and instrumental rules will lead to a ceaseless search for higher and still higher levels of perfection that, however, will ever elude humans. Instrumental rules will be born and then die out, but basic values will survive in some form or the other. Instrumental rules will have to pass the test of human experience for determining their efficacy to promote the desired values in the ever-growing framework of factual knowledge without any frontiers of race, religion, or region. This will require creative reflection and utter humility in the face of the inscrutable mystery of the cosmos. The Qur'an exhorts the entire human race to do so.

Muslims must reflect on the deeper significance of the Qur'anic verse that when the pre-human angelic creation expressed their concern at the Lord's disclosure to them of the Divine plan to endow humankind with reason and freedom of choice (which gifts had been denied to the angels themselves), God rejected their apprehensions that this would lead to great evils. This implies, in other words, that the capacity of analytical reason and spiritual autonomy are Divine blessings to humankind, despite involving the risk of evil. Humans have atrociously misused and abused these gifts in the course of history, but the truly virtuous among humankind can and do use them in the service of the Creator.[3]

May I close this section on a beautiful anecdote I heard from a remarkable Hindu social reformer and freedom fighter of modern India, Raja Mahendra Pratap (d. CE 1979) whom I was privileged to know personally. A saint going on a long pilgrimage to a distant place instructed his very dutiful son to water the house plants, without fail, twice daily at specified times. When the saint returned home after several months, he found that all the plants had died. What happened was that when the saint left home it was the peak of dry summer, but when he returned, it was the end of a long and wet rainy season. The son's literal obedience to his father's orders had led to the overwatering of the plants.[4]

The Qur'anic Approach to Gender Justice

Women form one half of humanity. Yet all religions have always given greater rights and privileges to the male. They regard the male as the superordinate and the female as the subordinate term in all interpersonal relations. For the first time in history, the modern Western metareligious value system (which is still evolving) has projected the ideal of complete polymorphous gender equality. This implies equal dignity of the sexes, quite irrespective of all natural biological and psycho-biological differences, and complete equality of opportunity and human rights in all spheres of human activity.

It seems to me that the Qur'anic value system is weighted in favor of the male in several respects. For instance, the share of the female in family inheritance is half the share of the male, the weight of the evidence of a female witness is less than a male, she does not have the right of unconditional divorce of her spouse, the female, unlike the male, is not permitted polygamy, she is not the natural guardian of her children and so on. Yet, the fact is that, among all the different world religions, the Qur'anic value system comes nearest to the modern concept of gender equality. For instance, it grants woman, single or married, to own, administer, and transfer property, the full freedom of entering into marriage contracts comprising stipulations and conditions of her own choice, and even to obtain divorce from her lawfully married husband with his consent, while no other religious tradition permits any such freedom of action even remotely similar to the aforementioned. Though women's empowerment in the above senses did not amount to complete gender equality, intellectually honest observers must concede that the Qur'anic value system was a great advance on the pre-Islamic social morality in the direction of the modern ideal. Yet, the Qur'anic idea of gender justice (in the operative sense) cannot be equated with absolute "polymorphous" gender equality (in the modern sense).

The Qur'anic prescriptions that discriminate against the female half of humanity, however, do not, necessarily, imply that the Qur'an prohibits women, *for all times to come*, from enjoying complete equality of status with men. How Muslim believers judge what is prohibited and what is permissible or desirable *at the present stage of human development* will depend on one's antecedent view in regard to the correct method of interpreting the prescriptive texts of the Qur'an, on one hand, and, on the other, an awareness of the distinction between the core fundamental spiritual and moral values of the Qur'an and the secondary or tertiary rules of conduct the Qur'an prescribed, under the conditions of Arab society in the 7th century, for realizing those values. I submit, the Muslim believer can, justifiably, hold that believers should not merely *adhere to* Qur'anic values and rules but *also promote and develop* them in the ever-changing human situation. Values develop not only in the sense of extension but also in the sense of intension, or inner depth. Development in the latter sense often requires a constructive modification of the existing rules or regulations that are a legacy from the past. To change an instrumental rule for the sake of increasing its effectiveness to promote the basic intrinsic value it was designed to realize, in the first instance, should not be regarded as a violation or rejection of the instrumental rule but, in fact, its more effective application under changed conditions, no matter how the change may have come about.[5]

Now what are the basic features of the Qur'anic value system in regard to sex morality and the place of women in society or their rights and duties in general? To my mind, the relevant Qur'anic texts and the Prophet's ﷺ example affirm the following values: mutual modesty, chastity, the principled regulation of the sexual instinct through free transparent contract, mutual respect, fidelity, and loyalty. Rape and irresponsible sex (even if consensual) without transparent public acknowledgment are major disvalues or vices. These values and disvalues apply in equal measure to both the sexes. However, in view of some obvious psycho-biological differences between the male and the female of the human species, the Qur'an does give the male a measure of greater freedom than to the female. The Qur'an also prohibits all homosexual contracts. These broad parameters of the Qur'an leave the Muslim believer with ample freedom to choose fresh patterns of dress and social and cultural behavior. In short, the Qur'anic value system, by itself, does not discriminate against women, but stipulates some qualifications (as an "affirmative" rather than discriminatory, measure) in applying an essentially common standard of sexual modesty for both men and women.

Muslim societies, however, have interpreted the Qur'anic ideal of sexual modesty in different ways. Thus, the extreme segregation of the sexes that prevails in conservative Muslim quarters, the various styles of "hijab" enforced on women, the multiple restrictions on women's rights and opportunities of self-realization, the restrictions on their free movement, etc., are not integral parts of the basic Qur'anic value system, but rather ill-considered interpretations of the Qur'anic texts or the result of ethnic customs and local practices. The discrimination against women in regard to their share in inheritance or human rights is another matter, which will be dealt with separately.

Complete gender equality, in the sense of equality of humanistic dignity and of consideration, is an ethical axiom for the modern mind. A believing Muslim as I am, I would be the last person to question this axiom. However, modern psychology of sex itself points out the difference between male and female sexuality and none should brush aside the implications of careful empirical research. Female sexuality is inextricably intertwined with the maternal instinct to give and receive love and care. As a consequence sexual interest and activity is never, or only seldom, a simple reflex physiological process. Male sexuality, on the other hand, is pretty much different. It seems the designed semi-nude exposure of the female body (that became the acme of women's fashion in the West after World War I and remains so to date) tends to propel the male onlooker into the world of unconscious erotic fancies. This is bound to devalue the sanctity and seriousness of the sexual bond and lead to a lighthearted disjunction between sexual engagement and the loving care and concern for one's sex partner. To my mind, this will amount to a greater loss for the female. I submit the Qur'anic value system takes into account these subtle realities. Muslim believers must respect them, but subject all instrumental rules to a continuing review in the ever-changing human situation.

Muslim believers must realize that they are fully competent and justified in revising all human interpretations of the basic Qur'anic values or the "Word of God." What is crucially important and desirable is that Muslims surrender their autonomous judgment neither to the traditional theologian or jurist, nor to the contemporary "Boston Brahmans" of the West. To my mind, modern Western permissiveness in sexual expression and the designed public display of the feminine body, as the acme of fashion, is as off-balance as is the traditional Muslim code of "*hijab*." Even if it be the case that the female quite innocently enjoys attracting male attention (as a part of nature's strategy to preserve the species), the bold and provocative public display of the feminine body cannot but trigger latent erotic fancies and associations in the male psyche, howsoever "gentlemanly" and "correct" his conduct might remain due to cultural conditioning. The fact is that, the continual titillation of the senses in the course of daily interpersonal contacts or through intrusive advertising cannot but reduce the sanctity and beauty of the sexual experience to mere physical sensationalism and a crude hedonism. The same remarks apply to the overt celebration of homosexuality.

Let me now turn to the theme of gender discrimination in the Qur'an in regard to female civil and human rights. Islamic apologetics on this issue do not at all convince me. To my mind, social distributive justice requires equal share of the male and female progeny in family inheritance, equal status in the eyes of law, equal human rights, and equal opportunities of self-realization. No matter how hard I try to justify the concerned Qur'anic prescriptions or regulations in respect of these matters, I cannot overcome my "conscientious objection" to giving to my daughter half of what I give to my son, or holding her testimony of less worth than her brother's and so on. The same remarks apply to the Sunni Islamic law of inheritance, which drastically reduces the share of daughters when the deceased has no male issue. In such cases, the daughter's normal share of one half of the son's gets further reduced. It is significant that the Shia Islamic law in this regard seems very equitable.

To my mind, these and similar Qur'anic texts do *not* refer to intrinsic values but belong to the category of instrumental rules whose validity is not absolute but conditional. Human dignity or status does not depend upon gender but upon the quality of life one attains through the ceaseless creative pursuit of values. Moreover, basic values grow and develop through the flowering of fresh dimensions on their stem, as mentioned previously. And Muslims must welcome, not obstruct, growth of values if they really care for Islam. This maxim applies equally to all other conceptual or cultural systems, whether religious or secular.

All thought and value systems (including religions) must ceaselessly grow in the organic sense for their effective survival in human society. The adherents themselves must review what may well be termed "deadwood" in the self-understanding of the creed and the morality of each religious tradition and what it means to be a good follower of the tradition concerned. Muslims have done this before several times. But they have not much traveled on this road, despite the clear and resounding Qur'anic exhortation to all believers to reflect on nature and seek wisdom. The Muslim community has "reduced" the Qur'anic stress on "righteous action" to unquestioning and ungrudging conformity to juristic interpretations of right and wrong as affirmed by the great *Imams* of the early period. In what follows, I shall mention, by way of illustration, a few beliefs I regard as "dead wood" in the self-understanding of Islam as a creed and as a concrete way of life.

1. *Shariah* is an all embracing and seamless body of canon law applicable to every sphere of individual and collective life. The true Muslim must actively strive to follow the *Shariah* in every individual or collective matter. Muslims living in an Islamic state must monitor the policies and activities of the state and censor the rulers if they violate the canon law in force. Muslims who live in a non-Muslim state must strive through rational persuasion and peaceful methods to convert it into an Islamic state. In any case, they must demand that the law courts administer *Shariah* law when the parties concerned are Muslim.

2. Muslims alone will attain salvation and enter heaven after undergoing proper penance and just suffering for their sins. Non-Muslims will be denied salvation and entry into heaven, though their good deeds in this world will be suitably rewarded.

3. Any Muslim living in an Islamic state who renounces Islam publicly and either converts to some other religion or rejects all religions should be given some time to reconsider his decision. If he persists, he becomes an apostate and must be executed.

4. Married persons who commit adultery should be stoned to death. All other *Shariah* penalties for sins or crimes must be strictly enforced, no matter what the findings of modern penology and sociology may be.

5. Muslims should keep minimum contacts with other communities and not fully trust them in preference to Muslims.

6. The charging or giving of interest on any money transaction is a violation of Qur'anic injunctions. Insurance also is sinful.

7. All talk of gender justice or equality of the sexes that go beyond the letter of the Qur'anic injunctions is anti-Islam.

8. The Creator has the power to sustain all creation without limit, and there is no need whatsoever for human intervention or efforts to regulate the growth of population.

9. Marriage is permissible between a male Muslim believer and a woman of the "people of the Book," but not between a female Muslim believer and a man of the "people of the Book."

10. A Muslim believer, who irrevocably divorces his wife, cannot remarry her at a later stage unless she marries another person and is irrevocably divorced by him.

11. A woman who charges a man of sexual assault will not get any relief but be presumed to be guilty of perjury unless four witnesses testify and corroborate the charge.

Out of the above eleven items (I have termed as "dead wood") only item No. 10 clearly confirms to the letter of the Qur'an. It is clear that the rest are either not stated or not necessarily implied by Qur'anic texts; they merely reflect the perceptions or interpretations of some distinguished Muslim jurists who reflected the "spirit of the age." I really wonder how "dated" human perceptions and opinions of individuals (however learned and sincere) could have been equated with the timeless values embedded in the Qur'an.[6]

Even in the case of item 10, which puts a severe constraint on "easy" remarriage with one's ex-wife, Muslim jurists themselves aver that the purpose was to counter the prevailing Arab custom of unilaterally divorcing one's wife without much thought or consideration to the wishes of the spouse, and then equally impulsively remarrying her at the pleasure of the male. Likewise, in the case of item 6, which prohibits usury, the purpose was to counter rich money lenders from charging exorbitantly on "distress loans" that committed the borrower to an extended term of "bonded labor" in cases of default. In other words, the term, "usury" in the Qur'anic and Biblical age had a, substantially, different (both qualitatively and quantitatively) meaning or "social significance" than from the word "interest" in modern economic parlance.

In all humility, therefore, I submit that the continuing review of the "instrumental rules," be they of Qur'anic origin, or part of the *Shariah*, be deemed as "creative fidelity" to the "Word of God," and "reflective obedience" to the *Shariah* (*bidat-e-husna*), not as their violation.

Candid Reflections on Some Practical Issues

The following brief observations on some topical themes and controversial issues that face Muslims living in the modern world are meant to round off the basic thrust and import of my own paradigm of Qur'anic Islam. I do desire that my candid submissions be widely considered and debated without fear or favor. Only when Muslims participate in free discussion, without any fear or threat from any quarter, whatsoever, will Muslim society throw up, in sufficient numbers, men and women having the clarity, courage, and integrity required to bring about lasting peace for the entire human family.

Spirituality, Religion, and Superstition

One often hears that so and so is very religious, or that he is an atheist. An amazing confusion and ambiguity lies concealed in such language. A person who is strongly critical of any organized religion or "Church," may be a deeply religious person in the sense of giving central importance to spirituality rather than to mere morality or to mere creed. Likewise, a person may think that he is an atheist and others may also believe that he is an atheist, when the plain truth is that he cannot honestly accept the particular conception of God or "*Theos*" current in his milieu. In other words he rejects a specific idea, or mental image of God, but is very sensitive and alive to "the sense of Divine Mystery" and is passionately drawn to a supreme Power that "creates" and sustains the Universe but cannot be further conceptualized through any creed. He honestly believes that "*there are more things in heaven and earth than are dreamt of in Horatio's philosophy,*" or, for that matter, in modern science. Still further, a person may believe he is very religious when the plain truth is that he is mighty afraid of omens, curses, witchcraft, the evil eye, and demons, etc., and seeks security and protection against them with the help of ritualistic practices or rites prescribed by some organized group or "holy personage."

Man reaches the level of spirituality when the simple goodness of the heart and universal kindness and compassion get impregnated with the gift of Divine grace or a mysterious inner purification beyond human effort and control. Spirituality, like music, beauty, intelligence, and the simple goodness of heart cuts across all creeds or religions in the narrow sense. Some would like to say that, to be religious, in the best sense, is to be spiritual, or that true religion is the same as spirituality. All this is pure semantics. Every religion admits of several versions of conceptual refinement and also of different levels of spirituality. Thus, I hold a *Manuvadi* Hindu to be at a lower level than a *Vedantic* Hindu. Likewise, all Muslims are not at the same level. Moreover, it is futile to grade religions, in the abstract, in view of the multiplicity of levels within each religion.

Superstitions come easily and naturally to the human family because infantile fears and illusions tend to persist in adult life. The belief in lucky numbers, incantations, charms, tombs, miracle performers, controller of demons, and wielders of supernatural powers, etc., are all different illustrations of this natural tendency. The belief in an all-powerful Divine Father or Mother also comes easily to the child when he realizes the limitations of his earthly father and mother. Religion in the sense of a body of theological doctrines also comes about easily due to cultural conditioning or indoctrination of the child. Spirituality, on the other hand, is the most difficult to attain, and in the final analysis, it remains a Divine gift, beyond human will and control.

Work Ethic in Muslim Societies

Muslim societies the world over place primary stress upon religious faith and ritual prayer, but not upon a strict work ethic. The modern Western approach is just the reverse. Society permits the individual to feel free to go to church or not to go, but penalizes him for shirking or violating the code of honest work. The practice of religion in the West is neither rewarded nor punished as it is deemed to be a very personal matter. Productive work is a social obligation and carries sanctions if it is not performed according to the terms of the contract. The West in medieval times was also creed-centered, and the individual was under considerable social pressure to conform to the prevailing faith. However, the ethical humanist revolution was the social correlate of the scientific and industrial revolutions of the West in the 18th century. This gradually led to tolerance of dissent in the sphere of religion, and the primacy of integrity and work ethic in society. Many centuries earlier Socrates, in the West, and Buddha, in the East, had done the same. Sufi Islam also lays tremendous stress upon work ethic through its doctrine of "akle halal." But the plain fact is that the modern Western value system represents a radical shift of priorities in the gradation of basic values. It leaves the individual quite free inwardly in the matter of religion, and this is a basic change in the human situation. Traditionally oriented religious persons tend to regard this modern approach as the rejection of religion. A more objective and accurate assessment is that the modern approach is the affirmation of inner freedom to choose any specific religious creed or thought system without fear of external sanctions. Muslim societies must do the same, not in imitation of the dominant West, but because of the intrinsic wisdom of giving primacy to work ethic and granting autonomy to the individual in all transcendental matters.

The World of Fatwas

I found Arun Shourie's recent work, *The World of Fatwas*, so lucid and powerful that I am using the title to express my own views on related issues. Shourie quotes extensively from original Muslim sources, and the thrust of his critique of traditional Islam, at the levels of *fatwas* and *hadith*, is quite valid. I wish Muslims candidly accepted this fact. However, the learned writer says rather little about the pure Qur'anic Islam, Sufi Islam, and the several well-known philosophically oriented versions of Islam down the ages. He hardly mentions the contributions made by, say, a Sir Syed, Iqbal, and Azad, *et al*. It may be that he wanted to focus on the weaker side of the Islamic tradition, or it is possible he argued that to enlarge the scope of an already voluminous work would make it rather forbidding for the general reader. I find Shourie's critique so powerful and incisive that I can honestly say that traditional Islam at the level of *hadith* and *fatwas* stands bruised and bleeding before the eyes of any honest observer, irrespective of his religion. Long back Shourie had done the same for traditional Hinduism through the pages of his remarkable *Hinduism: Essence and Consequence*. I, therefore, hesitate to blame him, in view of the author's penchant for calling a spade a spade. However, several other instruments are also available for inspection. Thus, neither Muslims nor Hindus need lament over the merciless probing eye of Shourie, the critic. Those who care for their cultural legacy but are honest enough to admit its limitations and to renew it from within can and should learn from those who, for some reason or other, are inclined to throw away the baby with the bath water.

It seems Shourie lacks empathy for Islam and the Muslims. Perhaps, when he wrote his probing work on Hinduism, he also lacked empathy for the Hindu tradition, but the gift of empathy grew upon him as he matured and evolved with the passage of years. But empathy must be universal and humanistic rather than for any segment of the human family. I find Sudhir Kakar's approach to Indian culture and mythology both critical and sympathetic, hence fruitful.

The Hold of Prejudice

Prejudice, conscious or unconscious, against the out-group, based on religion, caste, region, or some consideration or other continues to influence our behavior in unsuspected ways. When we were selling some land adjacent to our family house at Aligarh some well-meaning friends advised us to prefer Muslim purchasers, on grounds of security in these troubled times. Thanking them for their friendly concern, I pointed out that for me integrity of character came before everything else, including the religion one professed. The simple goodness of heart knows no religious or caste divisions, and the fellowship or fraternity of the good and honest souls is the most important brotherhood or caste for me. Consistently thinking and acting on these lines is quite compatible with remaining good Muslims and Hindus or Christians in the best sense.

On Religious Conversion

Looking from a global perspective, the 19th century was marked by Western imperialism, Christian apologetics and missionary activities, rapid growth of science and technology, atheism or positivism, belief in progress, and cultural pluralism. All these currents and movements coexisted and ran their own course, reinforcing or clashing with each other. The 20th century consolidated the same trends minus political imperialism and Christian apologetics. It has now become almost patently clear that religious faith is a matter of cultural conditioning and that the dream of converting the entire human family to the one single true faith is futile, since no religion can be proved objectively or logically true. Informed and practical religious leaders and missionaries have, therefore, reconciled themselves to the program of general betterment of the deprived and weaker sections of the human family, without aiming at their formal conversion. If the educational, medical, and other forms of service rendered by constructive social workers and missionaries to the weaker sections attract the latter to some religious tradition or other, this is not the same thing as the previous missionary goal of religious conversion to the one true religion. Indeed, the missionaries themselves are continually revising and renewing their own interpretations of the Christian faith. The best among them have advanced from the level of Christian apologetics and polemics to Christian Existentialism.

The idea of converting from one religion to another had no appeal for Gandhiji. All religions have elements of truth and some limitations. Every religion is a particular language of the spirit. One can well-draw upon the beauties and charms of different languages and their literature without giving up one's own mother tongue. This is what Gandhiji actually achieved. In some exceptional cases, however, the honest and perceptive person may hear an inner irresistible call or whisper of the soul to adopt a different language of the soul and to identify oneself in totality with some spiritual or linguistic fraternity, whatever the reasons. In such cases the inner voice represents a higher wisdom. However, what must be preserved at all costs is utter humility, inner transparency, and respect for all true believers, whatever their faith.

Respect for All Religions and Value Systems

Muslims feel deeply hurt and feel offended if anybody shows disrespect to Prophet Muhammad ﷺ. Muslims hold that the rank of the Prophet ﷺ is next only to God Himself. While Muslims may reluctantly tolerate a person who blasphemes or denies the Creator, they get enraged and are apt to become violent if anyone dares to blaspheme God's messenger. This sensitivity of the Muslim believer is, by itself, commendable provided he concedes the same right to others. Unfortunately, traditional Muslims do not realize that they barely concede the same right to others. I wonder if Muslims ever gave thought to this contradiction in their thought and value system when the Taliban government demolished the Bamian Buddha statue or sculpture in Afghanistan. Nor do they hesitate in resorting to retaliatory demolition of/damage to places of worship of other non-Muslims for whatever reason. There can be little doubt that behind the real or alleged veneration for the Prophet ﷺ, or for getting even with the enemies of God and His messenger, a mix of politics and group conceit gets the better of genuine religious piety. This critique of violent response in human affairs in general applies with equal force to other religious groups as well. In short, it is politics rather than piety that engenders and fuels religious slogans in such intergroup conflicts.

Since matters of faith can never be conclusively proved as true or false, the only rational and valid approach for all religious groups is to accept, unconditionally, the ethic of mutual respect and reciprocal active tolerance for the human family in totality. Freedom of expression is, without doubt, an integral part of human rights and of the full meaning of democracy as such. However, this right must be exercised in the atmosphere of mutual respect for each other's value system. Lampooning, ridiculing, debunking of heroes, saints, sovereigns, remote ancestors, may be permissible in one society, but others may view this as utterly repugnant and outrageous. To my mind, there is a clear distinction between sober and reasoned criticism (in the course of autonomous evaluation of any belief, truthclaim, or the character of any person, living or dead) and the act of humiliating, ridiculing, or debunking the same, for whatever motive. While sober criticism should never be suppressed, even if it results in causing hurt to the religious sensibility of this or that group, ridiculing, or abusing what is sacred for others cannot be deemed to be an integral part of the meaning of democracy and freedom of expression.

The Indian Constitution is admirably clear on this point. I submit it is in this light that we must see the infamous Salman Rushdie episode some years ago and the Danish cartoon episode in the recent past. As I see the above and other similar episodes, both the provocation, and the response to provocation come about because the parties concerned suffer from spiritual myopia and a deficit in self-understanding and basic humanistic empathy. The politically motivated triggering of mass emotion through slogan raising processions only deepens mutual misunderstandings and distorted perceptions. All such techniques carry the seeds of mass violence. The human family needs interfaith dialogue and sympathetic understanding of different perspectives. And this process is on, though it may not be very visible, due to the storms in teacups that power seekers engineer, be they priests or politicians.

The Modern Value System

Traditional norms governing arranged marriage and divorce, chastity, male dominance, female roles, double standards of sex morality, alternative sexuality, etc., have broken down in large sections of urban Indian society under the impact of Western industrial society and culture. It is not that Indians or Westerners have become immoral scoundrels. Rather the content of the moral law acceptable to them has undergone a radical change. The most positive and welcome feature of the modern value system is the concept of "authentic being" or "authenticity." In other words, this means that "being truthful" or inwardly honest has become more important than possessing or "having truth." I am quite convinced that the sphere of morality is different from that of legality, and the two should not be mixed up just as religion and politics should not. Some matters are best left to the conscience of the individual without any effort, direct or indirect, at "moral policing" in the public interest.

Empowering the individual conscience and giving freedom to responsible adults will not lead to anarchy or indifference to moral values or sexual ethics, provided that the individual is not only free and responsible but is also well-informed. In fact, when these conditions are jointly present, the concern for values and the sense of accountability are much greater than in the case of externally imposed moral codes.

Interreligious Marriage

The occurrence of mixed marriages is bound to increase in modern secular societies where young people of all religions and castes are thrown together in a common social space. The recent economic independence and the ever-growing empowerment of women cannot but encourage them to choose their own marriage partners instead of following old ways. Many parents either barely tolerate a mixed marriage or just break off family ties. This approach must go.

As is well known, the traditional Islamic law permits interreligious marriage of a male believer with a Jewish or Christian woman, but not with women of other religions, unless they first convert to Islam. I find this morally repugnant since this amounts to a sort of coercion to change one's religion for the sake of love or marriage. Moreover, it is quite feasible to interpret the Qur'anic texts on marriage in a humanistic manner without twisting or stretching the plain meaning of Arabic words and expressions.

The Qur'an categorically prohibits Muslim men and women to marry from among those who totally deny God. But it is plain that all non-Muslims cannot be said to be atheists as such. The traditional Islamic law is one among several possible interpretations of the Qur'anic texts concerned. The humanist interpretation I am suggesting is certainly a departure from the traditional, but I submit, that it is not as radical as it appears at face value. It is my faith that much earlier than we imagine, the humanist interpretation will cease to bother the Islamic conscience of enlightened Muslims committed to the universal values of tolerance and cultural pluralism in the modern age. Just as several restrictions and prohibitions imposed by traditional Islam on birth control, photography, music, and so on, have, or are in the process of withering away, the idea of interreligious marriage will no longer remain in the category of the "unthinkable" for good Muslims. The present Islamic restrictions on such marriages are certainly not an integral part of the essential Islamic value system. Indeed, the historical role of Islam in this respect, as in so many other social matters, has been quite innovative.

Muslim Personal Law

The directive principles of the Indian Constitution require that the government should bring about a common civil code for all citizens. A judgment of the Supreme Court in the late eighties in connection with the Shah Bano case against her husband made this issue a major public controversy. A large number of prominent Muslim individuals and organizations held the judgment of the Supreme Court of India as an interference with their personal laws, which they deemed to be an integral part of their religion.

The British rulers had deliberately refrained from such interference both in the case of Hindu and Muslim subjects, despite making far reaching changes in the constitutional, civil, and criminal laws of the land. This approach had won almost universal acceptance. Liberal quarters in all the different religious groups had initiated internal movements of social and religious reform according to their own lights. The great Indian patriot, Tilak, was an outspoken critic of outside agencies initiating reform in such matters. Muslims took legitimate pride in the fact that in many spheres of social justice (including rights of women), the legal system of Islam represented a great advance upon pre-Islamic ideas and norms. It is also a fact that several features and aspects of Islamic law, like the idea of marriage as a civil contract, right of divorce, and interreligious marriage (with some restrictions), etc., have gradually become integral parts of the modern value system. Muslim public opinion, therefore, merits respect, though much could also be said in favor of a quick enactment of a unified civil code.

I believe personal or family laws in Islam do deserve special treatment even in a secular dispensation or state. It is worth analyzing the central importance of personal laws in the Qur'an, which is the ultimate authority for the Muslim. The Qur'an has approximately 6,200 verses. Out of these, approximately 175 verses are clear imperatives that constitute the nuclear core of the *Shariah*. Now, of this number, a mere twenty deal with political, economic, and administrative issues, and twenty with moral rules or regulations. Approximately forty-five verses deal with prayers, fasting, and pilgrimage, etc., while as many as fifty-five with laws pertaining to marriage, divorce, and inheritance, etc. The *Shariah* also provides for fresh reasoning and reinterpretation of the legal system to meet new situations in a changing world. It should not be deemed outrageous for a "Muslim Gandhi" to arise and say: If stoning as a punishment for adultery, death penalty for apostasy, unilateral divorce, some statutory procedures of divorce, remarriage, and inheritance, etc., being integral parts of Islam, I am not prepared to call myself a Muslim. As is well-known, Gandhi had spoken in this very vein against the evil of untouchability, as practiced by orthodox Hindus in the past. In short, effective secularism and emotional integration of the diverse elements of the human family will not get diluted if a permissive approach be followed in the sphere of personal or family laws, as had been the British practice.

I sincerely believe that, when the British rulers adopted a permissive approach in respect of personal laws of their Indian subjects, their primary objective was not to divide and rule, but to show genuine respect for the religious convictions of the people in this sphere. The real empowerment of women and the removal of social injustice cannot be stopped in the long run for the simple reason that women constitute half the electorate in the world at large. No matter what the orthodox might say, gender equality is the destiny of the human family.

Muslim Names and Social Customs

Muslims generally hold that there are Islamic proper names, and those who convert to Islam should, therefore, adopt an Islamic name, customs such as circumcision, the dress code, mode of slaughter of animals for food, disposal of the body after death, and laws of marriage, divorce, and inheritance, and so on. Mere acceptance of monotheism, prophet-hood of Muhammad ﷺ, and life after death, etc., is not supposed to be enough. This approach to Islam is valid up to a point, but the issue is not so simple. The reason is that, it is essential to make a distinction between the core fundamentals of the thought and value system of any historical religion and its natural prevailing social and cultural matrix. In the case of Islam, Arabic was the natural language of the original Arab audience and reference group of the Prophet ﷺ. The names of his contemporaries, as well as his own name, were neither Islamic nor non-Islamic but simply Arabic; both before, as well as after Islam entered their lives. The same holds good of their dress, general food habits, marriage and divorce regulations, funeral rites, modes of entertainment, and numerous other social customs. Only such among the pre-Islamic laws and customs were modified or abrogated as God or His Prophet ﷺ judged to be wrong and harmful. It follows that social customs are primarily ethnic rather than based on religion or ideology. If so, pre-Islamic Arab customs can hardly claim to be essential ingredients of Islam as a universal religion.

There does not appear to be any justification for holding that, when any person or persons convert to Islam, they should discard their cultural heritage in general in order to become or to function as true and full Muslim believers. Why should Chinese, Iranian, African, or Indian Muslims exchange their original cultural legacy and deny their ethnic and historical roots to embrace Arabic social and cultural features of pre-Islamic origin? Some matters must be left to individual taste or the group ethos. In other words, Muslims themselves should make a distinction between Islamization and Arabization. By the same token, there is a clear distinction between genuine Indian nationalism and Hindu "majoritarianism."

Music and Fine Arts in Islam

As is well known, the traditional Islamic value system has an extremely puritanical complexion. However, the Qur'an nowhere prohibits music and other forms of artistic expression. One or two schools of Sufi thought did practice simple religious music or the chant, but this was not music in the full artistically developed sense. The ancient Hindu value system, on the other hand, glorifies music and dance, making them an integral part of the good and blessed life. I have no doubt that Islam in the modern age will have to accommodate and assimilate the aesthetic dimension of life far more deeply and comprehensively than the traditional approach. It is a plain fact of history that, despite all restrictions imposed by the tradition, Muslim musicians in India have been second to none in enriching Indian music. It is time that the creative Muslim thinkers and leaders review the Islamic ethos in regard to this matter and repudiate the excessive puritanism of the orthodox Muslim mind.

Prohibited Foods in Islam

As is well known, the traditional Islamic value system holds that animals whose flesh is permissible as food be slaughtered in a specific manner. If the slaughter does not conform to the prescribed manner, the food becomes unlawful for the Muslim. The Islamic modernists and reformers in the 19th century in India, Egypt, and elsewhere had adopted a much more liberal stance in this regard. However, due to various factors, social and political, a counter reform movement has emerged in several parts of the Muslim world. Some persons very near and dear to me, for instance, object to eating chicken or mutton in restaurants, unless they can be sure that the slaughter was made in the prescribed manner. It is worth pointing out that Sir Syed had repudiated the above approach, but many Aligarians today readily repudiate this "lapse" of the architect of the Islamic liberalism in modern India. I sincerely regret what I call the retreat of Islamic liberalism in the midst of the political emancipation and industrialization of Muslim peoples the world over.

I have no doubt that the Islamic liberals of the 19th century and their successors in the 20th were quite right in this as in most other matters. Unfortunately their "fundamentalist" critics have been seduced by what they call "scientific" arguments proving the overall superiority of "halal" meat to the "non-halal." I am rather amused by their claim that "halal" meat not only tastes better than "non-halal," but leather goods made from animals slaughtered in the Islamic way are more durable.

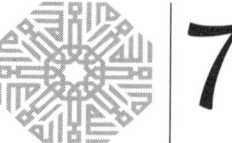

7

The Perennial Message of the Qur'an and the Human Situation

Introductory Remarks

HAVING PRESENTED THE BASICS of the vision, piety, and injunctions of the Qur'an, I shall attempt to describe its perennial message to Muslims and the followers of other religions alike. As a believing truth seeker, I can only convey what I earnestly find in or my "authentic take" from the Qur'an without any accretions of folklore or of learned tradition. Of course, I cannot help seeing or judging through the lens of my own authentic conceptual framework. This has emerged gradually, thanks to my Islamic heritage and the study of modern philosophy and social and natural sciences. This limiting condition holds in all cases of linguistic communication. However, I hold that the search for clear thinking, intellectual honesty, freedom from bias, and awareness of different points of view all converge to reducing the margin of possible distortion in understanding any piece or body of communication.

In the foregoing chapters I have already explained the semantic problems and difficulties that arise in the proper understanding of several portions of the Qur'an. Perhaps, the most commonly felt difficulty or intellectual uneasiness is caused when one applies the term "Book" to the collection of verses or "surahs" that comprise the Qur'an. A good book is expected to be a systematic, consistent, concise, non-repetitive, informative, critical, and elegantly phrased document or presentation. But do these criteria apply to the Qur'an? Not to my mind, though I have no doubt whatsoever that the Qur'an is a revealed Scripture. Indeed, I am overwhelmed by the beauty, elegance, and power of the Qur'an and am convinced that it is a Divine message to the Prophet ﷺ for his Arab audience and for all mankind. But I also know on good authority and empirical evidence that the Qur'an was not revealed, or publicly published, as are books in the ordinary sense. The verses of the Qur'an were revealed in stages and in different situations, and they address different needs and problems of the age in which the Prophet ﷺ and his contemporary audience lived and moved. Indeed, this is eloquently clear from the patent difference in the tenor and contents of the *surahs* revealed at Mecca and those at Medina. I am, therefore, quite indifferent to the charge that the Qur'an is not a systematic book. To my mind, the traditional Muslim theologians who passionately try to rebut the charge indulge in shadow boxing.

The Qur'anic language is Arabic because all Divine revelations are in the language of the people of the Prophet ﷺ concerned. In all humility, I submit that the Qur'an is in Arabic not because the language of God is Arabic, but because the language of the Prophet's ﷺ community was Arabic, not Persian or Sanskrit. In addition, the revelation had to be in the framework of orthogenetic ideas and images so that the people could readily understand the message. However, they were free to accept or reject the message. The Qur'an, therefore, should not be looked upon as a storehouse of advanced knowledge or a complete map of the good life, or as a rosary of *mantras* for obtaining specific objectives, say, victory over enemies, bumper crops, or male issue, etc., but rather as a source of inner light and fortitude of spirit.

Muslim believers must be clear on the above issues rather than indulge in sentimental glorification of the status of the Qur'an. No honest Muslim can question the veracity and the complete sincerity of Prophet Muhammad ﷺ. When the Prophet ﷺ clearly and repeatedly said that he did not compose the verses, and the Qur'an also confirms this statement, Muslim believers are committed to accepting that the Qur'an is not the word of Muhammad ﷺ, but that it is, in some sense or other, the "Word of God." However, to my mind, Muslims need not adopt any particular view or interpretation of the above expression. To give a clear meaning to or explanation of this belief is not an integral part of the Islamic faith that the Qur'an was received, and not composed by the Prophet ﷺ.

What then is the proper approach for the intelligent and honest Muslim believer? Admitting that the Qur'an is, in some sense or other, the "Word of God," the believer must realize that whatever be the ultimate Divine nature or mystery, humans can understand the "Word of God" only through language. Authentic believers are therefore called upon to understand the nature, functions, and limitations of human language, as such, particularly the semantics, usage, and stylistics of the Scripture itself. I have discussed these issues in the text and notes of earlier chapters. More details can be found in my earlier works, *Quest for Islam* and *The Call of Modernity and Islam*.

The Qur'anic Message in Capsule Form

1. All things that exist and all happenings that occur flow from the sovereign will of one Supreme self-existent eternal Being whose nature and purposes no finite being can grasp. He creates, destroys, sustains, rewards, punishes as He wills in His inscrutable wisdom. He is the Supreme Judge of what is good and bad, right and wrong. He is all merciful and master of the final Day of Judgment when He will rectify all wrongs and establish full justice. None can defy or defeat His plan nor understand it. Had He willed, wrongdoers would have met with instant punishment, but it is part of His plan to give a long rope to the evildoers.

2. His created beings are countless, but man is the peak of His creation. He guides His creatures in the way most appropriate for their created form and functioning and every creature glorifies the Creator in the appropriate way. He guides humankind by showering His special grace and blessings upon some chosen individuals from amongst themselves and charges such enlightened souls to guide their people to felicity in this life and the life to follow after death. These are the messengers, givers of good news, and the Warner's of God, but they are fully human and the true servants and slaves of the Sovereign Lord. God has sent His messengers to all peoples at different times, but He has mentioned by name only some in the Qur'an. However, they all have taught the same basic truth and the same basic spiritual and moral values, though different ethnic or regional groups followed different rituals for praying and adoring the one Supreme Creator, and also had their own social customs and practices.

3. In His inscrutable wisdom, the Supreme Creator first created the animal kingdom and also angelic beings who were all perpetually engaged in different ways in the adoration of their Supreme Creator. God then created the first man, Adam, and endowed him with knowledge beyond the ken of the angels. All the angels except one, bowed before Adam in deference to the Divine command. Again, in His inscrutable wisdom, the Creator punished the hubris and defiance of the angel, not through his annihilation, but through his expulsion from Divine grace. At the same time, He granted the angel, now turned into Satan, enormous kinetic power to tempt humankind into evil. On the other hand, the Creator gave immense potential power to humankind to resist and defeat Satan, the cursed Tempter. Thus began the drama of the cosmic conflict between good and evil, and it will continue till the Day of the final Divine Judgment. God and God alone know when the Hour of Judgment will come. But that, it will come, is an integral part of the faith in the Creator.

4. The history of the human race, as such, clearly shows the enormous power of Satan and the enormous delusion and weakness of humans who fall so easily into temptation. This resulted in corrupting the record of the scriptures revealed to the long line of Divine messengers who appeared before Prophet Muhammad ﷺ. However, the Creator, in His wisdom, willed to protect forever the accuracy of the Scripture revealed to Prophet Muhammad ﷺ. The Qur'an is, indeed, a reminder and confirmation of the past revelations rather than a new phenomenon or creed. However, it is the last and final revelation and marks the completion of the periodic showering of Divine blessings and grace that started with Prophet Adam's advent on the earth. Prophet Muhammad ﷺ is the last messenger of God, just as he was the first major messenger to appear after Prophet Jesus. However, Divine grace and blessings may well accrue in other forms and ways to all who have faith in the Supreme Creator and the final Day of Judgment and are virtuous and righteous in conduct. This holds good not only of Muslims, as an exclusive community, but of all believers in one Supreme Creator and the Day of Judgment. In any case, Prophet Muhammad ﷺ has a unique status in all creation as the Qur'an declares him to be a "*mercy to the worlds.*"

5. Prophet Muhammad ﷺ is the eternal exemplar and guide for the body of Muslim believers. They are strongly exhorted and enjoined to follow God and the Prophet ﷺ and those in authority, provided the latter observe the limits set by God. The Qur'an exhorts the faithful to follow the method of consultation in all collective matters, but does not prescribe any concrete legal or constitutional framework for governance. It is certainly not a code of conduct covering all spheres of life. Nor does it provide any legal penalties for civil wrongs or crimes with a few exceptions. The stress of the Qur'an is on "*righteous action,*" but it does not spell them out in their concrete details. This work has been done in the body of the *Shariah*. However, the Qur'an does spell out the content and meaning of "righteous action" in the "I-Thou" or spiritual sphere of human life (*ibadat*), though here, too, their details and concrete implementation comes from the *Shariah*. This is quite understandable.

6. The Qur'an lays the greatest stress upon accountability to the Creator on the Day of Judgment and the performance of righteous action. In the "I-Thou" sphere, this means guarding obligatory prayers of adoration, fasting for thirty days in Ramadan, paying purification tax (*zakat*) for collective welfare on savings, if any, pilgrimage to Mecca, if affordable, fighting in self-defense if called upon by the state.

7. There is no compulsion in religion. Had the Creator willed so, humankind would all have professed the same faith, but He has endowed them with the power to choose. Hatred of and violence against the rejecters of God or the followers of other religions, whether in the name of Islam or for the sake of power and wealth is hateful to God and prohibited to the Muslims. Islam is the religion of universal peace and justice. The Qur'an cites moving examples of non-Muslims who are virtuous and have faith and will be amply rewarded by the Creator.

However, it is the duty of Muslims to fight in self-defense, if attacked, and also to defend their legitimate interests if injustice be meted out to them.

8. The Creator is all loving and compassionate to His creation. But He is also just and inflicts punishment on the wrongdoers. Punishment is meted out both in this life and the afterlife as God pleases. Humans can never fully understand God's inscrutable wisdom and justice. Whenever good befalls them, they feel good about themselves; whenever they meet with harm or suffering, they are inclined to blame others or feel bad about the Creator. But those whose faith is strong remain steady in their fear and praise of the Creator.

9. The Qur'an clearly affirms that though the life and rewards of this life are fleeting and inconsequential in relation to the life and rewards of the afterlife, humankind must work in right earnest for success and felicity in both the worlds. The concern for piety and love of God should not deprive the faithful from enjoying the healthy joys and satisfactions that the Creator provides for this world. *Surah* 55, Al Rahman, is notable for describing the joys and beauty of the various physical creations. The ideal is to live in the "presence of God" and to be full of joy and gratitude to the Creator at all times and in all situations.

10. The human family is one. Different racial, linguistic, or religious groups should abjure mutual conflict and enmity, cooperate with each other and try to excel each other in serving the common Creator in their freely chosen way and work for the inclusive welfare of all of God's creatures in this world. Only the Creator knows the full truth of matters relating to the "world of the unseen" and on the Day of the final Judgment, He will inform the different religious factions about what is the real truth and also establish full justice for all creation.

A Believer's Response to the Message

Following the established tradition, Muslim believers are extremely reluctant to arrive at their own authentic understanding of the Qur'an, not only because they do not understand the Arabic language but also because they are averse to pursuing free inquiry in the Socratic sense. Muslims are brought up in a manner that they begin to dread the habit of free inquiry lest this step might push them into the pit of heresy, or apostasy, or blasphemy. Moreover, they find it extremely difficult to come out of their sectarian grooves of thinking whatever their sect might be. Shia Muslims mainly rely on Shia sources and authorities, and have scant respect for and knowledge of Sunni learned opinion, and Sunni Muslims stand in the same relationship to Shia perspectives. The Ahmadi Muslims are in the worst possible predicament since orthodox opinion not merely rejects their stand, but totally rejects their Islamic identity. Pakistan and Saudi Arabia do not permit them to visit the sanctuaries at Mecca and Medina for religious purposes.

The Perennial Message of the Qur'an and the Human Situation

There are some other unexamined assumptions that are uncalled for. One such assumption is that the Qur'anic language is very simple and straightforward Arabic entirely free from all ambiguity, or that sectarian controversies over their meaning or import, are the work of the Devil who misleads or confuses believers. The proponents of this approach further hold that belief in the infallibility and perfection of the scripture logically implies that its language must have one and only one true meaning. They further claim that this true meaning is none else than what one's own hallowed tradition says.

To my mind, the above is a regrettable over simplification of the nature and function of language, be it any natural language like German or Persian or Arabic. In fact, ambiguity and plural functions are inbuilt into all linguistic systems by the very nature of the case. Words and expressions of any natural language never have fixed atomic meanings; they gradually in the course of time, acquire or are given different meanings or uses in different contexts. I have discussed this issue in the third chapter at some length. I have given several examples of Qur'anic verses that just cannot be accepted as true in the literal sense of the words used. In some cases, the literal sense is clear, yet it hardly makes sense to accept it at face value; in other cases, the literal sense is not clear at all. To refresh the reader's memory, the Qur'anic verse that says that God "blinds the eyes or block the ears" of the disbelievers has a relatively clear meaning, yet, if we accept it as true in the literal sense, then how can we blame humans when they are unable to see or hear properly? However, the Qur'anic verse that says that when the devils try to sneak into the vicinity of God's presence to gather hidden knowledge, the angels strike them with lightning does not have any clear meaning at all for common mortals. In some it is quite evident that the verse is a metaphor rather than a literal truth. A good example is the verse that says that when the Creator offered the gift of revelation to mountains, they refused, but man was foolish enough to accept it.

Similar difficulties arise when we try to apply some Qur'anic injunctions, in the literal sense of the terms used. This happens in the case of the Qur'anic penalty for theft, the Qur'anic law of inheritance in some cases, such as when there is no male heir to property, or when a husband grants irrevocable divorce to his wife. Literal adherence in such cases lands believers into conflict between competing values, and this generates painful moral dilemmas. The acceptance in the literal sense of some Qur'anic verses that describe the horrors of hell or the pleasures of heaven also fall in the same category. To my mind, the proper response is to understand such verses in the figurative/metaphorical, rather than in the literal sense. The Qur'an itself says that it uses parables, similes, fables, and stories for conveying basic ethical and spiritual truths or insights rather than for describing actual events or incidents. This is a common didactic practice in all cultures and societies. Such cases do not imply any adverse criticism of the Qur'an, but only show that the language of the Qur'an performs plural functions just as this happens in the case of natural languages. Once we accept or realize this feature of the Qur'an, we also realize that those Muslims who honestly hold that every true believer must accept every Qur'anic expression or statement as true, in the literal sense, fall into a semantic error or language trap. The faith that the Qur'an is the "Word of God" and is infallible is quite different from any particular theory of meaning or truth.

Likewise, the faith that the Qur'an is the last and perfect Scripture or Divine revelation does not imply that the polity that was inaugurated and established by Prophet Muhammad ﷺ at Medina had achieved the apex level of growth and perfection, so that there is no need or possibility of further growth in the concepts and values of the Qur'an. Indeed, the need of Muslims is just the opposite. Orthogenetic growth of and growth in Qur'anic concepts and values or in the body of sublime instructions of the Prophet ﷺ that charmed the violent, raw and proud tribal Bedouins must go on and on. A ceaseless quest for perfection (which will never be achieved) is essential for preserving every thought or value system and institutional structure, be it spiritual or secular. I have pointed out in some detail in the relevant notes how concepts and values evolve in society. This process must never stop. Those Muslims who aspire to stop at some point in the cosmic journey of Islam in time, be it the age of the Prophet ﷺ, or the golden period of the pious Caliphate, or at any subsequent stage whatsoever, hardly do justice to the perennial beauty and power of the Qur'an and the character of Muhammad, the servant and messenger of the Lord of the worlds ﷺ.

The Qur'an is, certainly, the supreme source of truth and authority for the Muslim believer. Yet, I submit, it misleads Muslims when they are taught to believe that every truth is already contained in the Qur'an. Indeed, it is wrong and harmful if Muslims are encouraged to look up to the Qur'an as an infallible textbook of the natural and social sciences. It is equally harmful not to accept any scientific or cosmological theory unless it is corroborated by Qur'anic texts.

Indeed, all humans, be they Muslims or otherwise, should freely and readily follow common procedures (established through cumulative human experience and consensus) for investigation, reflection, confirmation, and justification of truthclaims that are appropriate to the subject matter of inquiry.

It also misleads Muslims believers when they are systematically indoctrinated into giving practically equal importance to the Qur'an and the *Shariah*, but they are not taught the basic primacy of intrinsic values over instrumental rules in every sphere of human activity. As a result, the traditional Muslims generally bracket the Qur'an and the *sunnah*, and even more importantly, they fail to distinguish between the core and the secondary contents of the two. This naturally results in the birth of the idea of unquestioning obedience and adherence to the

Shariah as the highest level of Islamic piety. However, once we accept the basic distinction mentioned above, Muslims get empowered to strive for basic values, yet remain free to make fresh rules best calculated to reach the basic values of the Qur'an or the Prophet's ﷺ objectives in the most effective manner.

This is not the proper place to discuss the various social and moral issues that face Muslims and others today in Muslim countries and all over the globe. What is significant is that Muslims should be aware of this basic distinction and its tremendous latent power and utility for reforming Muslim society without deviating from genuine Islamic or Qur'anic piety. As things stand today, Muslims are just being pushed into making adjustments to modern pressures and conditions of life without having any clear and consistent understanding of the complex issues, as such. For instance, family planning, desegregation, higher education for girls, entry into professions, and so on are on the increase, while child marriage, polygamy, the veil, parental control, joint families, and so on are on the decline. Yet, Muslim religious sensibility and their concept of Islam as a total code of life still remains broadly the same as it was several centuries ago. In contrast, the Christian, Hindu, Buddhist, and Sikh religious sensibility has undergone an inner transformation.

To my mind, the message of the Qur'an supports and confirms that there are plural paths to God, that salvation is not the monopoly of any single religious group, that loving tolerance is as essential as faith itself, that violence in the name of religion is a denial of faith, that fighting is permitted only in self-defense, that moral goodness and evil cut across all religious boundaries, that hubris destroys the soul, that compassion, justice, truth, and universal love bring about man's nearness to God, regardless of the language and symbols, or rituals that may be used.

The Qur'an is not a book in the ordinary sense of being a systematic and well-justified extended exposition logically divided into chapters and sections. It is a collection of revealed passages of varying length that deal with various themes, metaphysical, spiritual, ethical, social, and political events in the life of the Prophet ﷺ, or in earlier times. The Qur'an does not engage in polemics or argumentation; it speaks in a language that is remarkably simple, direct, elegant, and powerful, and its tone is authoritative and commanding, yet full of compassion and mercy. The Qur'an does not aim to convert or persuade by giving detailed reasons: it invites humans to open their hearts and to reflect directly at the beauty, power, and marvel of nature all around and the depths of one's own soul in silent wordless contemplation. It aims to illumine the existential anxiety and darkness in the inner space of individuals who yearn for peace and security. Parents, teachers, and the custodians of traditional wisdom do give some measure of inner security and guidance to their wards, but they themselves are perplexed souls, and their information and wisdom is circumscribed. The Qur'an beckons them to hear and ponder over the inspired messages delivered by different messengers in the past and the latest Message delivered by Muhammad, which confirms and completes them all.

The Qur'an is the written collection of the Divinely inspired or revealed communications to Prophet Muhammad ﷺ on various matters over a long period of twenty-three years. These communications, by and large, do not give information or knowledge in the ordinary or scientific sense, and reading or listening to them is no substitute for the study of history, humanities, and the natural and social sciences. Humankind, in order to live the good life, at its best, will have to pursue the above disciplines to their utmost abilities. What the Qur'an and all other revealed Scriptures, such as the Torah, Gospel, and Gita, *et al.*, do is to awaken and "quicken" the soul and lead it from the night of darkness and doubt into the glorious dawn of authentic faith. The contents of the Scriptures are not pieces of inquiry, research, and reasoned justification, nor are they like *mantras* of occult magic that many believe produce desired results just by plain recitation. The Qur'an calls its verses signs. All signs have to be respected. Indeed, all prescriptions of the Qur'an and the authentic instructions of Prophet Muhammad ﷺ have to be heeded. But the Qur'an itself exhorts believers to reflect and pursue wisdom that is a Divine gift. All injunctions and prescriptions of the Qur'an or the Prophet ﷺ should be used with intelligence and prudence rather than mechanically or blindly. And I submit that this task requires that a distinction be made between the believer's active concern for promoting fundamental spiritual and moral values in our conduct of life, and his concern for strictly adhering to instrumental rules contained in the Qur'an, or the *sunnah*, as the case may be.

In the final analysis, the study of semantics and the sociology of knowledge and world history is of profound importance for the proper understanding and appreciation of the Qur'an. If the believer remains content merely with the literal meaning of Qur'anic texts, without acquiring a background awareness of the plural functions of all natural languages, he is very likely to fall into the "idolatry of literal meaning," as it were.

The danger of this type of idolatry is greatest in the case of Qur'anic verses that describe persons or events in the world of the "Unseen"; angels, devils, the creation of Adam and Eve, and their temptation, the fall of Satan, the end of the cosmos, the Day of Judgment, and so on. These verses constitute the Mystique of the Qur'an. The relationship, if any, between mystique and myth is very problematic, since myths abound in all human cultures. Perhaps, pre-Islamic Arab society is the poorest, while ancient Indian society, the richest in this particular regard. In any case, for all practical purposes, two basic insights, namely, (*a*) the inner growth of new dimensions in basic spiritual values due to several factors and (*b*) the distinction between fundamental values and instrumental rules for their promotion, are, by far, more fruitful for human universal welfare than the study of myths. I have discussed these issues in Chapter 3 of the present work, though my reference to myths is rather sketchy.

The Qur'an, in brief and scattered passages of remarkable simplicity, beauty, and penetration into reality, reveals the coordinates and the essential structure of the human situation, and gives the assurance that the seeming chaos of the Universe is a Divine macrocosm, and not an accident or a jest of some malignant power. Muslims should look up to the Qur'an as the supreme mystery and miracle of Prophet Muhammad ﷺ. Its primary and main function is to inspire, impart wisdom, guide, sustain faith, console, warn, heal, illumine our unknown self-depths, prepare us for our return journey and the Day of Judgment, and give the message of ultimate felicity and salvation to all who engage in righteous action, whatever may be its form. To treat the Qur'an as a complete code of conduct or rigid laws covering every aspect of human life is not to enhance, but rather to diminish its blessings and status.

Concluding Reflections

Reciting or reading my favorite *surahs*, or verses of the Qur'an, in the original Arabic profoundly moves me. However, other scriptures can and do inspire others in the same way. I accept this with a sense of wonder and humility at the power of different "sources of inspiration and inner light," but the apex Source is one. The crucial factor is not where the inner light of the individual comes from; the crucial question is whether the inner light is present or shines in the individual. Any deeply committed believer who acts righteously (according to his authentic values) and knows that his own faith or "conceptualization of the Supreme Mystery of Being" is not the only window to the mystery as such is, to my mind, a fellow pilgrim on the journey of the spirit. An analogy from the realm of human love might explain better what I am trying to convey. If one truly loves another human being, no matter whom he loves, one enters the portal of the Divine and tastes bliss and blessedness.

The fruit of spirituality may blossom on different theological creeds. But the mere profession or verbalization of any creed, by itself, does not bring about the state of blessedness and bliss that are marks of spirituality. The essence of Islamic spirituality is the authentic conviction that there is only one supreme and eternally Self-existent Being and the Source Who creates, sustains and guides humankind through messengers who are human but blessed by Divine communications (*wahy*) and that Muhammad ﷺ was truly a messenger of God. This is an inclusive rather than an exclusive approach to the faith that the Self-existent Being not merely creates but also sustains and guides created beings in appropriate ways.[1]

Creeds and dogmas of any historical religion may appeal to one, but leave others indifferent. But the flame of wonder and mystery and the inner need of prayerful wordless surrender to the cosmic mystery that brings about the total silence of the spirit (*shoonya* in Sanskrit) is the only "jewel that shines by its own light" in the human search to fathom the cosmic mystery, as such. Different creeds or thought patterns are just different languages or alternative modes of conceptualizing the mystery beyond human comprehension. The essence of spirituality is keeping alive the sense of wonder and mystery of the cosmos and to be ever engaged in "righteous action." Islamic spirituality implies the additional faith that the Qur'an represents the completion of Divine blessings to humankind through revealed verbal messages (*wahy*).

The human family is gradually realizing that the diversity of religion, language, and culture is quite natural and is not, necessarily, harmful to humanity. It causes harm only when diversity breeds intolerance or fear. The ancient Indian Brahmanical tradition of the Vedic Upanishads, particularly the Gita, the wisdom of China, the Qur'an, uncontaminated by human gloss, the great mystics and poets of all times and regions all speak out this truth with one voice. Eminent scientists agree that man cannot live by science alone, but needs spiritual food for integrated human welfare. Loving tolerance of all creeds and according freedom of thought, expression, and propagation and equality of opportunity to all groups under democratic auspices is the only road for humanity.[2]

If so, how can enlightened and well-informed Muslim, Christian, Hindu, or Sikh believers think or act in terms of "saving the souls of heathens and nonbelievers"? To authentically and fully live one's own truth rather than to convert others to one's own view or line of thinking becomes the central challenge and concern of all reasonable and committed believers, no matter what religion they profess. After all, the fragrance of the rose spreads without its asking.

It is true that children are not born enlightened or cultured but stand in need of education and training by parents and teachers. However, what the child really needs is not creedal indoctrination or precepts, but rather high moral integrity and examples of righteous action by parents and teachers. The child learns quickly to walk on the path set by elders. But its inner growth comes, not through imitation or conformity, but through the nourishing of its soul. Its spontaneous sense of wonder and mystery of Being is in danger of getting choked if the food be overcooked. What he needs more than anything else is care, love, concern for truth, and right action.

Many children will just remain content to tread the path shown by the parents, but some will aspire to search their own. These are the blessed ones, but their paths may well differ. No harm is done should this happen.

The Perennial Message of the Qur'an and the Human Situation

Western thinkers and even liberal Christian theologians concede that religious faith can never be established logically or scientifically. A religious dogma or belief is a truthclaim, no doubt. But the nature of the truthclaim qualitatively differs from ordinary or scientific truthclaims, or even mathematical or purely logical truthclaims. I have discussed these points in earlier chapters. The religious belief is existential just like ethical or aesthetic judgments. Therefore, what is important is not proof but authenticity of conviction. Judgments of taste also can never be proved, but they fall in an entirely different category.[3]

This basic approach to religion and spirituality underlies the American Constitution as also the Indian. Both the documents are based on the principled separation of the state and religion. Neither of the two is anti-religion as was the Communist Constitution of Soviet Russia. The American and Indian Constitutions are neutral to all religions. The principled separation of religion and politics does not even remotely imply any hostility to religion or indifference to ethical values. The amoral pursuit of power without caring for right means is not a part of the connotation or essential meaning of secularism. Indeed, numerous secular politicians are more given to ethical politics than many religious politicians. Amoral politics is a human failing, as such. Indeed, secularism has many shades of meaning, and it means different things to different people. However, the concept of a secular state has a clear meaning and all religious groups, sooner or later, will have to come to terms with the modern preference of secular democracy and secular states to theocracy and ideological states, no matter which religion may be involved.

Al Ghazali, Rumi, Khwaja Nizamuddin Auliya, Ibn Khaldun, Dara Shikoh, Sir Syed Ahmed, Iqbal, Abul Kalam Azad, and also some other Muslim luminaries had won the above insights and practiced them in their lives. But a combination of factors—vested interests of the rulers and the priests, fear and intolerance of cultural plurality, and cultural lag or resistance of common folk blocked further progress of the said line of thinking. Ancient verities, therefore, cry out for repeated reiteration. Just as every individual breathes with his own lungs, rather than the lungs of his ancestors, every generation needs to understand the ancient verities afresh in its own idiom.[4]

Islam, in the literal sense, means the state of peace through willing surrender to some Higher Authority Who overwhelms the individual with His power and holiness but Who is inscrutable and mysterious. The message of the Qur'an is that mortals should become Muslims in the functional sense. This message is timeless and perennial, but mortals are temporal, and severely caught in the web of various diversities. No one individual, not even a Buddha, or a Shankar, or a Ghazali, or a Rumi, or an Iqbal, or a Plato, or a Kant, or a Darwin, or a Marx, or a Freud, or an Einstein, can claim access to every dimension of awareness. Nor can any *rishi*,

Sufi, sage, or savant. Nor can any prophet or Divine incarnation. Nor can any Revelation or Scripture. God alone is *Samad*, the fully Transcendent, and the fully Immanent, Self-Existent, eternal Reality.

Every truth seeker must learn to face dissent and active opposition coming from others with utter humility: without any loss of love or respect. Only then do one's own search for truth, and the final commitment, become free from conceit and self-importance.

Afterword

Working on *Living the Qur'an in Our Times* has been for me a labor of love and a great education. The fruits of my labor taste very sweet to me, but I remain very conscious of their limitations. While my work was in progress, many excellent works on Islam and related topical problems, both academic and generalist, appeared in Western circles. They came to my notice much after my own work was done. However, I acknowledge their high quality and utility, in particular, the magisterial work of Hans Kung, *Islam: Past Present and Future*; Muhammad Arkoun's *Islam: To Reform or to Subvert*; Abdullahi Naim's *Towards Islamic Reformation*; Tariq Ramadan's *Radical Reforms*; F.E. Peters's *The Voice, The Word, The Books*; Tarek Fatah's *Chasing a Mirage*; Hamid Ansari's *Travelling Through Conflict*; and also some others.

Turning to my own work *Living the Qur'an in Our Times*, my objective was to put in black and white, among some other ideas, my in-depth response to what I term *"the mystery of the Qur'an,"* which expression I prefer to the traditional *"miracle of the Qur'an."* While fully recognizing that no religious conviction can be fully proved or disproved (logically or scientifically), I do claim that religious convictions can be held to be authentic or inauthentic, as the case may be. In this sense I do believe deeply and unequivocally in the mystery of the Qur'an as the defining dogma or faith axiom of Islam.

Like any other person born and bred in a Muslim family, I was conditioned to say that the Qur'an was the supreme miracle of Prophet Muhammad ﷺ. I also held that the Qur'anic contents in their totality as well as the reported sayings and doings of the Prophet of Islam ﷺ (provided they were absolutely authentic) were infallible. As my thought developed, I was forced to make a distinction between the infallibility of the Qur'an and that of the Prophet ﷺ. I also came to realize that the expression *"mystery of the Qur'an"* more accurately described my in-depth response to the Qur'an than the traditional expression. Likewise, the concept of creative fidelity to the injunctions of the Qur'an better described my authentic response to the Qur'an than the traditional concept of unreflective adherence to Qur'anic injunctions. Gradually I realized that though every Qur'anic word or sentence may well be accepted as revealed and thus sacrosanct to the believer, the different verses perform different functions for the believer and satisfy different needs of the faithful. And these needs and purposes were not one, but many.

What was the implication of this insight? Well, it squarely clashed with the traditional idea of literal obedience to Allah and His Messenger ﷺ without raising any *ifs* and *buts* or taking into consideration the situational context of the revelation. This was and remains the predicament of Muslim believers who honestly accept the Qur'an as a revealed scripture without taking into account the plural functions of discourse in the language of the Qur'an. I have dealt with these problems in considerable detail in Chapter 3 of my main work.

To my mind the distinction Western philosophers make between intrinsic spiritual and moral values and instrumental rules for preserving and promoting them in society at any given time is the key to solving the predicament of the Muslim believers. I see no reason why this distinction should not be applied to the Qur'anic scripture. Why should such application be supposed to subvert the sanctity of the Qur'an? Once we realize that the Qur'an is the Word of God addressed to a human being for human beings of all times it is natural and inevitable that the revealed text be understood in the light of this basic distinction of intrinsic values (that are permanent) and instrumental rules (that are situational).

To hold that Qur'anic injunctions are directive principles that are meant to be wisely and judiciously interpreted before being applied to concrete situations in an ever-changing world by no means minimizes the status of the Qur'an or reduces its mystery and majesty in the eyes of the believer, provided he or she sincerely believes in Qur'an as "mystery." Millions of people down the ages have joyfully said yes to this claim. And I am one of them.

While I concede that every aspect of life must be governed by ethics, I fail to see why orthodox Muslims or Muslim theologians like Hasan al Banna, Sayyid Qutb, Maududi, and Khomeini, *et al.*, should insist that Qur'anic injunctions or the Prophet's ﷺ judgments in the literal sense must be regarded as a rigidly binding code in an ever-changing world. In this respect, the catholic and permissive approach of Sir Syed, Iqbal, Abul Kalam Azad, Ali Abdul Raziq, Ali Shariati, and Zafarullah Khan, *et al.* is far more insightful, valid, and relevant to the modern age.

I, therefore, in all humility hold that belief in one Supreme Being as Creator of all that exists and Qur'an as the mystery of Divine communication or revelation to the Prophet of Islam suffices to validate the claim that one is a Muslim or that one accepts Islam as his or her religion. This, of course, presupposes that the person desires to call himself a Muslim and also desires to be recognized as such. If so, both civil society and the state should respect the individual and protect the individual's freedom of choice, no matter what religious orthodoxy might declare.

What is the significance of choosing the word "mystery" rather than "miracle"? Well, the expression "mystery of the Qur'an" retains the air of "ontological mystery" and feelings of reverence on the part of the believer without importing theological images, ideas, and beliefs that by no means are necessarily true. The use of the word mystery leaves space for accommodating different views or human perspectives on transcendental truthclaims, such as the nature of God, revelation, details of happenings after death and afterlife, and other dogmas or faith axioms of Islam, apart from one single and simple belief. This is the belief in the total veracity of Muhammad ﷺ as a human being even before the momentous happening of "the event in the cave" and ever after his passing away.

Having accepted the unity of God and the mystery of the Qur'an, the complete integrity and sincerity of the Prophet ﷺ, the truth of his mission, the unknown and unseen dimensions of the Universe, and a final Day of Judgment free from any admixture of myth or folklore (be it pre-Islamic or Islamic), yet I cannot honestly accept the traditional paradigm of Islam in history. This paradigm includes the attribution of miracles to Prophet Muhammad ﷺ and bracketing his reported sayings with the Qur'anic text in the category of infallible truths or as unchanging and rigid injunctions in every walk of life. This approach patently results in a static morality both individual and social, and obstructs the creative growth and flowering of the human spirit. The fear of innovation puts a stop on multidimensional progress of the human spirit.

Orthodox custodians of the Islamic tradition may well accuse me of the audacity of spiritual conceit or charge me with hypocrisy and deceit. But I submit I am vocalizing the inner response of millions of Muslim believers living in the modern age. On hearing or reciting the Qur'an they cannot help being overwhelmed by the power and beauty of the "ontogenetic" verses of the Qur'an in Arabic. Yet these believers remain deeply and firmly aware of the fact that the idea of evolution applies not merely to the human store of knowledge but also to the realm of ideals and values. These latter admit of continuous growth and evolution. These Muslims love to identify themselves as loyal believers, but they also yearn to participate (along with the human family as a whole) in its evolutionary march toward goals, as yet, beyond our present imagination. They are thus inevitably led to accept a plural human society where Muslims and others can function as equal partners rather than one or the other being the boss. The goal of the dominance of Islam as a spiritual dynasty or exclusive super power, thus, turns into the goal of interfaith brotherhood and peace.

Islamic orthodoxy does not empathize with this vision and legitimate aspiration. The fear of the unknown pushes the traditional custodians of the Islamic faith into the intolerance of all dissent, whether inside, or outside the community. This attitude of intolerance has a very long history in the Muslim tradition as is evident from the fact that an unduly large number of Muslim political, spiritual, and intellectual leaders in the creative era of Islamic history were persecuted, tortured, or assassinated by their own folk. It is a truism to say that intolerance leads to a violent temperament and also acts of violence. The next step is obviously terrorism, as we know it today.

The mother of all evils is the evasion of truth and the fear of others. Tarek Fatah puts it very well when he affirms and approves of "*the state of Islam*" but rejects the idea of "*the Islamic state.*" Abdullahi Naim covers very useful ground for the Islamic reformation of the *Shariah*. Arkoun touches the heart of the problems relating to the language of Islamic discourse in a marvelous manner. Tariq Ramadan and Hussein Nasr are already being acclaimed for their creative vision of Islam. Many Western writers and humanistic observers have also made fruitful and profound observations on the Islamic vision as different from Islamic orthodoxy. Hamid Ansari's work is an extremely illuminating area study of Muslim peoples.

God alone knows the full truth, and we humans should ever beware of possessing exclusive truth and falling into the pit of spiritual conceit and the delusion of self-sufficiency.

We started this work by invoking the name of Allah and we now conclude it with one Qur'anic *surah* describing the human situation, and two Qur'anic prayers for guidance, for blessings, for protection, and above all for forgiveness.

Surah:103

By (the Token of) Time (through the ages), Verily Man is in loss, Except such as have Faith, and do righteous deeds, and (join together) in the mutual teaching of Truth, and of Patience and Constancy.

Surah:113

Say: I seek refuge with the Lord of the Dawn. From the mischief of created things; From the mischief of Darkness as it overspreads; From the mischief of those who practice secret arts; And from the mischief of the envious one as he practices envy.

Surah:114

Say: I seek refuge with the Lord and Cherisher of Mankind, The King (or Ruler) of Mankind, The Allah (or judge) of Mankind, From the mischief of the Whisperer (of Evil), who withdraws (after his whisper),— (The same) who whispers into the hearts of Mankind —Among Jinns and among men.

Ameen

Quotable

There have been fierce warriors as well as great champions of peace among devoted members of each religion, and rather than asking, which one is the "true believer" and which one a "mere impostor," we should accept that one's religious faith does not in itself resolve all the decisions we have to make in our lives, including those concerning our political and social priorities and the corresponding issues of conduct and action. Both the proponents of peace and tolerance and the patrons of war and intolerance can belong to the same religion, and may be (in their own ways) true believers, without this being seen as a contradiction.

—Amartya Sen, winner of the Nobel Prize, quoted from his book
Identity And Violence, The Illusion of Destiny.

Notes

Notes to Chapter 1   Perennial Islam: A Qur'an Based Paradigm

1. Consider the following texts from the Qur'an:

17:90–93

They say: "We shall not believe in thee, until thou cause a spring to gush forth for us from the earth, 'Or (until) thou have a garden of date trees and vines, and cause rivers to gush forth in their midst, carrying abundant water; 'Or thou cause the sky to fall in pieces, as thou sayest (will happen), against us; or thou bring Allah and the angels before (us) face to face: 'Or thou have a house adorned with gold, or thou mount a ladder right into the skies. No, we shall not even believe in thy mounting until thou send down to us a book that we could read." Say: "Glory to my Lord! Am I aught but a man,—an apostle?"

7:188

Say: "I have no power over any good or harm to myself except as Allah willeth. If I had knowledge of the unseen, I should have multiplied all good, and no evil should have touched me: I am but a Warner, and a bringer of glad tidings to those who have faith."

6:50

Say: "I tell you not that with me are the treasures of Allah, nor do I know what is hidden, nor do I tell you I am an angel. I but follow what is revealed to me." Say: "can the blind be held equal to the seeing?" Will ye then consider not?

Though this denial has had little effect upon popular beliefs and sentiments, several Islamic religious thinkers of eminence have accepted the Qur'anic approach. Sir Syed went one step further and attempted to explain away (through ingenious and rather far-fetched interpretations of the Qur'anic text) several Qur'anic verses, which ostensibly, describe the miracles performed by God's messengers before the advent of Prophet Muhammad ﷺ. Sir Syed's position on this particular score fails to convince me. But here I shall not pursue the exact Qur'anic position on miracles prior to Prophet Muhammad ﷺ.

As regards the infallibility of the Prophet ﷺ, once again, the Qur'anic texts do not warrant this approach. Indeed, several verses of the Qur'an directly or indirectly gently chide the Prophet ﷺ for some act of commission or omission, or show Divine disapproval of some impulse, or inclination of the Prophet ﷺ. Indeed, he was in the habit of tearfully praying night long for Divine forgiveness for his lapses or limitations. Several Qur'anic verses show that he was subject to tensions and anxieties as is the common lot of humanity. Here are some relevant verses from the Qur'an:

9:43

Allah give thee grace! Why didst thou grant them until those who told the truth were seen by thee in a clear light, and thou hadst proved the liars?

66:1

O Prophet! Why holdest thou to be forbidden that which Allah has made lawful to thee? Thou seekest to please thy consorts. But Allah is Oft-Forgiving, Most Merciful.

80:5–10

As to one who regards Himself as self-sufficient, To him dost thou attend; Though it is no blame to thee if he grow not (in spiritual understanding). But as to him who came to thee striving earnestly, And with fear (in his heart), Of him wast thou unmindful.

6:35

If their spurning is hard on thy mind, yet if thou wert able to seek a tunnel in the ground or a ladder to the skies and bring them a sign,—(what good?). If it were Allah's Will, He could gather them together unto true guidance: so be not thou amongst those who are swayed by ignorance (and impatience)!

9:80

Whether thou ask for their forgiveness, or not, (their sin is unforgivable): if thou ask seventy times for their forgiveness, Allah will not forgive them: because they have rejected Allah and His Messenger. And Allah guideth not those who are perversely rebellious.

9:84

Nor do thou ever pray for any of them that dies, nor stand at his grave; for they rejected Allah and His Messenger, and died in a state of perverse rebellion.

There is no contradiction in holding that though Prophet Muhammad ﷺ was Divinely inspired, he was subject to human limitations, afflictions, and trials. Indeed, the Qur'an itself describes such episodes in his life which should not have occurred at all in case he were perfect in the literal sense of the term "perfection." Absolute perfection just cannot be predicated of any created being. Absolute perfection belongs to God alone.

The belief that God favored Muhammad ﷺ with Divine revelations from time to time does not imply that he, as a human being, was infallible in all his judgments. Nor does the belief imply that Prophet Muhammad's ﷺ choices and preferences in all matters, including personal likes and dislikes, or matters of taste should be binding upon all believers. Indeed, the distinction between what is obligatory (*farz*) and what is merely recommended (*masnoon*) in the *Shariah* partly reflects the position I am taking.

What the Qur'an highlights is not the superhuman or miraculous powers of Prophet Muhammad ﷺ but God's sovereign power and transcendental majesty and the Prophet's ﷺ sense of total dependence, submission, and trust in his Creator. The Qur'an also highlights the exalted human character of God's messenger as a gift of Divine grace. The human quality, which stands out most prominently, is the Prophet's ﷺ awe of the Creator and compassion for humanity. That God's messenger possesses extraordinary powers is nowhere mentioned or even remotely suggested. Indeed, the accent of the Qur'an, in its references to Prophet Muhammad ﷺ, is not on his superhuman powers but rather on his limitations as an ordinary mortal. Here are some relevant Qur'anic verses:

28: 56

It is true thou wilt not be able to guide every one, whom thou lovest; but Allah guides those whom He will and He knows best those who receive guidance.

27: 65

Say: None in the heavens or on earth, except Allah, knows what is hidden: nor can they perceive when they shall be raised up (for Judgment).

40: 77

So persevere in patience; for the Promise of Allah is true: and whether We show thee (in this life) some part of what We promise them,—or We take thy soul (to Our Mercy) (before that),—(in any case) it is to Us that they shall (all) return.

3: 144

Muhammad is no more than an apostle: many were the apostles that passed away before him. If he died or were slain, will ye then turn back on your heels? If any did turn back on his heels, not the least harm will he do to Allah. But Allah (on the other hand) will swiftly reward those who (serve Him) with gratitude.

13: 40
Whether We shall show thee (within thy life time) part of what we promised them or take to Ourselves thy soul (before it is all accomplished),—thy duty is to make (the Message) reach them: it is Our part to call them to account.

3: 79
It is not (possible) that a man, to whom is given the Book, and Wisdom, and the prophetic office, should say to people: "Be ye my worshippers rather than Allah's": on the contrary (He would say) "Be ye worshippers of Him Who is truly the Cherisher of all: For ye have taught the Book and ye have studied it earnestly."

18:110
Say: "I am but a man like yourselves, (but) the inspiration has come to me, that your Allah is one Allah. Whoever expects to meet his Lord, let him work righteousness, and, in the worship of his Lord, admit no one as partner.

4: 113
But for the Grace of Allah to thee and his Mercy, a party of them would certainly have plotted to lead thee astray. But (in fact) they will only lead their own souls astray, and to thee they can do no harm in the least. For Allah hath sent down to thee the Book and wisdom and taught thee what thou knewest not (before): And great is the Grace of Allah unto thee.

17: 73–75
And their purpose was to tempt thee away from that which We had revealed unto thee, to substitute in our name something quite different; (in that case), behold! They would certainly have made thee (their) friend! And had We not given thee strength, thou wouldst nearly have inclined to them a little. In that case We should have made thee taste an equal portion (of punishment) in this life, and an equal portion in death: and moreover thou wouldst have found none to help thee against Us!

69:38–47

So I do call to witness what ye see, and what ye see not, That this is verily the word of an honored apostle; It is not the word of a poet: little it is ye believe! Nor is it the word of a soothsayer: little admonition it is ye receive. (This is) a Message sent down from the Lord of the Worlds. And if the apostle were to invent any sayings in Our name, We should certainly seize him by his right hand, And We should certainly then cut off the artery of his heart: Nor could any of you withhold him (from Our wrath).

The above Qur'anic verses show that the Qur'an does not give support to the traditional view regarding the Prophet's ﷺ infallible judgment in every walk of life. The approach of Caliph Umar to Prophet Muhammad ﷺ in decision making is very instructive. I shall refer merely to four out of several well-documented decisions or actions of the second Caliph. These clearly reflect his approach and attitude to the Prophet ﷺ, in his lifetime and after his death. All these facts have been taken from Shibli's monumental biography of Umar.

1. Prophet Muhammad ﷺ had built a small mosque adjacent to his modest residence at Medina where the faithful congregated every day for the obligatory prayers. There were different views on the best method of summoning the believers at prayer time. The Prophet ﷺ had his own suggestion, but the suggestion of Umar was accepted by the Prophet ﷺ. Umar's reverence and closeness to the Prophet ﷺ did not stand in the way of his independent thinking.
2. The Prophet ﷺ used to distribute war booty equally among his companions who had participated in the fighting. When Umar became the Caliph, he made the share proportionate to the contribution made by each fighter.
3. The Prophet ﷺ had allowed the Arab Muslim fighters to occupy the rich agricultural lands of the Jews of Khyber and other places after their surrender. But Caliph Umar did not permit Arab victors to displace the tillers and owners of land in the fertile Nile valley. In the above two cases Caliph Umar modified or amended the Prophet's ﷺ practice on the declared ground that changed conditions required a fresh approach. Umar thus stood for creative fidelity, not mechanical obedience or literal conformity to the example of the Prophet ﷺ.
4. While the *Kabah* was still under the control of the non-Muslim Meccan chiefs, they had permitted a small body of Muslim pilgrims to visit the shrine after the treaty of Hudaibiya. Under instructions from the Prophet ﷺ the pilgrims vigorously stamped their feet while performing the traditional circumambulation of the *Kabah*. This rite termed *"ramal"* in Arabic was a show of strength and high spirits rather than any spiritual exercise. Later on, the same practice continued. When

Umar became the Caliph, he held that the stamping of the feet was a temporary device to boost the self-confidence of Muslims when they were numerically small and the rite or practice could well be dispensed with in the changed conditions. However, the Caliph had second thoughts on this issue and decided not to change a practice the Prophet 鮥 had initiated.

Umar, thus, made a clear distinction between purely religious or spiritual matters and worldly or secular issues. While he felt free to innovate in worldly matters dealing with administration, economy, and war, etc., the Caliph conformed to the Prophet's 鮥 practice in religious or spiritual matters. The stamping of the feet while circumambulating the *Kabah* was a borderline case, and the Caliph preferred restraint and caution to his own independent thinking.

It may be pointed out that Hazrat Ali who occupied a very special position in the eyes of the Prophet 鮥 for several reasons disagreed with the Caliph. Ali stood for strict adherence to the "example of the Prophet" 鮥 in all matters. However, he deferred to the position adopted by Umar. This, I submit, was a happy decision, which has an important bearing on the subject under discussion. It is rather unfortunate that traditional Shiite quarters interpret Umar's independent approach as evidence of his disloyalty to his leader and preceptor and deviation from Islam. However, there is no denying the fact that, while the Prophet 鮥 was extremely tender hearted and gentle to women and children and also "soft" in judging others, Umar appears habitually to have been rather stern and strict both to himself and to others.

How and when did the popular belief in the infallibility and perfection (in the literal sense) of the Prophet 鮥 and his example arise? It seems to me that it was the result of three factors, (*a*) the powerful impact on Prophet Muhammad's 鮥 contemporaries and later generations of the charismatic personality and the extraordinary spiritual and moral excellence of the Prophet 鮥, (*b*) the manner in which several reputed religious leaders interpreted and drew inferences from some Qur'anic verses, and (*c*) the influence of the Shiite doctrine of the spiritual supremacy of Hazrat Ali. I shall first deal with the Qur'anic verses, which probably, lent themselves to this interpretation:

4:80

He who obeys the Messenger, obeys Allah. But if any turn away, We have not sent thee to watch over their (evil deeds).

59:7

... So take what the Messenger assigns to you, and deny yourselves that which he withholds from you. And fear Allah for Allah is strict in Punishment.

3:31,32
Say: "If ye do love Allah, follow me: Allah will love you and forgive you your sins: For Allah is Oft-Forgiving, Most Merciful." Say: "Obey Allah and His Messenger.: But if they turn back, Allah loveth not those who reject Faith.

48:10
Verily those who plight their fealty to thee do no less than plight their fealty to Allah. The Hand of Allah is over their hands ...

The above and similar other Qur'anic verses, understandably, suggested the belief that any argument with or difference of view from Prophet Muhammad ﷺ would amount to blasphemy or the rejection of the faith. This approach gradually culminated in the *Sunni* Muslim view that the polity at Medina, as introduced by the Prophet ﷺ and developed by the first four Caliphs, is the permanent Islamic norm. However, the verses concerned do not entail this conclusion, as should be clear from the example and approach of Caliph Umar himself.

The other factor, which generated the belief in question, is the much later Shiite doctrine of the infallibility of the Divinely ordained spiritual guide (*Imam*). If the first *Imam*, Ali, was an infallible or perfect leader and guide, and if all other *Imam*s who succeeded him were also perfect, Prophet Muhammad ﷺ also must have been perfect, since his was the original spiritual flame of Prophethood that had lighted the candle of Ali's faith and his high spiritual status as the first *Imam*.

The doctrine of Ali's infallibility appears to have crystallized in the religious thinking and tradition of a section of first and second generation Arab Muslims who felt rather disillusioned and frustrated when Ali was out-maneuvered by his senior colleagues and comrades in the choice of successor to the Prophet ﷺ. Indeed, he and other members of his family became the sad victims of internecine intrigues and civil war in the struggle for political power in the nascent Islamic state. When for reasons (which are quite irrelevant for our purpose here) Ali did not succeed politically, his closest admirers in the successor generations of Arab Muslims felt powerfully moved to glorify, at the spiritual and moral plane, their hero who had been politically sidelined. This was a case of genuine admiration and adulation of a great man who, in any case, was outstanding as a scholar, poet, and orator, besides being a fearless and dedicated warrior in the defense of Islam from its very inception. These subtle intellectual and spiritual gifts were, obviously, not conspicuous in Ali's three senior predecessors in the office of Caliph. Hence, his sincere admirers and close supporters, in combination with objective social and political factors or developments soon after the Prophet ﷺ gradually developed the doctrine that despite being denied his "due" right to be the first

Caliph, Hazrat Ali, nevertheless, remained and still remains the direct spiritual successor to the Prophet ﷺ and the supreme and infallible *Imam* of the entire body of true Muslim believers.

The spiritual glorification of Ali must have provided profound satisfaction and consolation to those who felt lost and forlorn in a selfish and cruel world where, from their perspective, might rather than right had prevailed. It was quite natural for them to gravitate toward the belief in a future redemption in historical time and of total victory of true Muslims (the lovers and votaries of *Imam* Ali) through Divine grace and intervention. The concept of the *Imam* became the vehicle of Divine grace and the promise that the Hand of God will, one day, set right the wrong course history had taken immediately after the passing away of the Prophet ﷺ.

Shibli Nomani's monumental Urdu work, *Seerat un Nabi (The Character of the Prophet)* published in India in the early years of the 20th century remains to date the classic study on the subject. Authored by an "insider" who was a great literary figure, historian and an eminent colleague of Sir Syed Ahmed Khan (d. CE 1898), the work is a model of objectivity, impartiality and rigorous critical scholarship. Among Western writers Montgomery Watt, Annemarie Schimmel (d. CE 2003), and Karen Armstrong have dealt with the theme with remarkable sympathy and impartiality.

2. A reliable and balanced recent work, *No God but God*, by Reza Aslan, London, 2005, briefly but brilliantly surveys the career of Islam right from the times of the Prophet ﷺ to the present from the perspective of a modern liberal Muslim, equally well-versed in the ideas and values of both Islam and the West. He judges men and matters without fear or favor. See also the many writings of Arnold Toynbee (d. CE 1975), H.A.R. Gibb (d. CE 1971), A.J. Arberry (d. CE 1969), and Hussein Nasr (b. CE 1933).

3. The American savant, Will Durant, in his multi-volume magisterial survey, *The Story of Civilization*, has done signal service to all humanity by highlighting in one full volume the contribution of eminent Muslim thinkers, scientists and savants to world culture. The best study on Ibn Khaldun is, of course, by Franz Rosenthal. The UNESCO has included Ibn Khaldun's classic *Prolegomena to World History* in its sponsored publications.

4. In modern times the pride of place to the impartial comparative study of religions belongs to such eminent Western historians of ideas and culture, as have honestly "deconstructed" their own cultural heritage with the conscious aspiration to transcend all cultural conditioning as far as this may be humanly possible. To the best of my knowledge, French and German scholars come on top with the British and American two steps behind. To my mind Islamic scholars are way behind them in the pre-requisite methodological task of "deconstructing" one's own cultural and religious tradition prior to entering the portals of one's own authentic faith, whatever it might be. Among my own countrymen, I admire the conceptual sharpness, intellectual honesty, and tolerance of several liberal Hindu intellectuals as well as the common man. In the medieval era, however, the Muslim Sufi saints, poets, and even thinkers attained high levels of cultural "deconstruction" and transcendence and also did pioneering work in the sphere of cross-cultural studies. The Arabic work of Al-Beruni (d. CE 1048) *Kitabul Hind* remains, to date, a classic study of Indian Brahmanism and its variants.

5. Every thinker, historian, and dispassionate observer of the human scene is agreed on this issue. Al-Beruni, who spent several years in India learning Sanskrit and carefully scrutinizing the beliefs, rituals, and customs of Hindu "polytheists" and idolaters concluded that, in the ultimate analysis, they too subscribed to the idea of one Supreme Creator and Sustainer of all that exists. Modern anthropologists have come to a similar conclusion. See Bhagwan Das: *The Essential Unity of All Religions*.

6. See the following Qur'anic verses:

2:62

Those who believe (in the Qur'an), and those who follow the Jewish (scriptures), and the Christians and the Sabians,—any who believe in Allah and the Last Day, and work righteousness, shall have their reward with their Lord; on them shall be no fear, nor shall they grieve.

22:67

To every People have We appointed rites and ceremonies, which they must follow: let them not then dispute with thee on the matter, but do thou invite (them) to thy Lord: for thou art assuredly on the Right Way.

21:92–94

Verily, this brotherhood of yours is a single brotherhood, and I am your Lord and Cherisher: therefore serve Me (and no other). But (later generations) cut off their affair (of unity), one from another: (yet) will they all return to Us. Whoever works any act of righteousness and has faith, His endeavor will not be rejected: We shall record it in his favor.

Some Qur'anic verses that refer to wartime prohibitions run as follows:

3:28

Let not the believers take for friends or helpers Unbelievers rather than believers: if any do that, in nothing will there be help from Allah: except by way of precaution, that ye may guard yourselves from them.

136

But Allah cautions you (to remember) Himself; for the final goal is to Allah.

3:118
O ye who believe! Take not into your intimacy those outside your ranks: They will not fail to corrupt you. They only desire your ruin: Rank hatred has already appeared from their mouths: What their hearts conceal is far worse. We have made plain to you the Signs, if ye have wisdom.

5:51
O ye who believe! Take not the Jews and the Christians for your friends and protectors: They are but friends and protectors to each other. And he amongst you that turns to them (for friendship) is of them. Verily Allah guideth not a people unjust.

7. An "authentic" person is one who can see into and through his "existential abyss" without any distortion or deception. Existentialist thinkers may be theistic, atheistic, or agnostic. The Danish thinker Kierkegaard (d. CE 1855) and the French thinker Gabriel Marcel (d. CE 1973) are the leading existential theists, the French thinkers Albert Camus (d. CE 1960) and Sartre (d. CE 1980) are the leading atheists, while the German thinkers Heidegger (d. CE 1976) and Karl Jaspers (d. CE 1969) are more or less agnostic. Existential analysis has similarities with Sufi theory and practice of prayerful deep introspection of the contents of the deepest self (*nafs*) and the Buddhist concept of "*vipasna.*" They all aim to reach the goal of non-conceptual authentic being.

8. Authentic Hindus are known to have accepted Muslim saints as their mentors, while authentic Muslims have turned to Sikh, Hindu, or Christian spiritual guides.

9. Guru Nanak (d. approximately CE 1539) and Mahatma Gandhi (d. CE 1948) are symbols of authenticity and tolerance in the history of India. Both were born Hindus who, in a spirit of humility, authenticity, and loving acceptance of spiritual plurality "deconstructed" their own cultural heritage and arrived at their own unique angle of vision of the human situation. Guru Nanak transplanted Islamic Monotheism in the Brahmanical conceptual framework after completely rejecting the Hindu ideas of caste and the belief in myth as history, but firmly retaining the idea of "*karma.*" Likewise, Gandhiji (d. CE 1948) created his own version of modern Hinduism under the influence of ancient Indian, Islamic and Christian values and concepts.

10. See Qur'anic text, 2:190–193 quoted in the text of Chapter 5, "The Piety of the Qur'an."

11. See Qur'anic verse:

9:72

Allah hath promised to believers—men and women Gardens under which rivers flow, to dwell therein, and beautiful mansions in Gardens of everlasting bliss. But the greatest bliss is the good pleasure of Allah: that is the supreme felicity.

Also see Chapter 5, "The Piety of the Qur'an."

12. See Chapter 2, "The Qur'an as a Revealed Book: Some Issues."

13. The most reputed liberal theologians and philosophical thinkers, no matter what their religion or philosophy, now concede the central importance of semantics for a fruitful study of all analytical, existentialist and epistemological, and theological issues. This is the only way to remove disagreement, which flows from confusion of terms and concepts. Semantic and conceptual analysis helps us to distinguish dogmas from beliefs. When one realizes that no "dogma" can be proved, one ceases to argue dogmatically, yet concedes space to oneself and all others to keep one's faith. If the faith was genuine, to begin with, it can well remain without the illusion or delusion that those who cherish other dogmas are not knaves or fools but simply have a "faith" that differs from ours.

14. One often notices that persons having deep and genuine faith in some creed have great humility and show great tolerance to others, while those whose faith is rather shaky tend to be loud in propagating their faith or creed. Many profound students of human nature and holy men interpret this phenomenon as a compensatory mechanism for overcoming their unconscious sense of inadequate faith.

15. This grand Indian tradition dating from very ancient times when Panchtantra and *Pitaka* tales were born is being continued by contemporary spiritual leaders from India, such as Sukhabodhanand, Sivananda, and Ravi Shankar, *et al.* They draw upon folklore and anecdotes from all over the world, and their wit is simply superb.

16. Unfortunately, Islamic spirituality seems to have lost its capacity for combining tradition with change. There is no Islamic counterpart of a Ramakrishna Paramhansa (d. CE 1886), Gandhi (d. CE 1948), Maharishi Raman (d. CE 1990), and Yogananda (d. CE 1952). The different Islamic movements today, and their main figures are focused on the *Shariah*, unlike the Islamic Liberalism of Sir Syed, Iqbal and Abul Kalam Azad in the Indian subcontinent, and Jamaluddin Afghani (d. CE 1897) and Muhammad Abduh in Egypt.

17. See the pioneering work, *A New Religious America*, by Diana Eck, 2002, and the several works by Karen Armstrong, the roving ambassador of the interfaith movement. Her latest work is, *Muhammad: Prophet for Our Time*, 2006.

18. See Chapter 6, "The Injunctions of the Qur'an: Some Issues."

19. The founding father of the idea of *Islamization of Knowledge* was (late) Ismail Faruqi, of Palestinian origin, and for many years a professor at Temple University, USA. He was assassinated under mysterious circumstances. He was well-familiar with modern thought, but it seems, from his writings, that he had only a superficial understanding of the European tradition of critical analysis, and the value system of the French and German enlightenment starting from the 18th century and still going strong. He overlooked semantics, existential analysis, comparative spiritualism in favor of the sociology of knowledge centered on the idea of "paradigm shifts."

20. The founder of Pakistan, M. A. Jinnah, was a vocal champion of secular parliamentary democracy and an ardent Indian patriot until his late middle life. He lost his way in the long march of India's fight for freedom from British colonial rule and became a powerful spokesman for a separate sovereign state for Indian Muslims.

The entire blame for this sudden reversal of direction should not be laid on his shoulders alone. However, the single largest share of responsibility for partition of the great Indian family on religious lines lies squarely on his shoulders. However, once partition was done, its architect made a u-turn in the National Assembly of sovereign Pakistan, and began speaking in the secular idiom of Gandhi (d. CE 1948), Nehru (d. CE 1964), and Azad (d. CE 1958). Had he lived longer, the history of Pakistan may well have been very different from the course it actually took.

Notes to Chapter 2   The Qur'an as a Revealed Book: Some Issues

1. The primary content or kernel of the Muslim's existential faith is the belief in one Supreme Creator and the absolute veracity of Prophet Muhammad ﷺ, even prior to as well as ever after the commencement of his apostolic mission. This mission started immediately after the "event of the cave" at Hira one fateful night in the latter half of the Arabic month of Ramadan in CE 610. I submit, in all humility, that this core or kernel of faith does not contain or imply any specific details of what exactly happened that night in the cave, beyond the five verses of *surah Qadr*, mentioned above. All the colorful details of the "event of revelation," the appearance or visitation of the Holy Spirit or angel Gabriel, the dialogue between God's angel and Prophet Muhammad ﷺ, his inner experience, and response are all part of the belief system of Muslims, rather than clear statements mentioned in the Qur'an as such. Likewise, the detailed stories, legends, myths, Prophet

Muhammad's ﷺ dialogues with other prophets and angels, at each stage of the Prophet's ﷺ journey from the first to the seventh heaven, during the "event of the ascension" (*meraj*) of the Prophet ﷺ, long after the "event of the cave," are not mentioned in the Qur'an. Yet, the fact remains that all the above secondary and tertiary beliefs and imagery have become integral parts of the Islamic faith at the most popular level. Even highly educated persons are liable to frown at a fellow Muslim who may be somewhat doubtful of the truth of any part of the colorful details of these sacred narratives that (quite obviously) are extra-Qur'anic. Even till today some highly educated Muslims severely castigate Syed Ahmed Khan (the Muslim reformer of the 19th century and founder of the world famous liberal Arts Muslim College at Aligarh) precisely because he rejected these details though he firmly believed that the Qur'an was a revealed Book.

The approach of the great Muslim thinkers and intellectuals of the classical Islamic times like Kindi (d. CE 873), Farabi (d. CE 950), Ibn Sina (d. CE 1037), Ibn Rushd (d. CE 1198), Al-Beruni (d. CE 1048), and, after a long break, Ibn Khaldun (d. CE 1406) was also very different from the popular belief system, and they also lived under a cloud of suspicion and mistrust as they had honestly and boldly deconstructed or "demythologized" the Islamic religious and spiritual tradition. They had sought to interpret and explain the "event of the cave" in the conceptual framework of pure spirituality without adding the alloy of myth or miracle. Their leading concepts were grounded equally in the Semitic religious tradition and Qur'anic spirituality as well as the ancient Greek wisdom and Indian spirituality. Their "root" concept was, perhaps, the idea that all values such as truth, knowledge, wisdom, love, goodness, beauty and so on flow from Divine grace and blessings, and that these Divine blessings are of different grades. The gift of "*wahy*" is the highest form of Divine blessings, and the recipient of this blessing is termed a prophet or messenger of God. These great Muslim sages and intellectuals did not repudiate the basic concept of "*wahy*." Rather, under the combined influence of Greek and Indian thought and spirituality, they tried to purge the grand tradition of Semitic monotheistic spirituality from all anthropomorphic contents or myths. However, due to social psychological reasons, the way in which the great Muslim savants and sages interpreted the "event of the cave" could not grip the imagination of Muslim believers at the popular level, and mainstream Muslims opted to remain and still remain at the level of myth and miracle rather than of reason and revelation. The attraction or charm of the religion of myth and miracle, and an anthropomorphic vision of Ultimate Reality or God is common to all religions. A believer cannot but believe in a certain way that corresponds to his or her level of understanding or fits in one's habitual and familiar conceptual frame. And no harm accrues if one's conceptual picture or faith does not generate any inner doubts or conceptual field-tensions in the individual and he or she does not try to impose one's own faith on others. I submit that Muslim society in general failed in regard to the latter condition. The Muslim thinkers, Sufi saints, and poets had inwardly assimilated the Qur'anic message of tolerance and its stress on authentic faith, and the pursuit of wisdom leading to righteous action. However, the great Muslim theologians and jurists, in their own wisdom, made strict and unquestioning obedience to their own interpretations of the Qur'an and the *sunnah* the exclusive test of being a good Muslim. This ethos hovers over the Muslim psyche even today.

2. The Qur'an refers to Prophet Abraham as a "*Hanif*" and a "*Muslim*." See the following texts:

2:135

They say: "Become Jews or Christians if ye would be guided (to salvation)." Say thou: "Nay! (I would rather) the Religion of Abraham the True, and he joined not gods with Allah."

3:67, 68

Abraham was not a Jew nor yet a Christian; but he was true in Faith, and bowed his will to Allah's (which is Islam), and he joined not gods with Allah. Without doubt, among men, the nearest of kin to Abraham, are those who follow him, as are also this Prophet and those who believe: And Allah is the Protector of those who have faith.

3:95

Say: "Allah speaketh the Truth: follow the religion of Abraham, the sane in faith; he was not of the Pagans."

4:125

Who can be better in religion than one who submits his whole self to Allah, does good, and follows the way of Abraham the true in Faith? For Allah did take Abraham for a friend.

"*Hanif*" is a general term in Arabic for referring to all who believe in one Supreme Creator, no matter what Book or Prophet one might follow. It means monotheist, be he Jew, Arab, Indian, or Chinese. Due to historical factors, this term never acquired wide circulation. But the contemporary situation is very different. In a world that is fast turning into a global city due to the irresistible impact of modern technology the "spirit of the times" is favoring the emergence of the concept of unity of "*deen*" in the midst of different organized religions. This concept implies that all believers in one God, irrespective of other differences of creed, symbol or scripture, form one fraternity.

3. The Arabic work of Ibn Ishaq/Ibn Hisham on the life and character of Prophet Muhammad ﷺ has been translated and edited by A. Guillaume (1955). It carries copious notes, and reference material, critically evaluated. Orthodox Islamists, however, do not set much store on the above two earliest works on the life and character of the Prophet ﷺ on the ground that they do not spring from or rely on *hadith* literature, which is (to their mind) the only authentic source material in addition to the Qur'an itself. The reluctance of the Sunni Islamic tradition to accommodate and appreciate the rich and well-researched contributions made by others, and an almost exclusive focus on their own circle of Qur'an and *hadith* scholars has ill served the ideals of free inquiry, critical objectivity, and conceptual clarity.

The crux of the issue is as follows: Muslim believers have generally "glorified" the life, character, and achievements of the Prophet ﷺ, indeed have looked upon him as the "Perfect Man" (*Insan-e-Kamil*). On the other hand, the Western world, almost right up to the 17th century, maligned and demonized the person they called "Mahund" (the distorted pronunciation of "Muhammad"). A new wind started blowing from the 18th century onwards, thanks to the great English historian, Edward Gibbon (d. CE 1794), the German savant, Goethe (d. CE 1832), the Scottish historian and man of letters, Carlyle (d. CE 1881), the French savant, Renan (d. CE 1892), and some other distinguished figures who rose above all pride and prejudice of race, region, religion, and the like. Now almost after 300 years of intellectual labor, free inquiry, and intercultural dialogue the world over, a consensus is steadily growing that the historical figure, Muhammad of Arabia, born, CE 570 at Mecca, was, indeed, a person of great integrity, intuitive wisdom, moral and physical courage, determination, organizing ability, very high qualities of leadership, sincerity, and faith in his sense of mission as a Divinely ordained messenger. This consensus certainly does not mean any convergence of the liberal humanist vision to the traditional or formal "ideology" of Islam. Indeed, all "ideologies," in the classical Marxist sense, are on the way out. To my mind, the growing consensus (that is still incomplete) is a sign that different human groups or nations which, hitherto, were "closed" ideological units, are moving toward the ideal of "open" and tolerant societies that respect cultural pluralism and liberal humanism. The so-called movement of "Islamic Fundamentalism" is a temporary backlash effect of Western or North American *realpolitik*. See the insightful works of the following illustrious writers: Montgomery Watt, *Muhammad at Mecca; Muhammad at Medina;* Annemarie Schimmel (d. CE 2003), *The Mystical Dimensions of Islam;* Martin Lings, *Muhammad: His Life based on the Earliest Sources;* Huston Smith, *The World's Religions;* Diana Eck, *A New Religious America;* Karen Armstrong, *Muhammad: Prophet for Our Time;* and Carl Ernst, *Following Muhammad, et al.*

4. In the Qur'an the Arabic verb *"yuha,"* derived from the same root as the Arabic noun, *"wahy,"* has been used not only in the context of the revealed Qur'anic verses, but also in a much wider context. See the Qur'anic verse:

16: 68
And thy Lord taught the Bee to build its cells in hills, on trees, and in (men's) habitations.

See also verse:
28:7
So We sent this inspiration to the mother of Moses: "Suckle (thy child), but when thou hast fears about him, cast him into the river, but fear not nor grieve: for We shall restore him to thee, and We shall make him one of Our messengers."

The Qur'an also uses the verb, *"yuha"* to refer to the secret signals some disbelievers sent to fellow disbelievers, while interacting with the Prophet ﷺ or other Muslims. The broad sense of the word *"wahy"* is, thus, the action of *"silently directing, guiding, communicating with, and hinting at somebody to say or do something as desired by some principal."* We all understand and use the term *"wahy"* in this broad sense. However, the "event of the cave" was not an instance of *"wahy,"* in the general sense, since, in this case, the guidance or communication came from the Supreme Creator through some mysterious agency or process beyond the Prophet's ﷺ own comprehension. The Prophet ﷺ himself felt bewildered and perplexed at the strange "event" and directly left for his home. All our knowledge of what transpired when his wife comforted him, or what she told her spouse is based on the earliest reports of what had happened. However, these reports themselves reflect the mental construction or understanding of the immediate contemporaries of the Prophet ﷺ and afterward of the earliest biographers. In short, it is extremely difficult, rather impossible for any human to claim clear and definitive knowledge of "the event of the cave." All that is certain, in the sense of historical certainty, is that Muhammad ﷺ (who was used to frequenting the cave of Hira and meditating there for long periods) one night underwent some very extraordinary experience that left him completely shattered and perplexed for some few hours after its occurrence in the cave. However, he soon recovered from the terrifying or awesome impact of a mysterious experience he never expected. The power of the "spiritual lightning," as it were, that befell him seems to have shaken him to the foundations of his existence for some time. After returning to his normal waking consciousness in the familiar comfort of his home and the ministrations of his trusted spouse, he realized that he had been blessed by the Supreme Creator and charged with the duty of guiding his own people steeped in pride and ignorance. At that moment there was ignited a burning sense of responsibility to perform the mighty task entrusted to him by the Creator Himself. He had not sought the task and he had no pretensions of ability or power or any ambition to act a hero or play to the gallery. A picture of humility, he thirsted to see the light and the truth and win a lasting peace of mind in "*the vale of ignorance and strife.*"

As soon as the Muhammad ﷺ of history proclaimed that he had been Divinely charged with a mission, he landed not only himself but also his fellow Meccans in serious trouble. The Prophet's ﷺ contemporaries were well-aware of his great integrity of character and his other abilities as a successful manager and social activist deeply concerned with public welfare. They could not deny his sincerity and truthfulness, yet they could not accept him as a prophet or his talk of God and the angels or the Holy Spirit. The pagan Bedouins, thus, concluded that the "event of the cave" did happen, and this did change Muhammad's ﷺ life pattern, but the truth was different from what Muhammad ﷺ thought. The pagan Meccan explanation or interpretation was that some "*jinn*" or evil spirit must have taken possession of Muhammad ﷺ, or that he had lost his mental balance. Some suspected that Muhammad ﷺ had turned into a soothsayer (*kahin*). Others likened his experience to the inspired poetic outbursts of poets in moments or phases of "inspiration." The pagans were familiar with these ideas or concepts and it was but natural for them to "fit" the "event of the cave" in their own antecedent conceptual framework or mindset. The more hardened and rather hostile opponents, however, accused him of downright fraud. Some accused him of being tutored in secrecy by some Jewish rabbi.

There was another reason for the conflict of interpretation made by the Prophet's ﷺ followers (who, mainly belonged to the weaker section of the populace) and that made by the dominant section of Meccan traders who controlled the market economy and the *Kabah* itself. To accept that Muhammad ﷺ was the messenger of God logically implied that he must be obeyed, and this meant losing their own superior status and also losing their freedom of choice in all social, political, and economic matters. Moreover, the nascent Islamic thought and value system itself had not yet fully crystallized and was not transparently clear to anybody, not even to the Prophet ﷺ himself. The revelation of the Qur'an was a continuing process and the revealed verses were quite often in response to some objection or query raised by the disbelievers. Moreover, according to the reports contained in the *hadith*, collections of the venerated *Imams*, Bukhari and Muslim, themselves, there was no uniform and fixed mode in which revelations came to the Prophet ﷺ. At times he heard the ringing of bells, at other times he had a vision of the Holy Spirit or Gabriel, at yet other times Gabriel appeared and conversed with him in a human form. I submit, in all humility, that if the disbelievers had been told or had come to know about the different modes or forms of "wahy," this must have increased their initial contumacy and doubts.

To my mind, therefore, the response of the Meccan contemporaries was quite in line with the normal human tendency to explain any paranormal event one comes across in terms of one's habitual conceptual framework. Ibn Khaldun points out this fact in his monumental *Prolegomena to World History*. This tendency will ever remain the same. The question is what is or ought to be the proper conceptual framework in *our* times in view of the immense growth of factual knowledge and of new disciplines of knowledge based on appropriate methodologies of study and research.

Today, there is a vast store of carefully investigated record of paranormal phenomena comprising automatic writing, extra sensory perception (ESP), precognition, multiple personalities, hypnotism, hypno-therapy, yogic control over bodily functions, and so on. William James' (d. CE 1910) classic, *The Varieties of Religious Experience*, and C. D. Broad's classic, *Lectures on Psychical Research*, 1962, and C. G. Jung's pioneering work, *The Concept of the Collective Unconscious*, 1936, make it imperative that one should overcome the "reductive scientism" of the previous two centuries. And, indeed, this way of thinking is on the rise.

The classical Muslim thinkers and scientists had never rejected the dimension of spirituality from their worldview despite solidly and strongly relying on the scientific method of observation and experiment. They were also sensitive to the dangers of uncontrolled speculation and of the unwarranted injection of anthropomorphism in religious or theological language. But they found it difficult to express openly their remarkable insights and refined interpretations of God, "wahy," the Holy Spirit, angels, mystical experience, "meraj" of the Prophet ﷺ and other spiritual concepts and values because the orthodox *ulema* and jurists frowned upon what they deemed to be "ajami" distortions of the pure Qur'anic Islam.

In short, the prevailing restrictions on free inquiry and unhampered expression of ideas prevented the full flowering and growth of the critical and rational Qur'an studies in the Islamic East, especially, after the Mongol sack of Baghdad in 1256, and subsequently in the Islamic West after the death of Ibn Khaldun. A relatively more free and liberal intellectual culture flourished in Mughal India right up to the advent of British rule. But the creative *élan* of the classical Islamic age had withered away.

The crux of the matter is that all conceptual interpretations of transcendental beliefs (that, by definition, are unverifiable or logically indemonstrable, such as the nature or existence of God, Divine attributes, Divine revelation, life after death, Divine incarnation, transmigration of souls, angels and the Devil and so on) are made in an antecedently accepted broad framework of ideas and assumptions. This framework is the matrix or the rock bottom seabed in which arise the waves of ideas and beliefs of individuals and groups when they try to respond to the mystery of the Universe. Thus, it is sheer folly for anybody to claim that his or her perspective or resolution of the mystery of being is the sole truth. The sages and saints of ancient India and China had won and stressed this tremendous insight in their fables and scriptures alike.

Neither any Qur'anic text, nor any saying of the Prophet 鷺 , nor any description given by the companions of the Prophet 鷺 or others spells out the nature or mechanics of the revelatory experience (*wahy*) as such. The nature of the experience cannot be communicated to others who, themselves, have not had a similar experience. Analogies may help others to understand, up to a point, but will never be able to convey the actual concrete "feel" of the experience, as such. Hence, the futility of theorizing or proving any truthclaim regarding such matters as "revelation," "incarnation," "Day of Judgment," "pleasures of heaven," "tortures of hell," and so on. What, however, remains absolutely undeniable, is that all well-versed in Arabic literature testify to the unsurpassed literary beauty, power, simplicity, and economy of expression of the Qur'an. This becomes all the more remarkable and puzzling in view of the fact that the Prophet 鷺 was either illiterate or barely literate. This fact, however, does not amount to proving that the Qur'an is the "Word of God." This belief is, in the final analysis, the "dogmatic differentia" of the Islamic faith as one particular version of monotheism in general.

It may be asked what is wrong if one interprets or explains the "event of the cave" as one instance of "paranormal" phenomena along with the ones mentioned above, whose genuineness is, increasingly, being accepted but whose explanation or etiology is yet problematic. A hardened positivist or agnostic might say that the Prophet's 鷺 "unlabored" recitation of Arabic verses or sentences of superb beauty and power could very well be just another case of the larger family of psychic or paranormal phenomena. Thus, the positivist might say that what the Muslim believer calls "revelation from God through Gabriel" may well be a benign outpouring or unlabored "linguistic expression" of Muhammad's 鷺 unconscious, at its deepest level. The positivist may then say that, since the Qur'an's temporal genesis involved no labor on Muhammad's 鷺 part, he was quite truthful and sincere in holding that the Qur'an was "revealed" to him from above, or from God.

I submit there is no one clear explication of the mystery of "the event of the cave" on that fateful night of Ramadan. The positivist's interpretation itself may well be true, provided one views the "Unconscious" as a "Supermind" or "Oversoul" (after the manner of a Jung), rather than as an "Id" (after the manner of a Freud). Indeed, the great thinkers and mystics of Islam in the classical era held that the Creator had endowed different forms of His creation, such as stones, plants, birds, insects, water and land animals, angels, *jinn*, and finally, humankind, with different grades of gifts or capacities. They further held that the "capacity for receiving revelation" was the highest form of several gifts or powers, such as the power of sense perception, memory, making logical, moral and aesthetic judgments, creating music and poetry and other works of art, understanding the Divinely ordained patterns of cause and effect in the cosmos.

According to the above line of thinking, humankind was the apex of Divine creation, and God's messengers, (scattered all over the human family) were the recipients of the apex gift of Divine revelation. This gift was a kind of inner light that enabled the messengers or prophets to see and understand the basic spiritual and moral truths of supreme importance for human welfare and salvation in accordance with the Creator's Will and Wisdom, as such. To my mind, the above line of thinking was a remarkable attempt to "demythologize" the great spiritual heritage of Semitic Monotheism and to define, effectively and consistently, the core of the Islamic faith within the parameters of a pure ethical theism whose differentia was faith in Divine revelation (*wahy*) to the messengers of God, in general and Prophet Muhammad ﷺ, in particular. It was an attempt to transcend the mythical, theological, and legalistic approach to Monotheism and to view faith in God and the "Word of God" in a conceptual framework that could stand on its own inner logical consistency and power rather than blind conformity to parochial ideas or local conceptual patterns.

The Vedantic view that the individual mind or soul (*Atman*) is organically connected with the Absolute Mind or Soul (*Brahman*) and that the existential realization of this supreme truth leads to the highest wisdom, bliss, and salvation can *also* serve as a conceptual model to clarify (partly) that the source of the "revelatory process" was internal rather than external. In short, there can be many ways of looking at the mystery of the "event of the cave." What, to my mind, really matters is not the explication of the mystery, but the authentic acceptance of the total sincerity and integrity of Muhammad ﷺ.

5. Two examples of prima facie internal contradiction are the Qur'anic texts, which prescribe, respectively, the punishment for theft and the punishment for mocking at the "Signs of Allah."

5:38, 39

As to the thief, male or female, cut off his or her hands: a punishment by way of example, from Allah, for their crime: and Allah is Exalted in power. But if the thief repents after his crime, and amends his conduct, Allah turneth to him in forgiveness; for Allah is Oft-Forgiving, Most Merciful.

17:45,46

When thou dost recite the Qur'an, We put, between thee and those who believe not in the Hereafter, a veil invisible: And We put coverings over their hearts (and minds) lest they should understand the Qur'an, and deafness into their ears: when thou dost commemorate thy Lord and Him alone in the Qur'an, they turn on their backs, fleeing (from the Truth).

18:57

And who doth more wrong than one who is reminded of the Signs of his Lord, but turns away from them, forgetting the (deeds) which his hands have sent forth? Verily We have set veils over their hearts lest they should understand this, and over their ears, deafness, if thou callest them to guidance, even then will they never accept guidance.

The issue of prima facie internal contradiction in the Qur'an has been dealt with more fully in Chapter 3, "The Semantics of the Qur'an."

6. The Qur'an refers to itself by several names other than "Book," such as "Statement" (*Bayan*, 3:137), "Criterion" (*Furqan*, 25:1), "Guidance" (*al-Huda*, 72:13), "Light" (*An-Noor*, 7:57), "Reminder" (73:19), and many other names. English and other languages also use the word "book" in varying senses, such as reading the "book of nature." To my mind, therefore, both those who allege that the unsystematic and rambling style or arrangement of the Qur'an are inherent defects in the Qur'an, and those who reply in defense (using dubious arguments) that the Qur'an is a highly systematic book are equally wrong.

7. Parchment/papyrus was used as a writing surface in China and Egypt several centuries before the birth of Christ. The Jewish Bible was also written on these surfaces. The Dead Sea scrolls were discovered from caves near the salt lake between modern Israel and Jordan near the West Bank. The Jewish rabbis had buried them there to protect them from being destroyed by Roman armies. They were written between the second century BC and the first century CE. However, these facts do not clearly indicate that during the Prophet's ﷺ time, Arab society had easy access to paper, unless there be some other positive evidence in support. See *www.wikipedia.org*.

The division of the Qur'an into thirty parts (*paras*) of exactly equal phonetical length independently of subject matter/name of the 114 *surahs* was done to help the accurate memorizing of the Qur'anic contents, probably, under the Caliphate of Uthman in the 7th century CE. Diacritical marks or vowels were inserted in the text, probably, toward the close of the 9th century CE.

8. Among the eminent and impartial non-Muslim scholars of the Qur'an the pride of place, to date, goes to the German scholar, Noeldeke (d. CE 1930). His multi-volume *Textual History of the Qur'an* is hardly likely to be surpassed by any other work. However, on a much smaller scale, John Burton's, *The Collection of the Qur'an* (Cambridge, 1977) appears to me as the most well-informed and balanced contribution to the subject.

Burton concludes that the Prophet ﷺ himself had given directions and instructions in regard to the proper sequence of the verses and the *surahs* to his close companions, Abu Bakr and Umar, to prepare a full proto-copy of the Qur'an in its present arrangement. The Sunni Islamic tradition generally attributes the collection and dispersal of the Qur'an (as we know it today) to the third Caliph, Uthman. Burton concludes that Uthman had merely consolidated, and mass circulated the proto-copy prepared earlier and ordered the destruction of spurious versions that had come into being due to the rapid and far reaching political expansion of Islam in the regions of Asia and Africa. The learned Islamic scholars of the Qur'an, Muhammad Ali (d. CE 1951) of Lahore and Hamiedullah (d. CE 2002) of Paris are also of the same view.

To the best of my knowledge and belief, the dominant version of Shia Islam, as represented by its most enlightened and sincere protagonists in the modern age, concurs with the Islamic faith that the Qur'an, as it now exists, is entirely free from any human tampering or corruption. The vast majority of the large Shia fraternity in the world, however, does persistently regret (expressed in rituals of public lamentation) that the person who was most qualified to succeed the Prophet ﷺ was denied his due because of *realpolitik* as well as personal ambitions. I, respectfully, submit that the house of Islam ought to be big and broad enough to admit many mansions.

Some minor alternative Shia traditions actually nursed (in the middle ages) and may well continue to nurse even now "conspiracy theories" that the enemies of *Imam* Ali actually managed to remove some Qur'anic texts and sayings of the Prophet ﷺ that favored *Imam* Ali's direct succession to the Prophet ﷺ. Some of these phantasies were to the effect that God intended to appoint Ali as His messenger but the angel Gabriel mistook Muhammad ﷺ for Ali. The inherent absurdity of many such phantasies or beliefs do not bother the simple folk whose credulity knows no limits and who seldom, if at all, try to think consistently. Such believers are found in all religions and sects.

The most crucial point to be kept in mind is that the core of the faith, as such, is, unavoidably and essentially, "nebulous", and this core just does not have any inherent fixed or precise "meaning" that can be communicated, explained, or "proved" as the "real" meaning of the dogma. The concrete content of the abstract dogma partly comes alive for the individual or the group due to cultural conditioning effected by parents, teachers and the life situation of every individual. Thus the dogma does not function as an ordinary linguistic tool used for pointing out, referring to, or manipulating things or directing/ negotiating/ cooperating and performing the whole range of cognitive and other social activities and tasks of life. The dogma functions, basically, as a life giving and sustaining bond that unifies a particular group and gives it a collective identity and stability. This is, indeed, a very vital function, but it should not be confused with the other functions of human language and reasoning in the enterprise of individual and collective life. Nor should the believer in any dogma inadvertently "reduce" the potential plurality of its concrete interpretations or formulations to any one particular interpretation or formulation. However, this reductive fallacy is extremely common, and, obviously, the most natural step is to suppose that "the" and only "right" interpretation of the dogma is the one, which is upheld by one's own in-group.

9. The Western theory of knowledge has always laid much stress upon the distinction between subjective and objective judgments. This distinction, indeed, is fundamental. However, it is now widely accepted that there are types and subtypes within the broad category of "objective judgment" and "subjective judgment." Thus, autonomous, ethical judgments are not "objectively certain" like methodologically grounded scientific judgments (usually regarded as the model of an objective judgment). Yet, scientific judgments themselves are not "objectively certain" in the still more rigorous sense of a mathematical/ logical certainty. The ethical judgment "murder is bad" is certain (provided we use murder in the sense of unprovoked/ illegal killing), yet it is not certain in the sense of the certainty of the scientific judgment, "the specific gravity of ice is less than that of water." And this scientific judgment is less certain than the mathematical judgment, "$3 + 2 = 5$."

Metaphysical and religious beliefs fall in yet another category that has its own unique kind of criteria of validity or acceptability. I have discussed this issue in great detail in my earlier work, *Quest for Islam*, 1977.

Notes to Chapter 3   The Semantics of the Qur'an

1. I can do no better here than to quote a rather extended excerpt from the preface of the recently published six-volume *Encyclopedia of the Qur'an*, which is a very valuable addition to some other excellent works of reference on Islam:

"Other questions quickly arose: When and in what circumstances, were certain verses revealed? Who or what is intended by an ambiguous term or phrase? To whom or to what does a particular pronoun refer? Who is being addressed by a specific passage, and to whom should it apply: to all believers, present and future, or to a restricted set of individuals? Is the intended sense metaphorical or should the verse be understood literally? Are all parts of the Qur'an equally comprehensible or are some parts more inherently obscure or problematic? Are there connections between verses, either within a *surah* or across various parts of the Qur'an? Can a passage elsewhere in the text help to explain the one under present examination? Are there levels or layers of meaning in the text and are they accessible only to individuals with special intellectual or spiritual training?"

2. The well known theologian, Abu Musa Ashari (d. approx. CE 940) and his followers held that the entire corpus of the Qur'an was eternally present with God, and the angel, Gabriel, under God's command, merely transferred the eternal Qur'an to the consciousness of the Prophet. To the best of my knowledge, his view was based on his interpretation of the Qur'anic texts,

85:21, 22
Nay, this is a Glorious Qur'an, (inscribed) in a Tablet Preserved!

43:3–5
We have made it a Qur'an in Arabic, that ye may be able to understand (and learn wisdom). And verily, it is in the Mother of the Book, in Our Presence, high (in dignity), full of wisdom. Shall We then take away the Message from you and repel (you), for that ye are a people transgressing beyond bounds?

The earlier Mutazilite theologians, Huzail (d. CE 841), Nazzam (d. CE 845), and Jahiz (d. CE 868), had held that the Qur'an was not co-eternal with God but was created by God. The dispute became very bitter indeed, and some of the Caliphs themselves persecuted scholars and theologians who disagreed with the Caliph's own view on this issue. I submit that such speculative interpretations of Qur'anic verses or expressions are not an integral part of the simple Islamic faith or dogma that the Qur'an is the "Word of God." Indeed, it is impossible for any one to explain and conclusively prove any dogma or article of faith of any religion or value system. Modern linguistic analysis and semantics reveals that such debates are not about facts as such, but how to label them and are thus, essentially, language games theologians or others play for satisfying extra-logical needs or value judgments. In this particular case the Asharite interpretation serves the purpose of "glorifying" the Qur'an, ad infinitum, while the Mutazilite view is based on a more realistic and functional approach to the Qur'an.

In all humility, I would like to give two clear, rather glaring examples of playing linguistic games to satisfy extra-logical needs/glorify what one venerates.

Christian theologians right up to the beginning of the modern era seriously discussed the issue as to how many angels could dance on the head of a fine needle. Muslim theologians and popular folklore mentioned the number of guardian angels God deputed to accompany Gabriel when some especially important verse or *surah* was to be revealed to the Prophet ﷺ. See the section *Mystique of the Qur'an* later.

3. Human communication in general combines the different functions of language or rapidly shifts gears from one function to the other. To pinpoint different functions is only an analytical device to achieve a clearer understanding of what we do with language in different life situations. A clearer understanding of the different functions prevents or reduces the chances of our falling in language traps or getting "bewitched" by the inherent "plasticity" and other limitations of human language and of linguistic symbols. This is the lasting insight and message of the German speaking analytical thinker, Ludwig Wittgenstein (d. CE 1951).

According to this line of thinking, linguistic communication uses concepts that are inherently plastic or indeterminate and static, while reality is inherently concrete, vibrant and dynamic, or changing. This is also the liberating insight of the vastly influential and still growing existentialist approach to religion and philosophy under the impact of Kierkegaard (d. CE 1855), Nietzsche (d. CE 1900), Heidegger (d. CE 1976), Karl Jaspers (d. CE 1969), Gabriel Marcel (d. CE 1973), Sartre (d. CE 1980), and others. In the context of Qur'an Studies the Japanese thinker, Izutsu (d. CE 1993) remains, perhaps, the lone eminent pioneer, among the modern scholars of the Qur'an (see his remarkable works, *God and Man in the Qur'an*, 1964, and *Ethico-Religious Concepts in the Qur'an*, 2002).

4. In Babylonia the quantum of the "increase" or charge on the quantum of the loan was calculated on the analogy of the natural growth, in one year or any fixed period, of the commodity concerned. The borrower was also subject to bonded labor extending to a maximum period of seven years, in case of default. This was the functional meaning of "*riba*" in pre Qur'anic times and the Qur'an strongly prohibited the same. See, entry on "*riba*" in *Encyclopedia of Religion and Ethics*, 13 volumes, edited by James Hastings, 1927.

5. There is no contradiction in believing that all created beings obey the Creator's commands without fail (except humans) and also holding that all events are subject to the principle of uniform causality. Science only discovers the exact uniform and quantified connection between the cause and the effect. But pure science does not raise or seek to answer who decreed or fixed the connection in the first place. Ghazali (d. CE 1111) and even earlier Muslim theologians had clearly anticipated Western thinkers like David Hume (d. CE 1776) and Immanuel Kant (d. CE 1804) in pointing out this significant point and also in showing there was no logical connection or necessity that the cause-effect connection (as it obtains in the present) shall ever remains so in reality. Indeed, science itself accepts the principle of mutation in natural phenomena.

6. Qur'anic verses give different values to "*one day*" in the sight of the Supreme Creator. This figure ranges from one thousand to fifty thousand years. Qur'anic verses also say that after completing the creation God "*sat on the Throne of Power*," that on the Day of Judgment He will place some on His "*Right Hand*" and some on the "*Left Hand*." It should be perfectly obvious that in these and all similar contexts the sense or use of words and expressions is not literal but figurative.

7. The same remarks apply as above.

8. The Qur'an states that everything has been created from water, that God created all things in pairs, that all living creatures are "*communities*" like humans, that God creates the embryo in the female "*in three stages of darkness*," that everything shall perish "*except the countenance of the Lord*."

> 6:38
> *There is not an animal (that lives) on the earth, nor a being that flies on its wings, but (forms part of) communities like you ...*

> 36:36
> *Glory to Allah, Who created in pairs all things that the earth produces, as well as their own (human) kind, and (other) things of which they have no knowledge.*

> 11:7
> *He it is Who created the heavens and the earth in six Days—and His throne was over the waters ...*

> 21:30
> *Do not the unbelievers see that the heavens and the earth were joined together (as one unit of creation) before We clove them asunder? We made from water every living thing. Will they not then believe?*

> 39:6
> *... He makes you in the wombs of your mothers, in stages, one after another, in three veils of darkness ...*

9. The Qur'an says that nothing happens without God's permission. If so, natural calamities and disasters involving deaths of millions of innocent children and other living beings happen with God's permission. Human atrocities against innocent fellow humans would also have to be so viewed. In the latter case, it is plausible to explain that such atrocities against innocent fellow humans or others happen because God gives a long rope to humans to defy the Creator for a fixed period as part of a grand Divine Plan. But does not this plausible explanation break down in the case of natural calamities where human perversity and defiance of God's will is absent. Such defiance is also absent in the case of ghastly accidents and tragedies. I think the plausibility does break down. This creates a paradox for conventional theists who believe that the existence of tragedy, pain, and suffering can be reconciled with the conventional belief that God is all powerful and all merciful in heaven above and all is well and would be well on earth below if one just believes firmly and acts righteously.

Another major paradox arises when we understand the words and expressions (in the literal sense) of the Qur'anic story of the Divine Plan to create humankind, God's dialogue with prehuman angelic creation, including Satan, the subsequent expulsion of Satan from God's presence, and the final Divine creation and placement of the first human in a pre-terrestrial garden blessed by God. A host of difficulties crop up: God is all-knowing, and all-powerful, yet, He entered into a dialogue with angels. Again He is all-powerful, and yet He entered into a sort of truce with Satan. Furthermore, God is all-knowing and all-powerful, yet He permitted Satan to corrupt Adam and Eve even in the pre-terrestrial and blessed garden from which both were expelled even as Satan had been expelled earlier from Divine presence. The paradox is why should God take so long when He is all-powerful and why should He permit so much suffering for so long when He is all-loving.

But can a Muslim believer or, for that matter, any monotheist reject such stories as fairy tales or downright nonsense? My answer is in the negative. In all humility, I submit that, along with the various functions performed by Qur'anic verses, some of them perform the function of a Mystique. Such verses create an air of mystery about matters concerning human origin and destiny and awaken the individual to look within for unsuspected latent human capacities for spiritual growth. Many creative and well-informed Western scholars who are no apologists for any formal or organized religion or cultural tradition have come round to the view that some of the enduring myths of the human family, if interpreted symbolically, do yield deep and fruitful psychological and moral insights and practical wisdom and guidance, despite their grotesque absurdities, pure phantasies, and pre-scientific cosmologies. C. G. Jung (d. CE 1961) and Joseph Campbell (d. CE 1987) are, perhaps, the most well-known names in this list.

Obviously, the negative elements mentioned above are totally absent from what I respectfully call the "Mystique of the Qur'an." Indeed, the Qur'anic Mystique is the model of sobriety, dignity, elegance, and brevity. Given this semantic caution, I submit that Muslim believers may well explore, in a spirit of prayerful humility, the hidden meaning or wisdom embedded in the Mystique of the

Qur'an, and remain fully receptive and open to other views or interpretations instead of understanding such verses in their literal sense and then excluding all other variant views as heretical.

10. "Bakka" is another name for "Mecca." The verse says the "*Kabah*" was the first shrine dedicated to Monotheism. This is, clearly, a descriptive historical statement.

11. This is also a historical statement. To the best of my knowledge, some enlightened and informed quarters in the West are coming round somewhat close to this view in the light of continuing research.

12. The last verse ends on an "evaluative" note, and this is the main "point" or message of the long descriptive portion.

13. Here again, the earlier part of the text is descriptive, but the last portion is an "elliptical" explanation of how and why one rebels against God. See the text and notes on the elliptical style of Qur'anic verses in Section B later.

14. See note 14 to Chapter 4, "The Vision of the Qur'an."

15. See note 15 to Chapter 4, "The Vision of the Qur'an."

16. See note 15 to Chapter 4, "The Vision of the Qur'an."

17. See section on Gender Justice in Chapter 6, "The Injunctions of the Qur'an: Some Issues."

18. This Qur'anic verse prescribes the penalty for killing a fellow Muslim in an age when slavery was a universal practice. The freeing of a slave as atonement and as a part of the punishment acted as a lever for speeding up the total abolition of this grave social evil. From the perspective of our present moral and social sensibility, however, one must concede that the Qur'anic value system fell short of the modern ideal of human rights or universal polymorphous equality. However, the text does not, necessarily, exclude the idea that human concepts and values grow and develop fresh dimensions and depth in the course of history. See the text and notes of Chapter 5, "The Piety of the Qur'an."

19. This prescriptive verse affirms the primacy of truth and justice over the bonds of blood, family, self, class, or any other material gain. This is ethical idealism at its best.

20. This verse sounds a note of caution and moderation to those inclined to go to extremes of Puritanism or Hedonism.

21. This verse also extols the wisdom of the middle position or the "golden mean" in human affairs.

22. Note the suggestive power and scope of this verse. However, the expression "*nothing have We omitted from the Book*" should be understood, not literally, but in the broad sense only. See note 23 below.

23. This verse affirms the basic unity of the cosmic process in an elliptical manner or style. The faith of God's knowledge and control of the entire cosmos stimulates and sustains the human quest for discovering what God's *"clear record"* contains. Leading creative scientists like Einstein (d. CE 1955) and thinkers like Alfred Whitehead (d. CE 1947) testify to the mystical and religious source springs of their intellectual or scientific curiosity and passion.

24. The *"Religion of Allah"* mentioned here should be understood in the broad sense that all created beings follow, per force, the laws of their own nature, as created by the Supreme Creator. He, however, granted to humankind a measure of freedom to choose between surrender (*Islam*) to the Creator or defiance and denial (*kufr*).

25. This verse further clarifies Qur'an, 3:83.

26. Several verses dealing with the same theme are given in Chapter 4, "The Vision of the Qur'an."

27. The reader may note that the Qur'an gives a very high rank, indeed, to the gift of wisdom to humankind. The popular or folk version of Islam, on the other hand, hardly appreciates this point in its single point agenda of blindly conforming to what the religious leaders say or command.

28. The text clarifies the theory and practice of *"living in the presence of the Lord."* People of all faiths or organized religions can do so. To my mind, these liberating words apply to all who have faith in the Supreme Creator and the ultimate triumph of good over evil.

29. The scope and power of the text is tremendous, indeed.

30. The same remarks apply to this verse.

31. This is the "verse of the throne" (*ayat-ul- kursi*). Millions of Muslim believers display this verse in their homes or carry it on their persons and the beauty and power of this famed verse inspires faith in their hearts, which begin to vibrate with ecstatic joy and surrender to the Lord of all creation.

32. This text is one of the several that clearly show the Qur'an accepts the idea of religious plurality as part of God's plan for the human family scattered in different parts of the globe.

33. This Qur'anic text points out the supreme importance of developing an integrated and consistent outlook or vision of life. Mere lip profession of any creed or faith is not enough. Likewise, mere conceptual consistency is not enough if it is not followed by consistent corresponding action.

34. See note 7 to Chapter 4, "The Vision of the Qur'an."

35. See notes 11 and 12 to Chapter 4, "The Vision of the Qur'an."

36. See note 18 to Chapter 4, "The Vision of the Qur'an."

37. The deep and powerful sexual attraction is, indeed, a matter for profound wonder and reflection. Note the depth of the expression that the Creator has put *"love and mercy between your hearts."* This applies not only to the love of the sexes, but primarily (to my mind) to the love of the mother for her offspring. The unconditional and literally irrepressible mother's love for her baby is, perhaps, the most moving of the numerous "*Signs of Allah*" in the entire creation. But for maternal love and tenderness no species could have survived in the cosmos.

38. See notes 17, 18 to Chapter 4, "The Vision of the Qur'an."

39. See note 17 to Chapter 4, "The Vision of the Qur'an."

40. See note 24 to Chapter 4, "The Vision of the Qur'an."

41. See note 16 to Chapter 4, "The Vision of the Qur'an."

42. See note 11 to Chapter 4, "The Vision of the Qur'an."

43. See note 2 to Chapter 6, "The Injunctions of the Qur'an: Some Issues."

44. See note 5 to Chapter 6, "The Injunctions of the Qur'an: Some Issues."

45. See note 3 to Chapter 4, "The Vision of the Qur'an."

46. See the section "Mystique of the Qur'an."

47. See the section "Mystique of the Qur'an."

48. It is extremely difficult, if not impossible, to determine the exact meaning of the text. See note 49 below.

49. The traditional school understood the text in the literal sense. Some went to the other extreme of understanding much or most of the Qur'anic texts in the metaphorical sense to escape prima facie contradictions or objections that arose when the text was understood literally. The modern mind must avoid all extreme positions and apply the well-established principles of semantics in interpreting the Qur'an.

50. The same remarks apply.

51. The same remarks apply.

52. The same remarks apply.

53. See the text and notes of Chapter 2, "The Qur'an as a Revealed Book: Some Issues."

54. The German philosopher Immanuel Kant (d. CE 1804) is, to my mind, the most illustrious thinker of the modern age to do full justice to science, religion, and spirituality. All Western thought after Kant (including the hugely influential approach of British linguistic analysis and the equally influential approach of European existentialist analysis) bears the stamp of his genius in some sense or the other. Kant looked upon religion as autonomous in its own proper sphere and created space for pure faith and the cultivation of genuine spirituality.

55. I can not help strongly suggesting to my readers who have given me a patient reading thus far to take the trouble of (in case they have not done so already) reading the following selected pages from Izutsu's great work, *Ethico-Religious Concepts in the Qur'an* (referred to already): Introduction, pp. 3–15, and Chapter 2, "The Method of Analysis and Its Application," pp. 24–41. I assure them they will be deeply rewarded. See also, note 30 to Chapter 5, "The Piety of the Qur'an," and note 5 to Chapter 6, "The Injunctions of the Qur'an: Some Issues."

Notes to Chapter 4   The Vision of the Qur'an

1. Perhaps the best example of this approach is the anecdote concerning Bibi Rabia Basri (d. CE 801), the most famous woman mystic in Islam. Some people saw Rabia walking on a street in Baghdad while holding a plate of burning coals in one hand and a jug of water in the other. When questioned for this strange behavior, she said that she wanted to destroy both heaven and hell so that people acted neither out of fear of hell, nor hope of heaven.

2. The fact that many good and innocent persons undergo great suffering while many evil persons have a good time until their final exit from the earth remains an enigma in the face of the belief or faith that the Creator is all loving and just as well as all powerful. The Semitic belief that the guilty will be duly punished and the virtuous amply rewarded after the final Divine reckoning does explain or resolve the prima facie paradox of faith and fact. So does the Indian belief or faith that human suffering is the inevitable consequence of one's own *karma* either in one's past or in some previous incarnation in the endless cycle of birth and death, but this cycle comes to an end when the balance of good and evil in a person turns to a zero sum.

While the belief in a Supreme Being or Power is almost universally held (in some form or other), the belief in *karma* is culture specific. Moreover, the *karma* hypothesis lacks the emotional appeal of belief in a Supreme God of love Who responds to human entreaty and tears. Whatever be the ultimate truth of the matter, the fact remains that these two beliefs can never be proved. They remain possibilities, and different individuals may have different authentic responses to them. The existence of a Supreme Being, as such, without any further qualifying beliefs about the nature and functioning of the Supreme also cannot be proved. This is also a matter of faith, but a faith that requires or demands no evidence or confirmation beyond the existential certainty as such. I think there is a crucial distinction between faith in a Supreme Power, as such, and faith in either the Semitic "linear" concept of just reward ending in final salvation of the individual, or the Indian "cyclical" concept of the repeated birth and death of the individual ending only when the individual consciousness merges with the Supreme Being.

3. There are numerous cases when we strongly believe a particular statement to be true, though we do not understand its exact meaning or sense in which it is true. This was the liberating insight of the Cambridge thinker, G.E. Moore (d. CE 1958) who along with Bertrand Russell (d. CE 1969) and Ludwig Wittgenstein (d. CE 1951) gradually transformed classical metaphysics into modern linguistic analysis. Kant had done the same earlier in his own way. This approach creates space for genuine authentic faith and spirituality without getting involved with endless and inconclusive speculative disputes between different religions, sects, or secular thought systems without any clear method of reaching agreement as is possible in the case of scientific truth.

4. See the Qur'anic verses:

99:1–5

When the earth is shaken to her (utmost) convulsion, And the earth throws up her burdens (from within), And man cries (distressed): 'What is the matter with her?'—On that Day will she declare her tidings: For that thy Lord will have given her inspiration.

5. See the following Qur'anic texts:

2:252, 253

These are the Signs of Allah: we rehearse them to thee in truth: verily, thou art one of the Messengers. Those Messengers We endowed with gifts, some above others; to one of them Allah spoke, others He raised to degrees (of honor); to Jesus, the son of Mary, We gave clear (Signs), and strengthened him with the Holy Spirit. If Allah had so willed, succeeding generations would not have fought among each other, after clear (Signs) had come to them, but they chose to wrangle, some believing and others rejecting. If Allah had so willed they would not have fought each other; but Allah fulfilleth His plan.

5:48

To thee We sent the Scripture in truth, confirming the scripture that came before it, and guarding it in safety: so judge between them by what Allah hath revealed, and follow not their vain desires, diverging from the Truth that hath come to thee. To each among you have we prescribed a law and an open way. If Allah had so willed, He would have made you a single people, but (His plan is) to test you in what He hath given you: so strive as in a race in all virtues. The goal of you all is to Allah; it is He that will show you the truth of the matters in which ye dispute;

6. The Qur'anic verse 2: 255 (the verse of *The Throne*), verse 24: 35 (the verse of *Divine Light*), and verses 112: 1–4 (*surah Ikhlas*) along with a few others are regarded as pearls of Qur'anic spirituality. It is impossible to capture, in any translation, their "ontogenetic" power in the original Arabic.

7. This, along with some other similar texts, beautifully illustrates the elliptical Qur'anic style of describing the reign of law and order in the phenomena of nature. To say that the sun and the moon obey the Commands of their Creator is a poetic way of describing that their movements are fixed and uniform, not random. And Astronomy gives an exact quantified graph of this movement in accordance with the Divine command. The function of the Qur'anic description is poetic or ontogenetic—the evocation of a sense of wonder and of participation in the cosmic process as if one were an insignificant but integral part of some tremendous Unity; the function of scientific description and explanation is the discovery of the abstract and quantified mathematical structure or graph of the movement of heavenly bodies. The motive of this striving to discover may be pure epistemic curiosity or the desire to promote human welfare in the broad sense.

8. See the sheer eloquence and power of the Qur'anic text. The verse does not prove any truthclaim but merely invites the truth seeker to look carefully at nature and into one's own soul with humility and receptivity and be a witness to one's authentic response. This is strikingly similar to the ancient Buddhist method of "*vipasna*" and the modern concept of "authenticity." The question arises what should one do if (for whatever reason) one's honest inner looking or search does not yield any positive result and leaves him as perplexed and spiritually thirsty as before. Personally speaking, I cannot come round to the view that such a person is an accursed soul who will attract Divine wrath on the Day of Judgment. God knows best.

9. The reader will note how accurate minute details blossom into moral exhortation and the glorification of the Supreme Being.

10. Humans have always yearned to convert hearsay belief or "faith" into direct vision or experience of Reality as it is in itself. This verse devalues this aspiration and extols pure "*faith in the Unseen.*" In the final analysis, the "operative core" of the Islamic faith is faith in the veracity and sincerity of Prophet Muhammad ﷺ, and the individual believes and acts as if he will be "accountable" to the Creator on the "Day of Judgment." The only test of one's faith is stable good will (in the Kantian sense) continually leading to righteous action.

11. These verses use the language of mystique and metaphor to extol humility and warn humankind against the evil of hubris and pride in one's own independent status without realizing one's inherent brittleness and dependence upon the Creator even in the very moment of denial as such.

12. These verses appear to be an indirect devaluation of the common human vice of self-glorification and will to power at the expense of others. It is very difficult to claim one has fully understood this and similar other Qur'anic texts. To my mind, this is a good example of the "Mystique of the Qur'an."

13. This verse, along with verses 2: 111, 112, 113, 252, 253 and verse 5:48, conclusively show that the Qur'an prescribes universal tolerance and respect for all religions. The actual behavior of Muslims should not be confused with the idea of Islam as found in the Qur'an. The chasm between Qur'anic doctrine and Muslim behavior in history should be a matter of deep regret for Muslim believers and concern for the human family as a whole. Sincere and honest Muslims must reflect on the reason or reasons for this unhappy situation. I submit, in all humility, that Muslims should stop blaming others.

14. These verses and those immediately following are powerful reminders that the cosmos is not an accident but a Divine act, even though humankind may not be able fully to grasp this truth or to prove it conclusively.

15. This verse and a few others state that the wrong-doer is one who takes his own passion or vain desire as his "god." The implication is that this amounts to polytheism (*shirk*); the most heinous and cardinal sin in the Islamic value system and one which the Creator never forgives unless the sinner totally abandons associating other gods with God. This shows the very great stress the Qur'an places on moral and ethical values and righteous conduct by saying that the wrong-doer turns into a polytheist.

16. Modern Biology shows that different parts or sections of the human embryo, such as muscles, bones nerves and other tissues, develop from three layers of the fertilized ovum inside the darkness of the mother's womb. Likewise, the Qur'anic description of the various stages of the development of the embryo is also corroborated by modern Biology. See Maurice Bucaille's well-known work, *The Bible, The Qur'an and Science*.

The Qur'an is not a book of natural or biological science. And it would be highly misleading and objectionable if any Muslim believer were to claim that the Qur'an is a compendium of all knowledge, and that it anticipates all factual knowledge and contains all truths worth knowing. The truth of the matter is simply as follows: The Qur'an is, indeed, a remarkable Arabic work whose sentences/verses perform several semantic functions mentioned previously. Some verses invite the reader to look at and observe the various phenomena of nature that all humans experience and confront in daily life. The Qur'an then describes these phenomena in very general terms within the broad conceptual framework of the age in which the Prophet ﷺ lived and moved. These descriptions are marked by a wonderful and compelling beauty of style and economy of expression and they have a high degree of "connotative plasticity." In other words the Qur'anic Arabic words and expressions can be variantly understood and interpreted.

Modern science, obviously, was unknown when the Qur'an was "revealed." The Prophet ﷺ, himself, was no scientist and he too, along with his contemporaries, must have interpreted the Qur'anic descriptions of the phenomena of nature in the then generally accepted conceptual frames of reference. However, both the modern conceptual frame, as well as the store of factual knowledge, vastly differ from the ancient and the medieval frame of reference. Yet, due to the remarkable plasticity of the language of the Qur'an, its contents are quite amenable to a different set of meanings and interpretation, and the words and expressions can be integrated with modern science. This point is best illustrated by the cycle of night and day, or darkness and light. The Qur'an describes and explains this cycle in terms of the sun obeying the creator's command to move as ordered, but modern science explains the same phenomenon in terms of the earth rotating on its own axis. The ancients interpreted the sun's movement according to plain visual perception. Modern science rejects this, yet it has to accept that the sun also moves along with the galaxy. So in this sense the Qur'anic description that the sun moves stands vindicated by modern science though not in the ancient sense as such.

One would go wrong if one claimed that an intensive and truly dedicated study of the Qur'an (as the "Word of God") is the best and surest way of acquiring perfect knowledge of every aspect or feature of the Universe. Reliable factual knowledge will accrue only by following the established scientific method—accurate observation, controlled experimentation, and verifiable explanation, etc. Creative and highly gifted minds may be granted flashes of insight or intuition as to what may be the case. But he (or she) will still have to travel the long road to scientific truth to grasp the complexities of natural phenomena and to prove or substantiate that his hunch, intuition or faith was valid and worth universal acceptance.

17. The above verses refer to a large range of natural phenomena—cattle producing milk, trees bearing fruits, bees producing honey, and so on. The Qur'an exhorts humankind to reflect on these "wonders of nature," to be grateful to the Creator and enjoy Divine blessings. The statement that God taught or *"inspired"* the bee *"to build cells in hills and on trees and in habitations,"* implies that laws and instincts are not accidental features produced in the evolving Universe but an integral part of the Divine *"telos,"* though it might be beyond human comprehension to grasp the same.

18. See the following excerpt from Bucaille's work, pp. 194–95, cited above:

It is only the existence of a migratory program in the genetic code of birds that can account for the extremely long and complicated journeys, which very young birds, without any prior experience and without any guide, are able to accomplish. This is in addition to their ability to return to their departure point on a prescribed date. Professor Hamburger in his [French] book, *Power and Fragility* [Paris, 1972] gives as an example the well-known case of the "mutton-bird" that lives in the Pacific, with its journey of over 15,000 miles in the shape of the figure 8. It must be acknowledged that the highly complicated instructions for a journey of this kind simply have to be contained in the bird's nervous cells. They are most definitely programmed, but who is the programmer?

19. These Qur'anic verses have a profound "appeal" to me though, I confess, I am unable to accept them in the literal sense. Extremely "malleable" in the semantic sense, as they are, they evoke a sense of a tremendous mystery when they proclaim the power and glory of a Beneficent Creator, beyond Human comprehension. This is a good example of the "ontogenetic function" and the Mystique of the Qur'an.

20. These verses express the innermost response and "state of mind" of a person having genuine faith when he/she contemplates the vast panorama of nature and lets himself go or lost in aesthetic admiration of its power and beauty as well as the overpowering sense of mystery of existence as it is without any concern to use, change or control even an iota of what is the case.

21. This verse expresses a brief but extremely powerful intimation of the end of historical time and the dawn of the Day of Judgment. There is no proof, nor can there be any. This is only a Divine warning, a wake-up call, as it were. Each individual is free to respond according to one's own inner lights, for there is *"no compulsion in religion"* either in the form of physical, logical, or emotional coercion.

22. The same remarks apply as in the previous note. Personally speaking, the power of the Qur'anic clause, *"by degrees shall We punish them from directions they perceive not"* shakes me to my foundations.

23. The verses in this section deal with the Qur'anic perspective on the general course of history, the rise and fall of human groups, and the struggle between good and evil, and the final destination of the human family. The Creator remains ever fully aware of all the phenomena of nature and the actions of humankind who have been granted a measure of freedom to choose between good and evil. The Creator could have punished the wrong doers instantly and He also could have denied them the power of choice, as such, in the first instance, or He could have preempted the occurrence of some ghastly accidents or deeds that result in enormous suffering to innocent humans. But the Creator has a Plan of His own and he gives a long rope, as it were, to all.

God's Plan cannot be grasped in full by humankind. However, the texts make this much clear that God "sends" warners and messengers from among the people themselves to guide the people to the right path. Thereafter, the Creator leaves the people free to choose and act. God generally grants success and happiness to the people who act righteously and protects them against the doers of evil. However, He also gives power and success to some evil people or wrong doers to keep other wrong doers in check. This is a Divinely ordained mechanism for keeping a measure of balance between the forces of good and evil. However, the Creator is all-powerful and He will dispense full and final justice to all on the Day of Judgment when the final reckoning will take place.

24. The above set of verses is, indeed, a clear and convincing refutation of the wild charges hostile critics leveled against the Prophet ﷺ. However, they do not constitute a logical refutation. The actual character and conduct of the Prophet ﷺ in the early years of his relative failure, and his character and conduct later on in the later years of his total triumph are a living proof of the integrity and moral excellence of the Prophet ﷺ. But even this is no conclusive proof of the Islamic faith "There is no god but God and Muhammad is His messenger." But does the absence of proof really matter at all?

25. This text is also extremely powerful, but does not prove the "truth-claim." The very nature of "existential" certainty is different from "logical/mathematical" certainty as pointed out by modern analytical philosophy. In the case of logical certainty of a truthclaim its denial involves a plain internal contradiction, but in the case of existential certainty its denial does not result in any internal contradiction but only a divergent interpretation of some fact or belief.

26. These Qur'anic texts should be taken as internal evidence that from the very commencement of the prophetic mission it was part of the Divine plan to preserve and protect the accuracy and purity of the Qur'anic revelation. Records show that the Prophet ﷺ saw to it that the revealed contents were written down by some scribe at the earliest. However, honest doubts or differences of opinion may well arise as to the date of some particular revelation and the time of its recording in writing.

The above Qur'anic texts affirm that its entire linguistic content was Divinely revealed to the Prophet ﷺ ,and he was also Divinely enabled to retain it accurately in his memory. However, his natural humility, sincerity, and intellectual caution, at times, made him anxious lest he might not be able to cope with the tremendous task of accurate retention of the entire unit of revelation. The verses concerned assure the Prophet ﷺ not to worry on this score but to trust fully in God. The text also assures Divine help in preserving and explaining the text as God knows best. This assurance, obviously, does not amount to any coercive proof that the Qur'an is the "Word of God," as Muslims believe. Yet, this explicit assurance greatly strengthens and fortifies the Muslim believer's faith that the original Qur'anic revelation stands preserved for all times. See section on the collection of Qur'an, in Chapter 2, "The Qur'an as A Revealed Book: Some Issues," together with notes.

27. It is generally held that the first six verses of the *surah* refer to the Prophet's ﷺ first revelatory experience in the cave at Hira, while the following twelve verses refer to the Prophet's ﷺ religious or mystical experience during his night journey from Mecca to Jerusalem and from there his ascension to the "seven heavens" *(meraj)*. True to the unique allusive and suggestive style of the Qur'an when it describes transcendental themes relating to God, revelation, angels, resurrection and so on, the text does not clarify the exact or real nature of the Prophet's ﷺ ascension. One can interpret it as a purely spiritual experience without any physical movement or transportation of the person of the Prophet ﷺ from Mecca to Jerusalem and thence to the heavens above. Or one may interpret the event in the physical sense as a miracle vouchsafed to the Prophet ﷺ. The debate can never be clinched. What is, really, important for a Muslim who honestly believes that the Qur'an is the "Word of God" is the honest belief that on the night of the *"meraj"* the Supreme Creator had blessed the Prophet ﷺ in a special way that differed from the intermittent revelatory episodes *(wahy)*. This is to say that while *"wahy"* was a recurring and continuing unsolicited Divine blessing or gift to the Prophet ﷺ, the *"meraj"* was a unique one time "outpouring" of Divine grace and blessings upon the Prophet ﷺ. The rest is silence.

28. These verses in *surah* 53 refer to the Quraish leader's misunderstanding that the Prophet ﷺ would have no quarrel with their continuing veneration for the three traditional Meccan goddesses, *Lat, Manat,* and *Uzza,* provided the Meccans affirmed faith in one Supreme Creator of all that exists. This was certainly not what the Prophet ﷺ had said or meant, but this is what the Meccan leaders thought he had said. The three verses of *surah* 22 state that Satan is ever busy disguising his own evil suggestions as Divine revelations, thereby confusing and trying to mislead God's prophets. Some hostile critics and opponents of the Prophet ﷺ as well as some commentators were led to combine the two sets of verses and to insinuate that the Prophet ﷺ had been guilty of confusing "Satanic verses" with Divine revelation. This was a double charge of fallibility or poor judgment as well as of a lack of integrity in the Prophet ﷺ.

To my mind, a careful reading of the concerned texts shows that the Prophet ﷺ was always keen to win over the entire body of pagans of Arabia together with the "people of the Book" into the larger family of the followers of Abraham; the great *"Hanif"* or believer in one Supreme Creator. But at the same time, the Prophet ﷺ was the first to subordinate his own desire or inclination to the contents of *"wahy"* whenever he received any revelation.

It is patently unjustified to think that the verses concerned affirm or imply that the Prophet ﷺ had been seduced by the so-called Satanic verses into diluting the Islamic faith just to please or appease the pagan opposition. As regards the general question of the Prophet's ﷺ fallibility as a human being or the possibility that he might err in judgment, several Qur'anic verses gently and lovingly "chide" the Prophet ﷺ to beware of his habit of excessive care, concern, and kindness toward his fellow human beings, irrespective of their human limitations or perversions. The Qur'an does not project the Prophet ﷺ as perfect or as possessed of miraculous powers. See Chapter 1, "Perennial Islam: A Qur'an Based Paradigm," and its notes for extended excerpts from the Qur'an dealing with this theme.

29. To my mind, the Arabic word *"iman"* (faith), in the present context, does not refer to being a formal member of any organized religion, but to sincerely believing in one Supreme Being, Day of Judgment and acting righteously at all times according to one's own cherished moral code. If this code differs (in some matters) from the Islamic code, why should the Muslim believer grieve for or condemn other good believers who are not troubled by any qualms of conscience concerning the controversial issue or issues? The Creator and Sovereign Lord of the worlds will judge all humankind on the Day of Judgment. The Qur'anic exhortation, *"die not except in a state of Islam,"* in its operational sense, does not refer to becoming a formal member of any exclusive group, but rather to abjure false pride, hubris, and blind bondage to the "herd," and, in all humility, try to respond to the mystery of all that exists.

30. See how the Qur'an describes good Christians (during the Prophet's time) with *"eyes overflowing with tears"* and saying *"Our Lord! We believe, write us down among the witnesses."*

31. To my mind, the Islamic tradition falls short of a proper understanding of this Qur'anic text. That is why the tradition sees nothing wrong in banning all non-Muslims from visiting the shrine in Medina where the mortal body of the *"mercy for all creatures"* was laid to rest. There are literally millions and millions of noble and enlightened souls the world over who have tremendous respect and admiration for the Prophet ﷺ, without having formally converted to Islam or without any inner need to do so. I pray for a genuine change in the Muslim mind set, and for the day to dawn when this restriction will cease. The Qur'anic verse 9:28, (*O ye who believe! Truly the Pagans are unclean; so let them not, after this year of theirs, approach the Sacred Mosque. And if ye fear poverty, soon will Allah enrich you, if He wills, out of His bounty, for Allah is All-knowing, All-wise*), which prohibits the entry of non-Muslims to the *Kabah* should have been interpreted as a temporary war time measure rather than as a permanent ban. In no case this ban should have been extended to the Prophet's ﷺ resting place at Medina. The opening of the Medina shrine to all pilgrims, pledged to respecting its sanctity, will allow millions of genuine admirers of the historical Muhammad ﷺ to come much closer to one who was sent as a *"mercy for all creatures."*

32. Islamic orthodoxy justifies the belief that Prophet Muhammad ﷺ is the last messenger of God and the Qur'an the last revealed Scripture on the strength of this verse along with the verse 5:3, *"… This day have I perfected your religion for you, completed My favor upon you, and have chosen for you Islam as your religion…"*

I submit, in all humility, that neither the above two Qur'anic texts, nor the standard Islamic creedal formula (*There is no god but God and Muhammad is His messenger*) explicitly state that Muhammad ﷺ is the last messenger. However, this belief, most certainly, is implicit in the grand Islamic tradition down the ages past Yet, if the inner lights of any committed Muslim truth seeker or seekers honestly and powerfully impel him or them to any fresh alternative interpretation of the Islamic creed that does not negate the minimum core of the Islamic faith—the unity of God and the prophethood of Muhammad ﷺ—such individuals or groups should be allowed full freedom of conscience to do so and to enjoy all human rights equally with all *other* citizens of the state, without mainstream Muslims "excommunicating" them from Islam.

The above approach is grounded in the democratic principle of "agreement to differ." It appears pretty simple and almost self-evident to modern sensibility. But humanity in general has come to accept this truth, if at all, by a very hard way, indeed. Many Christians and Muslims (who are very conscious of their denominational identity) still find it difficult to imagine how Christians or Muslims of other denominations could, possibly, win salvation? To my mind, this extreme approach flows from the common tendency to select a particular strand from one's value system, as a whole, and to treat it as its core without going through an initial honest "deconstruction" of one's tradition in a spirit of humility and a critical search for truth. This gives rise to fanaticism and fundamentalism, whatever the area of human concern might be; religion, morality, science, art, politics, economics, and whatnot.

33. This verse and Qur'anic verses 40:77; 17: 73–75; 18:110 highlight the essential humanity, fallibility, and mortality of the Prophet ﷺ. Indeed, the awesome directness and power of the verses 69: 43–47 (the last Qur'anic excerpt in this section) shakes the very foundations of my being. The rest is silence.

34. Qur'anic verses 12:103 and 88:21, 22 caution the Prophet ﷺ not to become overanxious that the entire human family should embrace (quickly) the Divine message. The function of the Prophet ﷺ was not to manage men's affairs or to bring about a world Islamic state or Islamic hegemony, but to *"give admonition"* and to exhort humanity to turn to the Supreme Being.

Notes to Chapter 5 The Piety of the Qur'an

1. History clearly records that, when followers of value systems (religious or secular) consciously or unconsciously begin to treat, what were originally intended to be instrumental rules, as rigid imperatives, the effectiveness and existential grip of the rules begin to decline. The community loses the inner dynamism and idealism of the founding fathers of the cherished tradition and the managers and magistrates are tempted to compensate for their lapses through threats and punishments. In the final analysis, all closed and unexamined instrumental rules breed the germs of hypocrisy inside the bloodstream of the value system concerned. Brahmanical Hinduism, Judaism, Christianity, Islam all (at some point of time or other) and Communism, in our own times, have fared precisely in the same way. After years or centuries of travail and hope arise "servant leaders" whose "leitmotif" is not domination over others, but service of ideas and ideals. They lovingly "deconstruct" the cherished tradition and then equally lovingly "reconstruct" their cherished cultural legacy and then hand over a never ending task to the coming generations.

2. The seven verses of the *surah* Fatiha could well be called the seed of the entire Qur'anic corpus, or "*the mother of the Qur'an.*" Its commentaries run from a thousand to several thousand words.

3. To my mind, the expression, turning "*your faces toward east or west*" refers not only to a particular Islamic rite while performing the five obligatory prayers, but to the entire "corpus of rites and rituals" of Islam, or of any other religion for that matter. Living in the presence of the Lord, practicing universal compassion and generosity, fulfilling contracts, being patient in adversity, and so on, are more important than "*facing east or west.*" The vast majority of Muslim believers are barely tuned in to this great truth.

4. This verse beautifully complements verse 2: 177. The simplicity, economy, and graphic directness of the words leave one in silent wonder.

5. To my mind, the expression "*your wives and your children*" should be understood as "your spouse and your children." Concern for one's kith and kin often makes one selfish or partial in one's social or professional dealings. Elsewhere also the Qur'an exhorts humankind to act equitably and give truthful evidence even when it might hurt one's own near and dear ones.

6. The tortures of hell described in the Qur'an are meant to strike fear in the reader or listener. But for one whose main aspiration is "*to live in the presence of the Lord*" the greatest fear and torment is to become alienated from his Creator. Such a person always invokes the Lord to be granted inner strength and wisdom to resist all temptation. This is the real meaning of the "fear of the Lord" and one who lives in fear (in this sense) is a good and virtuous soul, no matter what his religion or creed might be.

7. This verse clearly enunciates the Qur'anic principle of the "freedom of belief and conscience." The traditional Muslim concept of apostasy (*irtidad*) clearly violates this Qur'anic verse, apart from committing the fallacy of "double standards" while judging those who shift from one organized religion to another. According to the traditional Islamic view, a Muslim believer who converts to any other faith attracts the death penalty, while any non-Muslim who converts or reverts to Islam attracts infinite praise and honor. This approach is self contradictory and highly objectionable, since it violates the basic value (humanistic as well as Qur'anic) of the freedom of belief and of conscience.

8. This verse highlights "spiritual conceit" and belief in "exclusive salvation of the in-group" as root evils in society.

9. This verse is a beautifully clear snapshot of "the good life," according to the Qur'an.

10. This text prescribes that Muslim believers show full tolerance to believers who may have different religious convictions. However, religious pluralism, in the highest sense of the term, means much more than reluctant and bare toleration of some detestable or horrendous evil. Tolerance, at its best, is loving agreement to differ from others with full respect and friendly feelings unless they initiate armed hostilities and attempt the extermination of Muslims themselves. Sufi and *Vedantic* thinking as well as the modern interfaith movement all agree on this point. All who believe in One Supreme Creator can and should cultivate universal love and compassion, without giving up their own cherished traditions, holy places, and symbols.

11. These two short *ayats* show that fields of negative, dark, and destructive forces exist in the created world along with the positive and the good, as part of the Divine Plan. However, the Qur'an makes it clear that Divine Power is supreme and that God's will is bound to prevail in the end.

12. This verse points out the importance of maintaining a sense of proportion and proper balance between the "soft" virtues like, compassion, sympathy, forgiveness and the like, and the "hard" virtues like justice, firmness, deterrent punishment, and the like.

13. Charitable actions that spring from the inner beauty of the soul and the pure goodness of the heart, and the cultivation of unconditional love and generosity are far more desirable and valuable than when they are done for acquiring a sense of power and prestige.

14. This verse beautifully extols the value of kindness, respect for others, and genuine humility.

15. Muslims in general hardly suspect that speaking ill of others behind their backs is such a tremendous or cardinal sin as this simple but awesome verse affirms. They generally tend to think that consuming alcohol, eating pork and sexual promiscuity, etc., are the cardinal vices.

16. I hold that this verse clearly implies that Allah bestows His grace on all who are truthful, morally upright, and do good deeds, no matter to which organized religion or sect they might belong. The Qur'anic expression, *"beautiful fellowship"* (*hasano rafeeqa*) is not restricted to formal or declared Muslims alone but applies to all who are truthful and righteous. Indeed, to my mind, just as being a formal Muslim, by itself does not confer membership of this "spiritual club," not being a formal Muslim does not exclude one from being an equal member of this *"beautiful fellowship."*

17. The Prophet's ﷺ character and conduct is beautifully exemplified by the basic Qur'anic spiritual and moral values. However, the minutiae of his daily living, dress, food, social customs, entertainments, and similar other habits or practices were, obviously, culture bound, and should not be deemed to be permanently normative. Indeed, Muslim believers must carefully reflect on Qur'anic texts themselves to ascertain which prescriptions deal with basic values, as such, and which with instrumental rules. For instance, some Qur'anic prescriptions dealing with forms of punishment, such as stoning, flogging, wife beating, or some customs such as slavery, usury, child marriage, unilateral divorce and the like, to my mind, are instrumental rules, rather than affirmations of basic values. See Chapter 6, "The Injunctions of the Qur'an," for more details.

18. This verse beautifully mentions the rationale of the custom of the human dress—protection from the elements, elemental modesty, and the adornment of the body. But *"the raiment of righteousness"* is deemed the best. I respectfully submit that both the "Western pundits of modern fashion" and the *"muftis* of Islamic morality" reflect on the wisdom of the Qur'an instead of rushing to join their respective moral brigades and "play games with words." It seems this inevitably results in indulgence in spiritual conceit.

19. To my mind, the Qur'anic text does not refer to the humble and intellectually honest truth-seeker who is unable to resolve some inner perplexity or conscientious objection to some belief or practice connected with the thought and value system of his or her religious tradition. The warning is directed to those who are arrogant and bedeviled by hubris and scoff at the mere mention of *"the signs of God."*

20. If the high and mighty lords of the earth could have caught only a few glimpses into the ultimate truth only a few times in their life, half the problems of suffering humanity would have been over.

21. This text injects a healthy dose of intellectual honesty and realism into the sentimental one sided thinking of those who are prone to be selectively blind to facts of life that contradict their faith. Even when one deeply and sincerely "believes" in God one never "understands" the nature or attributes of the Creator and feels bewildered and puzzled by the extent of so much pain and evil in the world. All explanations break down for some reason or the other. Even our knowledge or understanding of other human beings is limited due to various reasons. If so, how foolish and unrealistic it is to aspire to conceptual transparency in our notions and ideas about the Creator. All that one can, possibly, aspire to is to be truthful in all situations, to act righteously and be consistently kind, loving and equitable. God alone knows the full truth and we humans will come to know the truth on the final Day of Judgment. That this Day shall dawn (though we know not when) is itself a matter of faith or of "existential certainty" rather than of knowledge.

22. These verses should dispel popular beliefs that some holy men can intervene or plead with God to waive the proper penalty for wrongdoing or evil deeds committed by Muslim believers. God alone forgives sinners and the guilty if they genuinely repent, and God accepts their repentance.

23. If we look upon our difficulties and sufferings as the result of our own acts, we stop accusing or blaming others. We begin to see clearly that the remedy lies in honest self analysis or review of our character or conduct in the past and in taking proper constructive action in the future. And lo! One gets healed and is rewarded with inner peace. All this is Divine grace.

24. The words of the text have an awesome effect on me, and millions of others. The word, "*soon,*" however, should not be understood in the literal sense.

25. Unfortunately, most of us remain unaware that we often have double standards in our dealings with others.

26. Goodwill, love, compassion, remain empty shells unless they lead to appropriate acts. Muslim believers readily accept this thesis. But it seems they have very great difficulty in accepting that this thesis applies equally to "faith in God." What is even still more difficult or puzzling for conventional Muslim believers is to judge righteous action without "faith in God." To my mind, all controversies centered on the issue of final "salvation after death" (*nejat*), are totally futile and they lead to "spiritual conceit." Why should Muslim or Christian believers bother about how the Creator will judge others, including atheists? It seems it is not so much love and compassion for others but rather one's ego and sense of importance that drives so many "loud" believers to strive so hard to "save" others instead of lovingly leaving others free to find their own authentic path to salvation.

27. These remarkably suggestive and pregnant verses pinpoint the attitude and behavior of a person who denies the Day of Judgment. The verses do not refer at all to the traditional description of the "pillars of faith." Instead they refer to the person's lack of social concern and indifference to caring for and actively helping the poor and the needy. Even more significantly, the Qur'anic text goes on to add that mere worshipping God in the mosque, without caring for and helping others, amounts to a "*desire to be seen or noticed*" rather than being a sincere submission to the Creator.

I submit that the "operative value system" of the vast majority of Muslim believers focuses on congregational prayers, ritual recitation of the Qur'an, avoiding non-halal meat and alcohol, and gives only a marginal importance to active social concern. But the above Qur'anic text reverses the "priorities" of faith and gives a new turn to what it means to deny the "*Judgment.*"

28. This Qur'anic verse points out that salvation is, essentially, spiritual growth without disturbing the sense of proportion as willed by the Creator. All humans (including the prophets) aspire to ascertain the ideal proportion as willed by God. But none can ever claim to have equaled Divine Omniscience.

29. Some misinformed critics of the Qur'an hold that Islam disparages poetry, music, and some other forms of art and cite the above Qur'anic text in support of their judgment. The Qur'an, however, does not disparage poetry, as such, but only points out the flaws in some bad poets who indulge in vain glory and "*say what they practice not.*" Nor does the Qur'an prohibit the drawing, painting, or sculpting of human or animal forms. These prohibitions form part of theological and juristic interpretations that reflect the "spirit" of the medieval Islamic mindset.

30. This Qur'anic verse clearly negates the myth of God's "chosen people." When Prophet Abraham wanted to know if after his death his descendants would also be Divinely favored with the mantle of leadership of nations, God said that His promise of help was "*not within the reach of evil doers.*" This verse affirms that the Creator is the "*Lord of the worlds*" not just of Muslims and that the Creator is just and compassionate to all, rather than to any race or group. What befalls individuals or nations is not arbitrary but the result of their own deeds. The Creator does not take sides. He helps only those who believe, and act righteously. If one believes but does not act righteously God's promise to help does not apply. But what happens if one acts righteously, but does not believe?

It is here and in similar cases that a proper understanding of the stylistics and semantics of the Qur'an helps to resolve confusions and perplexities that arise when one reads or hears the Qur'an. I submit, that the Arabic expression "*those who believe*" can be understood in both a wide and a narrow sense. In the wider sense the expression refers to all good and virtuous persons whether or not they are formal members of the Muslim community; in the narrow sense it refers to the latter group only. Therefore, formal Muslims should never delude themselves that no matter how morally elevated or virtuous a non-Muslim individual or individuals may be, they will never receive Divine help and favor at the expense of the Muslim individual or community. There is absolutely no doubt that one can believe in one Supreme Creator without being a formal Muslim. And if such a person acts righteously (according to his lights) why should God not help such an honest non-Muslim when he is ethically in the right and the formal Muslim, ethically in the wrong?

31. The Qur'anic text clearly explains that the religious obligation or exhortation of Muslim believers to fight or take up arms applies to the defense of Islam and the Muslims, if, and when, attacked by some enemy. The Qur'an prohibits all aggression or aggrandizement for political or material gains, or any forcible conversion of others to Islam. Even in the case of defensive war, Qur'anic texts lay down rules based on natural justice and humanitarian considerations. That the record of Muslim kings, rulers, or tyrants in history has often greatly deviated from the Qur'anic code of war is a different issue.

Notes to Chapter 6   The Injunctions of the Qur'an

1. Shibli Nomani's (d. CE 1914) Urdu work, *Al-Farooq* remains to date the unrivalled magisterial classic study on this important theme. There is a complete chapter entitled "The Firsts of Umar" that lists the innovations he introduced in the Islamic polity of his times. Shibli throws a flood of light on how different close companions of the Prophet ﷺ thought and acted in regard to different issues and how they differed without any acrimony. Unfortunately, the spirit of mutual respect and tolerance of dissent got dissipated in the heat and dust of power politics some fifteen years after the passing away of the Prophet ﷺ.

2. Some traditional Muslim quarters hold that Islam was completed and perfected in the time of the Prophet ﷺ himself, and therefore all talk of any change or development in the Islamic value system is out of question and even amounts to challenging the authority of the Qur'an and the Prophet ﷺ. They refer to the Qur'anic verse:

5:3

...This day have I perfected your religion for you, completed My favor upon you, and have chosen for you Islam as your religion...

I submit that this interpretation of the Qur'anic text is invalid. Perfection of religion (*deen*) and completion of God's favor refer to the basics of Islam, not to the possibility of inner growth in its thought and value system. Iqbal (d. CE 1938) has made illuminating comments on this matter in his famous "*Lectures on the Reconstruction of Religious Thought in Islam.*"

3. See Qur'anic verses:

2:30–34

Behold, thy Lord said to the angels: "I will create a vicegerent on earth." They said: "Wilt Thou place therein one who will make mischief therein and shed blood?—whilst we do celebrate Thy praises and glorify Thy holy (name)?" He said: "I know what ye know not." And He taught Adam the names of all things; then He placed them before the angels, and said: "Tell me the names of these if ye are right." They said: "Glory to Thee, of knowledge We have none, save what Thou hast taught us: in truth it is Thou Who art perfect in knowledge and wisdom." He said: "O Adam! Tell them their names." When he had told them, Allah said: "Did I not tell you that I know the secrets of heaven and earth, and I know what ye reveal and what ye conceal?" And behold, We said to the angels: "Bow down to Adam" and they bowed down. Not so Iblis: he refused and was haughty: He was of those who reject Faith.

4. Another illuminating anecdote runs as follows: Some guests unexpectedly arrived at a saint's house. The master ordered his servant to get some bananas from a particular vendor. The servant found the shop closed. Another shop close by had grapes but no bananas. The servant returned empty handed, feeling satisfied he had obeyed his master's instructions. But the master knew better.

Simple anecdotes like the above convey profound wisdom far more easily and effectively than piles of books. Some Indian spiritual masters are presently scattering pearls of wisdom before an enchanted world audience. See Sukhabodhanand's twin volumes, *O Mind! Relax Please* and *O Life! Relax Please.*

5. Consider the Islamic concept of an annual tax (*zakat*) on the believer's wealth (if any) after all normal expenditure. The classical quantum of this tax is 2.5 percent of the net wealth. Will it be reasonable to treat this percentage as permanently fixed and sacrosanct? Will imposing any new charge or tax be a violation of Qur'anic laws or the *Shariah*? Should the procedure of selecting or electing the Head of an Islamic state or of government follow exactly the procedure adopted fourteen hundred years ago? What about gender equality? What about the equality of human rights of non-Muslims with Muslim citizens in a modern state, whether Islamic or secular?

To my mind, all instrumental rules, whether mentioned in the Qur'an or included in the *Shariah* are, in principle, subject to change after careful collective reflection. This decision should be made in the light of free investigations, surveys, and the actual experience of the working of the previous instrumental rules in different societies and in different conditions. It is equally important to realize that even basic spiritual and moral values, which, certainly, are permanent and underpin the entire structure of the instrumental rules, also stand in the need of continuing reflection and redefinition in the unceasing human quest for value in an ever-changing and evolving Universe. The change required in the case of instrumental rules involves better social engineering and social mechanisms for promoting some basic values; the growth required in the case of a permanent value or values involves an enlargement and deepening of human vision. The need for deepening and enlarging human vision remains even when a Muslim believer surrenders or submits to the Qur'an and views it as the "Word of God." This is because the "Word of God" is interpreted by the mind of man with the help of human concepts and words that are born, grow, and develop in time and

174

space. Even basic values that are permanent have to be concretized and inter-preted before they can be applied in a world, which itself is concrete and determi-nate in so far as it exists as an object rather than as an idea in the sheer imagination of some human being or beings.

Consider the idea of "democracy" or "human equality." Not long ago the idea of human equality was that all humans have a similar physical shape and bodily organs and are born, breathe, grow, and die in more or less similar ways and also have similar passions and instincts, but there was hardly any hint of their pos-sessing equal rights. Half the population, namely, female humans was regarded to be congenitally inferior (in some sense or other) from the male half. When the idea of human equality emerged as a basic value, its proponents understood it as meaning that every adult male owning a defined minimum quantum of land or wealth, has the right to vote once every 3–5 years at the polls. There was no inkling of anything more than this "embryonic idea" of human equality. Gradually and by very well-known stages (for equally well-known sociological reasons) this "embryonic idea" developed into the idea or value of human rights, as we under-stand this concept today. The same remarks apply to the idea or value of "equality of opportunity," "social justice," "gender equality," "freedom," and the like.

The process of growth of a basic value or idea is long and twisted because humans are not equally situated or placed in the flow of individual and collective life and different life situations (including differences of gender) "breed" or gener-ate different interests and their corresponding different notions and interpreta-tions of basic value terms. Plato had long ago pointed out that most people tend to define justice according to what best serves their own interests. This is why there is so much tension and strife over the proper or real meaning of justice and other basic value terms. People, be they religious or secular, tend to "justify" or prove those meanings or views that best promote their own narrow and selfish interests. This is how Karl Marx (d. CE 1883) used the term "ideology," and there is a great deal of truth and wisdom in this approach. However, I submit that Marx failed to do full justice to the immense power of spirituality that enables authentic believ-ers to transcend "class interests" in the ceaseless pursuit of value as an integral part of human life.

The upshot of the above longish note is that all believers (no matter what their religion) and even secular Marxists and other theorists must concede that all basic ideas and values acquire fresh dimensions in the course of human life.

6. Even this Qur'anic text is not as simple as traditional interpreters of the Qur'an seem to believe. The relevant Qur'anic text is as follows:

2:230

So if a husband divorces his wife (irrevocably), He cannot, after that, re-marry her until after she has married another husband and He has divorced her. In that case there is no blame on either of them if they re-unite, provided they feel that they can keep the limits ordained by Allah. Such are the limits ordained by Allah, which He makes plain to those who understand.

This text, read together with other relevant texts, makes it quite clear that a husband forfeits his right *suo motu* to restore the marriage contract once the period of estrangement/temporary separation turns into irrevocable divorce thereby attracting the Qur'anic procedure mentioned above. But the question is, when does a "revocable" divorce become "irrevocable" in the absolute sense? Does it become irrevocable automatically after the expiry of a three-month period? Or is it permissible for the husband, even after the expiry of the three-month inter-regnum, to remake a normal contract of marriage with his wife-in-separation (without attracting the Qur'anic clause, as such)?

The point to consider is that a three-month period of temporary alienation or separation of a married couple is absolutely insufficient for turning a separation into an irrevocable divorce that can be repaired only when the woman has been duly married to another man and divorced by him. This way of looking at the marriage contract and the conjugal relationship is brutally harsh and unfair to the woman. This interpretation of the Qur'anic text reduces woman to a sex object instead of according her equal dignity and respect as the male. I confess to having a deep "conscientious objection" to this interpretation. However, this has been the traditional Muslim interpretation of the Qur'an.

An Arabic-speaking research scholar, however, informs me that some learned jurists (not well known at the popular level) hold that the Qur'anic text in Arabic does not entail the traditional view. According to these scholars, the husband is not barred from remarrying his ex-wife even after the lapse of three months of interim separation without attracting the controversial Qur'anic procedure. According to this view, the Qur'anic procedure becomes obligatory only when the husband has already abused, thrice, the male prerogative of unilaterally divorcing and (normally) remarrying the same woman.

Notes to Chapter 7   The Perennial Message of the Qur'an and the Human Situation

1. Here I would like to relate a personal conversation with Akbarbhai Chavada, an ardent Muslim follower of Gandhiji. Akbarbhai, twice member of the Indian Parliament (Lok Sabha) from Gujarat, told me that Gandhiji once asked him if he reads the Qur'an in the original Arabic. When Akbarbhai replied in the negative, Gandhiji insisted that, as a good Muslim, he should do so. Gandhiji added that all

religions were true, and one must cultivate one's own religion without, however, believing or doing anything, which might prick one's own authentic conscience.
2. The pluralistic approach to spirituality is deeply embedded in the *Brahmanical Upanishads*, Sufism, Sikhism, and has now penetrated into the modernist versions of Judaism and Christianity. Neutral Humanism is even more permissive since it does not focus on God. As a Muslim believer, I would not like to disparage any agnostic or atheist or deny their "goodness" simply because they have not been able to find God, or do not need God, provided they continue to seek truth and live their truth, as they see it.

Several eminent modern Christian theologians and thinkers like Reinhold Niehbuhr (d. CE 1971), Paul Tillich (d. CE 1965), and John Robinson (b. CE 1919), *et al.*, concede that the medieval "Scholastic Rationalism" of St. Thomas does not conclusively prove the truth of the Christian faith. Kant also was of the same view. The German thinker, Rudolph Otto (d. CE 1937)) in his classic *The Idea of the Holy*, had earlier affirmed the futility of trying to give coercive reasons for faith in God. The great Islamic thinkers such as Ibn Sina, Ghazali, Ibn Rushd, and in modern times, Iqbal (d. CE 1938), also laid primary stress upon the role of religious experience and intuition rather than of logic or reason in the sphere of religious, spiritual, and moral truth.

See Qur'anic verses 45:14 and 4:124

Tell those who believe, to forgive those who do not look forward to the Days of Allah: It is for Him to recompense (for good or ill) each People according to what they have earned.

If any do deeds of righteousness- be they male or female—and have faith, they will enter Heaven, and not the least injustice will be done to them.

3. A person who passes a judgment of taste, say, "chocolate is tastier than toffee" cannot "prove" this claim though he certainly believes that he is speaking the truth. But the significant point here is that he does not start a quarrel with someone who does not agree with his judgment. The case of some ethical judgments is entirely different. They also cannot be proved, but we just cannot be indifferent to a difference of opinion between one who says that murder or rape are evils and another who says that murder or rape are just acts of passion. In any case, when there is a clash of truthclaims, there must be an agreed method of settling disagreements.
4. The founding fathers of the first ever, secular state in the world, namely, USA, were not atheists, but deeply committed Christians. They, however, had come to believe, in the light of the bitter experience of interreligious tension and conflict

in the entire European continent that the state, as an institution, should be neutral to all the different organized religions, but give equal respect and consideration to all its citizens irrespective of their religious affiliation. As is well-known, the Catholics, Protestants, and the Jews stood in perpetual adversarial relationship, and the religious majority always felt like treating the minority or minorities as second class citizens, if not, plain enemies.

The American idea that the state should be secular was certainly not opposed to religion, morality, or spirituality. It is a plain fact of history that secular America acted as a haven of tolerance and peace to all who wished to escape from persecution on religious grounds. Indeed, the American people as well as the state in the early years of the 19th century warmly welcomed The Unitarian sect of Christians who were hated and persecuted both by Catholics and Protestants on European soil. Muslims and Jews were also welcome to settle down in the new world with full freedom of belief and conscience and equal rights.

The founding fathers of the Indian Constitution drew inspiration from the American precedent, in spite of the fact that the overwhelming majority of the Indian people were Hindu, in some sense or other, and the country had been partitioned on religious lines in the teeth of Hindu opposition. I submit that the choice was right. Indeed, all those who clamor for a religious state (Islamic, Christian, Sikh, or Hindu, as the case may be) hardly realize that a secular state, indirectly, promotes honest and genuine religious commitment instead of hypocritical and sham religiosity.

Annotated Glossary of Key Concepts

1. **Apologetics**: The general attitude and approach of different ideologues to explain prima facie intellectual difficulties, contradictions, confusions, or factual errors in the thought or value system of one's in-group by giving dubious arguments, reasons, or selective narratives and the like. This approach is quite different from an open and impartial review of the tradition. Religious apologetics thus gives birth to polemics.

2. **Authenticity/Authentic Being**: This means an individual's undistorted awareness of or insight into his/her depth feelings, attitudes, and responses to his own situation, and existence as a whole. To be an authentic person is, therefore, much more difficult than to be merely a sincere person, since a person might be sincere and loving to others without being aware of any negative or evil elements lurking in his inaccessible depth responses. See also "*Vipasna*."

3. **Connotative Plasticity**: This expression points out a basic feature of all natural human languages—that words have no inherent rigid use or meaning, quite unlike artificial or especially designed terms/words or symbols used in mathematics or pure or applied science. Creative, poets, thinkers and writers thus, project highly "catchy" out of the way meanings or uses upon the same words and expressions whose normal or traditional use was quite otherwise. This phenomenon throws into relief the fact that natural languages are "plastic" or "porous," and that words of any language can easily "absorb" a wide variety of meanings without violating its basic grammar or usage. This feature can also be termed as "malleability" of natural languages. That is why the approach of understanding the Qur'anic text in the absolutely literal sense in every case can be quite futile and misleading.

4. **Creative Fidelity**: This expression means a sense of commonality with and loyalty to an individual, group, book, or tradition without stopping at any fixed stage of the "ceaseless quest for value." The underlying assumption of this approach is that absolute perfection can never be achieved by any individual, society, or thought and value system. The ethos of creative fidelity therefore leads to the practice of "reflective obedience" to one's chosen authority in contrast with "mechanical obedience."

5. **Deconstruction**: The contemporary French thinker, Derrida, has introduced this word in philosophical discourse. The older word, which performed a similar function was "reconstruction" or "revision" of a thought or value system.

All these terms draw attention to the fact that words and expressions have no permanent and fixed meanings, and that creative poets, thinkers, and religious reformers give old terms ever fresh meanings in their authentic quest for values in the course of a critical reevaluation of the tradition concerned. In the process, they may also coin some apt, fresh expressions that may well become a part of new thinking. At times, creative minds bring about a decisive enlargement and deepening of the human vision and of piety. This also happens when Holy Scriptures are interpreted in the light of new paradigms.

6. **Demythologization**: This is the program or process of separating "myths" and secondary beliefs from the essential dogma and core beliefs and values of any religious tradition. Several religious thinkers of all the great religions have done this in the past. And this practice is likely never to end. To the best of my knowledge, the German philosophical theologian and religious thinker, Bultmann, was the first to use this word. In the modern Islamic period, Sir Syed Ahmed Khan of Aligarh, the philosophical poet, Iqbal, and the thinker and statesman, Abul Kalam Azad, undertook this task.

7. **Dogma**: It is any belief that is logically possible but not conclusively verifiable or falsifiable in this Universe but which may become manifestly evident in "eschatological time," and which is therefore accepted by a person or persons who honestly believe in the absolute veracity of a person or book that proclaims the said belief or because the belief springs forth from their own inner conviction or existential certainty.

8. **Existential Certainty**: This form of certainty differs from logical certainty as well as scientific certainty. Logico-mathematical certainty arises only in those cases where the denial of a truthclaim leads to plain self-contradiction. Scientific certainty arises in those cases where the opposite or contrary belief does not involve any self-contradiction, but human experience always confirms the belief or scientific truthclaim concerned. Existential certainty pertains only to those cases where the truthclaim in question is neither self-evident, nor logically certain, nor scientifically certain, nor universally certain in the sociological sense. Despite all this, a person may have existential certainty in the sense of a compelling inner conviction. This state of mind is "*sui generis*" and qualitatively very different from any inner demand for conformity with the "herd."

9. *Hindutva*: This term was coined by the Indian Hindu revolutionary freedom fighter, Veer Savarkar, in the first half of the twentieth century. The *Rashtriya Swayamsevak Sangh* (RSS), the right wing Hindu militant organization founded in 1925 subsequently adopted the term to pinpoint its own Hindu-centric concept of polity and governance of independent India to distinguish it from the prevailing secular democratic approach of the Indian National Congress Party and other secular organizations. *Hindutva* is, thus, an exclusivist approach to Indian politics.

It ignores the rich Hindu spiritual tradition represented by a long line of modern Hindu thinkers, reformers, statesmen, and patriots.

10. **Intrinsic and Instrumental Values**: It is extremely difficult to define the word "value" in a way that would satisfy all the different ways in which this key word is used. I will, however, explain as simply as possible my use of the expressions, "intrinsic/instrumental values."

Any state of affairs, in the widest sense, that in the judgment of any human subject, is worthy of being preserved/promoted/created/brought into existence for their own sake or as a final end is a value "for that human subject." When two or more humans agree on this core, we can say that they have common intrinsic values even though they may not fully agree on how these values ought to be preserved/promoted, etc. The reason why disagreement may arise in spite of cherishing the same intrinsic values is that the states of affairs desired for their own sake become real only though sustained human action that servers as an instrument for the said purpose. This in turn requires rules of behavior and management in the broad sense. Different human subjects usually have different views on how to promote the intrinsic values on which they agree. According to my usage, if and when this happens, we may say that the final ends on which all are agreed are intrinsic values or values in themselves, while the rules determining how the values can best be realized are the instrumental values. In actual practice however, there is much overlap between the two. Thus, distributive justice, freedom of inquiry, truthfulness, compassion, love, sense of duty, moral courage, reverence for life, benevolent caring for others, gratitude to benefactors, inner consistency, aversion to hurting others, and so on, are all intrinsic values. On the other hand, rules of conduct, such as rules and regulations governing taxation, charity, dress codes, food habits, marriage and divorce, etc., are instrumental values.

11. **Kantian "Good Will"**: The expression "good will" as used by the German thinker, Immanuel Kant, means that unconditional desire and active concern always to do what is ethically right and reasonable for its own sake without any expectation of reward or fear of punishment.

12. **Mystique of the Qur'an**: Several Qur'anic texts cannot be clearly understood or explained in the literal sense of the text. This fact can be interpreted in different ways. For a believer, the expression "Mystique of the Qur'an" is, to my mind, the most apt. It implies suspension of judgment on such texts, provided that the matters concerned do not involve any conscientious objections on the part of the believer.

13. **Ontogenetic**: Ontogenesis means the inner growth of the soul—the core controlling center of a living human being in continuous interaction with other souls or the environment in general. Physical/biological growth of the individual

stops after a certain stage has been reached. But, as is well-known, the individual continues to grow psychologically, cognitively, and emotionally. Ontogenetic growth refers to a distinct dimension of the individual's growth as a conscious and responsible actor on the human and the cosmic scene. This is the task of purifying and refining the source and ground of unconditional doing of duty and the cultivation of the inner beauty of the soul as a finite reflection of Divine perfection.

14. **Paradigm**: It means a radically new form or structured model of some basic belief or idea, whatever the subject of discourse might be. Thus, for example, in the discourse of Christianity, Unitarianism may be said to be a new paradigm of the faith of a Christian relative to the prevailing Trinitarianism. In the field of science, modern optics is a new paradigm of classical physics of light, just as Copernican astronomy was a new paradigm relative to the Aristotelian astronomy.

15. **Perennial Islam**: This means the essential core of the Islamic faith or belief system, which is the common denominator of the several concrete beliefs and value systems subsumed under the umbrella term, "Islam."

16. **Playing Linguistic Games**: This expression was most probably coined by the Austrian thinker, Ludwig Wittgenstein, to describe what philosophers functionally do when they propound philosophical theories describing the ultimate nature of "knowledge," "reality," "beauty," "truth," "goodness," and so on, when in fact there are no, and can be no, definitive answers to the "philosophical problems," which such theories try to address. The supposed problems arise due to the inherent inability of language to match the concrete richness and uniqueness of human experience as such. The fact is that humans are forced to use a limited stock of general/blanket words or expressions to cover a wide variety of situations. This generates typical problems when the same word is used in different senses without any clear awareness of the exact meaning of the same word in different contexts. This confusion creates unconscious fallacies and pseudo-problems, which results in unending philosophical perplexity. Every theory, which claims to be exclusively true and holds other theories to be false, is partly true in some sense, while false in some other.

Wittgenstein held that ordinary language is quite clear and effective since people follow agreed rules for the use of ordinary words. Philosophers, on the other hand, use ordinary language, but more or less unconsciously, give words radically new meanings and uses. It is in this sense that they play "linguistic games," in the words of Wittgenstein.

17. *Realpolitik*: This is the original German term for the game of power politics individuals or nations play to maintain/promote their interests in the ongoing struggle for dominance in society or politics.

18. **Semantics**: This is the systematic inquiry into the nature of meaning, as such, and the different meanings and uses of words and expressions of a language, the nature and types of agreement and disagreement in different fields of discourse and the methods of their resolution. Semantics also studies the way in which language grows in complexity and range. So viewed, semantics is the latest version of analytical philosophy in the wider sense.

19. *Shoonya*: It is a key concept and value in Buddhist thought. This Sanskrit word refers to the greatly coveted state of "non-conceptual pure awareness of undifferentiated reality," the nearest possible human approximation to Divine blessedness. This state may last only for a second or even a fraction thereof before it is dissipated by some fleeting idea, image, association, or memory arising in the individual's field of awareness.

20. *Telos*: The Greek word for purpose. I have used it exclusively in the context of Divine purpose. No human being can claim to understand and explain the Divine purpose, even if one cannot help thinking or believing that there was or must have been some purpose of God's creation.

21. **Theism**: This term, for all practical purposes, is interchangeable with monotheism. While the idea of the oneness of the Supreme Being is explicit in the case of monotheism, it is implicit in theism. Theism almost invariably implies that the Creator, not only creates, but in His inscrutable wisdom and compassion, continually helps, sustains, guides, and responds to human prayer and entreaty. Deism, which is closely connected with Theism, however, does not imply any such continuing Divine solicitude and concern for His creatures after the initial act of creation.

22. **Transcendental Sphere of Human Discourse**: Humans have different kinds of needs and concerns because of their complex nature. Reflecting this complexity, language also serves different human purposes and needs. Controlling and manipulating the physical environment is necessary for human life. So are social cohesion, security, sympathy, mutual assistance, rest and recreation, and (at higher levels) some sense of wordless wonder at the contemplation of the cosmos and speculation as to the origin of life and the phenomenon of death. The traditional culture of the group addresses these concerns and the vast majority of people follow their tradition almost automatically. But they cannot avoid learning from actual experience, especially in empirical matters, though the remote past and the distant future remain beyond their comprehension. However, science does not cover the totality of human concerns that include fear of death, basic anxiety, man's quest for power, beauty, inner harmony and peace—in one word, the complete final truth of what is and what will happen in the future to the individual and to the world at large. These basic issues remain as baffling as ever, and it is these issues, which may be called transcendental matters.

23. **Vipasna**: This is another Sanskrit word and a key value in Buddhist thought. It means the capacity to become aware of what lies hidden in the depths of the individual's awareness or response to the "Other." It may also be understood as the actual state of being so aware. Thus a fully authentic person is a person who excels in "*vipasna*."

Resources

This list does not cover the full range of topics discussed in this book. In fact, works by some of the most celebrated authors of the Muslim world are conspicuous by their absence from this list.

This is a list of high quality, in-print books, which are easily available at this time from www.amazon.com. Most of the references are to the more affordable paperback editions. All listed titles are serious, scholarly works, and should not be confused with the numerous "bestsellers" devoted to self-serving propaganda.

Each one of these titles will open a window into the reality of Islamic civilization. They are generally free of "scholarlese" and extensive background knowledge of Islam is not required. Let the reading begin!

BOOKS:

1. *In the Footsteps of the Prophet: Lessons from the Life of Muhammad* by Tariq Ramadan, 256 pages, ISBN–13: 978–0195308808, Oxford University Press, USA (December 11, 2006).

2. *Muhammad: His Life Based on the Earliest Sources* by Martin Lings, 384 pages, ISBN–13: 978–1594771538, Inner Traditions; Revised Edition (October 17, 2006).

3. *Meanings of the Glorious Qur'an* translated by Marmaduke Pickthall, 950 pages, ISBN–13: 978–9839154269, Islamic Book Trust (June 20, 2007).

4. *Approaching the Qur'an: The Early Revelations* by Michael Anthony Sells, 224 pages, ISBN–13: 978–1883991265, White Cloud Press (1999).

5. *Following Muhammad: Rethinking Islam in the Contemporary World* by Carl W. Ernst, 272 pages, ISBN–13: 978 0807855775, The University of North Carolina Press (August 18, 2004).

6. *Interpreting the Qur'an Towards a Contemporary Approach* by Saeed Abdullah, 192 pages, ISBN–13: 978–0415365383, Routledge; 1 edition (November 11, 2005).

7. *The Qur'an* (Oxford World's Classics) by M. A. S. Abdel Haleem (Translator), 502 pages, ISBN–13: 978–0192831934, Oxford University Press, USA; New Ed edition (May 26, 2005).

8.   *The Meaning of the Holy Qur'an* translated by Abdullah Yusuf Ali, 1759 Pages, ISBN–13: 978–1590080252, Amana Publications.

9.   *The Message of The Qur'an* translated by Muhammad Asad, 1200 pages, ISBN–13: 978–1904510000, The Book Foundation; Bilingual edition (December 2003).

10.   *Major Themes of the Qur'an* by Fazlur Rahman, ISBN–13: 978–0882970462, Bibliotheca Islamica; 2nd edition (June 1989).

11.   *Remembering God: Reflections on Islam* by Charles Le Gai Eaton, 256 pages, ISBN–13: 978–1930637085, Kazi Publications (April 11, 2000).

12.   *The Veil and the Male Elite: A Feminist Interpretation of Women's Rights in Islam* by Fatima Mernissi, 240 pages, ISBN–13: 978–0201632217, Perseus Books Group.

13.   *Mecca the Blessed, Medina the Radiant: The Holiest Cities of Islam* by Seyyed Hossein Nasr and Ali Kazuyoshi Nomachi, 192 pages, ISBN–10: 089381752X.

14.   *And Muhammad Is His Messenger: The Veneration of the Prophet in Islamic Piety* by Annemarie Schimmel (d. 2003), 389 pages, ISBN–13: 978–0807841280, The University of North Carolina Press (November 30, 1985).

15.   *Rumi's World: The Life and Works of the Greatest Sufi Poet* by Annemarie Schimmel (d. 2003), 224 pages, ISBN-13: 978–0877736110, Shambhala; 1st edition (May 22, 2001).

16.   *A Vanished World: Muslims, Christians, and Jews in Medieval Spain* by Chris Lowney, 352 pages, ISBN–13: 978–0195311914, Oxford University Press, USA (August 14, 2006).

17.   *Muhammad: A Prophet for Our Time* by Karen Armstrong, 256 pages, ISBN–13: 978–0061155772, HarperOne; Reprint edition (August 28, 2007).

18.   *Science in Medieval Islam: An Illustrated Introduction* by Howard R. Turner, 282 pages, ISBN–13: 978-0292781498, University of Texas Press (1997).

19.   *No God but God: The Origins, Evolution, and Future of Islam* by Reza Aslan, 352 pages, ISBN–13: 978–0812971897, Random House Trade Paperbacks (January 10, 2006).

20. *The Empire of the Great Mughals: History, Art and Culture* by Annemarie Schimmel (d. 2003), 352 pages, ISBN–13: 978–1861892515, Reaktion Books; 1 edition (October 2, 2006).

21. *The Oxford Encyclopedia of the Modern Islamic World* (4 Volume Set) by John L. Esposito (Editor), 1904 pages, ISBN–13: 978–0195148039, Oxford University Press, USA; New Ed edition (May 29, 2001).

22. *101 Questions and Answers on Islam* by John Renard, 192 pages, ISBN–13: 9780809142804, Paulist Press (May 3, 2004).

23. *Mystical Dimensions of Islam* by Annemarie Schimmel (d. 2003), 527 pages, ISBN–13: 978–0807812716, The University of North Carolina Press (April 1, 1978).

24. *Sufi Essays* by Seyyed Hossein Nasr, 204 pages, ISBN–13: 978–1871031416, Kazi Publications; 3rd. edition (January 1, 1999).

25. *With God on Our Side: Politics and Theology of the War on Terrorism* by John L. Esposito (Foreword), Aftab Ahmad Malik (Editor), Khaled Abou el Fadl (Introduction), 431 pages, ISBN–13: 978-0954054465, Amal Press; 1 edition (June 1, 2006).

26. *Speaking in God's Name: Islamic Law, Authority and Women* by Khaled Abou El Fadl, 384 pages, ISBN–13: 978–1851682621, Oneworld Publications (December 25, 2001).

27. *The Great Theft: Wrestling Islam from the Extremists* by Khaled M. Abou El Fadl, 336 pages, ISBN–13: 978–0061189036, Harper One (January 23, 2007).

28. *The Place of Tolerance in Islam* by Khaled Abou El Fadl, 112 pages, ISBN–13: 978–0807002292, Beacon Press (November 8, 2002).

29. *Holy War: The Crusades and Their Impact on Today's World* by Karen Armstrong, 672 pages, ISBN–13: 978–0385721400, Anchor; 2nd edition (November 27, 2001).

30. *Islamic Art and Architecture: From Isfahan to the Taj Mahal* by Henri Stierlin (Photographer), Anne Stierlin (Photographer), 320 pages, ISBN–13: 978–0500511008, Thames & Hudson (November 2002).

VIDEOS:

31.   *Islam: Empire of Faith*, Format: Color, DVD-Video, Widescreen, NTSC, Run Time: 160 minutes, DVD Release Date: March 8, 2005.

32.   *Lion of the Desert*, Starring: Anthony Quinn, Oliver Reed Director: Moustapha Akkad, Format: Color, DVD-Video, Full Screen, NTSC, Run Time: 93 minutes, DVD Release Date: November 1, 2005.

33.   *The Message*, Starring: Anthony Quinn, Irene Papas Director: Moustapha Akkad, Format: Color, NTSC, Run Time: 178 minutes, DVD Release Date: November 1, 2005.

34.   National Geographic—*Inside Mecca* (2003), Director: Anisa Mehdi, Format: Closed-captioned, Color, DVD-Video, NTSC, Run Time: 60 minutes, Studio: National Geographic Video, DVD Release Date: October 21, 2003.

35.   *Great World Religions: Islam*, 12 lectures, 30 minutes/lecture, Course No. 6102, Taught by John L. Esposito, Georgetown University. Course available from The Teaching Company www.teach12.com. They have many other interesting courses.

Index of Names

Abduh, Muhammad; *139*
(d. CE 1905). Pre-eminent Egyptian Islamic reformer and commentator of the Qur'an in modern times.

Abraham; *14, 70, 71, 90, 141, 165, 172*
The first of the Biblical patriarchs. Judaism, Christianity, and Islam consider him to be a prophet and trace their origins back to him.

Abu Bakr; *17, 20, 149*
(d. CE 634). Also called al-Siddiq (Arabic: "the Upright"). The Prophet's ﷺ closest companion and adviser. The first of the four rightly guided Caliphs.

Abu Musa Ashari; *151*
(d. CE 662 or 672). A companion of the Prophet Muhammad ﷺ and important figure in early Islamic history.

Abu Talib; *18, 53*
(d. CE 619). An uncle of the Prophet Muhammad ﷺ. He raised and supported him in his youth. He was the Head of the Prophet's ﷺ clan of Banu Hashim.

Afghani, Jamaluddin; *139*
(d. CE 1897). Islamic reformer of Iranian origin, and father of the pan-Islam movement in modern times.

Ali, Abdullah Yusuf; *xvii–xviii, 54*
(d. CE 1953). Renowned translator and commentator of the Qur'an. His English translation ranks as the most widely known and used in the world.

Ali ibn Abu Talib; *17–18, 20, 133–35, 149–50, 195*
(d. CE 661). A cousin and son-in-law of the Prophet Muhammad ﷺ. One of the earliest converts to Islam. Sunni Muslims consider Ali as the fourth and final Rightly Guided Caliph. Shia Muslims revere Ali as the first infallible *Imam* and consider him and his descendants to be the rightful successors to Muhammad ﷺ.

This political disagreement split the Muslim community into the *Sunni* and *Shia* branches.

Ali, Muhammad; *xvii, 149*
(d. CE 1951). He devoted his life to the service of the Ahmadiyya Movement. He produced a vast amount of literature in English and Urdu including a translation of the Qur'an.

Al-Tabari; *xx, 16, 195*
(d. CE 923). One of the earliest, Persian historian and exegete of the Qur'an. Most famous for his *Tarikh al-Tabari* (History of the Prophets and Kings) and *Tafsir al-Tabari*.

Ansari, Hamid; *123, 126*
(Born, 1937). Ansari started his career as a civil servant in the Indian Foreign Service. He is also a respected academician. A former Vice-Chancellor of the Aligarh Muslim University, he was elected the 12th Vice President of India in 2007.

Arberry, A.J; *135*
(d. CE 1969). British scholar of Islamic Studies and translator of the Qur'an.

Aristotle; *16, 182*
(d. 322 BCE). Eminent Greek philosopher, a student of Plato and teacher of Alexander the Great. He wrote on many different subjects.

Arkoun, Muhammad; *123, 126*
(d. CE 2010). Arkoun was born in 1928 in Algiers. He consistently advocated Islamic modernism and humanism. As the editor of *Arabica*, he broadened the journal's scope, and played an important role in shaping Western language scholarship on Islam. He is the author of numerous books in French, English, and Arabic.

Armstrong, Karen; *xii, xvii, 135, 139, 143*
A British author of numerous works on comparative religion, who first rose to prominence with her highly successful *A History of God*. A former Catholic nun, she is also the author of several respected books on the Muslim tradition.

Aslan, Reza; *135, 186*
An Iranian-American Muslim writer and scholar of religions. Aslan is also a regular commentator for American Public Media's *Marketplace*, and the *Middle East Analyst* for CBS News.

Attar, Fariduddin; *12*
(d. CE 1230) Pre-eminent Persian poet and Sufi mystic.

Azad, Maulana Abul Kalam; *xii, xvii, xx, 102, 121, 124, 139*
(d. CE 1958). Indian Muslim scholar and senior political leader. Worked tirelessly for Hindu–Muslim unity.

Basri, Bibi Rabia; *158*
(d. CE 801). Many spiritual stories are associated with her, and for centuries she has been a torchbearer for Sufis. Being a woman, she is the feminine voice in Sufi annals.

Beruni, Al; *3, 136, 140*
(d. CE 1048). Pre-eminent Muslim scientist. Author of an encyclopedic work on medieval India.

Broad, C. D; *145*
(d. CE 1971). An eminent English philosopher and writer on the philosophical aspects of psychical research.

Bucaille, Maurice; *161–62*
A French medical doctor, he was appointed family physician to King Faisal of Saudi Arabia in 1973. His book, *The Bible, The Qur'an and Science*, argues that the Qur'an is compatible with modern science, while the Bible is not.

Bukhari, Imam; *144*
(d. CE 870). Popularly known as *Imam* Bukhari; he was an eminent, scholar most known for authoring the *hadith* collection named *Sahih Bukhari*. Sunnis regard it as the most authentic of all *hadith* compilations.

Campbell, Joseph; *154*
(d. CE 1987). An American mythology professor, writer, and lecturer best known for his work in the fields of comparative mythology and comparative religion.

Camus, Albert; *137*

(d. CE 1960). French author and philosopher who won the Nobel Prize in 1957.

Carlyle, Thomas; *142*

(d. CE 1881). An essayist, satirist, and historian from Scotland, whose work was hugely influential during the Victorian era.

Chavada, Akbarbhai; *176*

A close associate of Mahatama Gandhi. Elected Member of the Indian Parliament.

Chishti, Baba Farid; *12*

(d. CE 1266) Indian Muslim Sufi saint.

Dara Shikoh, Prince; *121*

Dara (d. CE 1659) was the eldest son of Mughal emperor Shah Jahan, the world famous builder of the Taj Mahal. He was a patron of the fine arts and spent much of his time in exploring the commonalities between Islam and Hinduism. He commissioned the translation of the Upanishads from their original Sanskrit into Persian.

Das, Bhagwan; *12, 136*

(d. CE 1958). An Indian theosophist and public figure committed to freedom from British rule and interfaith harmony.

David (Dawood); *41, 65*

David was the second and the greatest of the Kings of the Israelites. Muslims believe that David was an honorable prophet of God. See Qur'an 17:55

Durant, Will; *135*

(d. CE 1981). A prolific American popularizer in the fields of history, religion and philosophy. He is best known for the 11-volume *The Story of Civilization*, written with his wife Ariel and published between 1935 and 1975. Durant's quote, "*A great civilization is not conquered from without until it has destroyed itself from within,*" resonates with Americans to this day.

Eck, Diana; *139, 143*

Professor of Comparative Religion and Indian Studies at Harvard University. Her work addresses issues of Christian faith in a world of many faiths.

Index of Names

Einstein, Albert; *121, 156*
(d. CE 1955). A German-born theoretical physicist. He is best known for his theory of relativity and specifically mass–energy equivalence. Einstein received the 1921 Nobel Prize in Physics.

Ernst, Carl; *143*
He is a specialist in Islamic studies, with a focus on West and South Asia. Ernst received his A.B. in comparative religion at Stanford University in 1973, and his Ph.D. at Harvard University in 1981.

Farabi; *3, 140*
(d. CE 950). One of the greatest scientists and philosophers of the Islamic world in his time. He was also a cosmologist, logician, musician, psychologist, and sociologist.

Faruqi, Ismail; *139*
(d. CE 1986). Palestinian-American philosopher who was recognized by his peers as an authority on Islam and comparative religion. He was one of the first to propose the idea of *Islamization of knowledge*.

Fatah, Tarek; *123, 126*
A Canadian political activist, writer, and broadcaster of Pakistani origin. Born in 1949, he is the author of *Chasing a Mirage: The Tragic Illusion of an Islamic State*.

Fatima, Bibi; *20*
(d. CE 633). Daughter of the Prophet Muhammad ﷺ from his first wife, Bibi Khadijah. She is regarded by Muslims as an exemplar for women.

Freud, Sigmund; *121, 146*
(d. CE 1939). Founder of the psychoanalytic school of psychology. Freud is best known for his theories of the unconscious mind and for creating the clinical practice of psychoanalysis.

Gabriel/Holy Spirit (Angel); *10, 16, 18, 21, 53, 140, 145–46, 149, 151–52*
Mentioned in both the Qur'an and the Bible.

Gandhi/Gandhiji; *xii, 12, 103, 107, 137–39, 176*
(d. CE 1948). He was a major political and spiritual leader of India. Gandhi practiced and advocated non-violence and truth in all situations. He is commonly known in India and across the world as the *Mahatma*, "Great Soul."

Ghazali; *xx, 47, 121, 152*
(d. CE 1111). He was a theologian, jurist, philosopher, psychologist and mystic, and remains one of the most celebrated scholars in the history of Islamic thought. He changed the course of early Islamic philosophy, shifting it away from the influence of ancient Greek, toward cause and effect that were determined by God.

Gibb, H. A. R; *xvii, 135*
(d. CE 1971). British Arabist and scholar of Islam. Gibb taught at Oxford for eighteen years. He served as an editor of the *Encyclopaedia of Islam*. His *Mohammedanism*, published in 1949, became the basic text used by Western students of Islam. In 1955, Gibb became the James Richard Jewett Professor of Arabic, and University Professor at Harvard University.

Gibbon, Edward; *142*
(d. CE 1794). An eminent English historian and Member of Parliament. Published in six volumes, *The History of the Decline and Fall of the Roman Empire* is a landmark.

Goethe, Johann Wolfgang von; *142*
(d. CE 1832). He is considered by many to be the most important writer in the German language and one of the most important thinkers in Western culture as well.

Goliath; *41, 65*
A Philistine warrior, famous for his battle with the young David, the future king of Israel, described in the Hebrew Bible and, more briefly, in the Qur'an.

Guillaume, Alfred; *142*
(d. CE 1965). Author of *Life of Muhammad: A Translation of Ibn Ishaq's Sirat Rasul Allah* and other works.

Hafsa, Bibi; *20*
(d. CE 665–666). Hafsa bint Umar, daughter of Umar ibn al-Khattab (the second Caliph) and wife of the Prophet Muhammad ﷺ, and therefore a Mother of the Believers.

Hambal, *Imam*; *3*
(d. CE 855). *Imam* Ahmad ibn Muhammad ibn Hambal, founder of the Hambali School of Muslim jurisprudence, is one of the great personalities of Islam. Through his disciple Ibn Taimiya, he is the distant progenitor of modern Wahabism.

Hamiedullah; *149*
(d. CE 2002). Professor Hamiedullah belonged to an illustrious family of scholars, jurists, writers, and Sufis. His contribution to the dissemination of Islamic teachings in the Western world is universally recognized.

Hasan al Banna; *124*
(CE 1906–1949). Egyptian schoolteacher, political activist, and *imam*. Best known for founding the Muslim Brotherhood (1928), one of the largest and most influential 20th century Muslim revivalist organizations. He deeply influenced the development of Islamic thought in the 20th century.

Hastings, James; *152*
(d. CE 1922). A Scottish Presbyterian minister and religious scholar.

Heidegger, Martin; *137, 152*
(d. CE 1976). An influential German philosopher. His best known book, *Being and Time*, is generally considered to be one of the most important philosophical works of the 20th century. Heidegger's work remains controversial due to his involvement with the Nazis.

Hisham, Ibn; *15, 142*
(d. CE 833). Edited the biography of Muhammad ﷺ written by Ibn Ishaq. Ibn Ishaq's work is lost and is now only known in the recensions of Ibn Hisham and Al-Tabari

Hume, David; *152*
(d. CE 1776). Considered among the most important figures in the history of Western philosophy. Hume was the first great philosopher of the modern era to carve out a thoroughly naturalistic philosophy.

Husain; *3*
(d. CE 680). He was the grandson of the Prophet Muhammad ﷺ and the son of Ali, the fourth Caliph, and Muhammad's ﷺ daughter Fatima Zahra. He is revered

as a martyr who fought tyranny. Revenge for Husain's death at Karbala was turned into a rallying cry that led to the rise of the Shia movement.

Hussein, Seyyed Nasr; *126, 135*

Professor of Islamic studies at George Washington University. Nasr is a renowned Iranian scholar of comparative religion. A lifelong student and follower of Frithjof Schuon, he writes in the fields of Islamic esoterism, Sufism, philosophy of science, and metaphysics.

Iblis (Satan); *37, 53, 60, 68–69, 81–83, 112, 118, 154, 165, 174*

The name of the primary Devil (*Shaitan* or Satan) in Islam.

Iqbal, Sir Muhammad; *xx, 102, 121, 124, 139, 173, 177*

(d. CE 1938). A prominent Muslim poet, philosopher, and politician of India. His poetry in Urdu, Arabic and Persian is considered to be among the greatest of the modern era. He was a strong proponent of the political and spiritual revival of Islamic civilisation. His vision of an independent state for the Muslims of British India was to inspire the creation of Pakistan.

Isaac; *71, 197*

According to the Hebrew Bible, Isaac is the son of Abraham and Sarah. His story is told in the *Book of Genesis*. Muslims honour Isaac as a prophet of Islam. The Qur'an views Isaac as a righteous man, servant of God and the father of Israelites. The Qur'an states that Isaac and his progeny are blessed as long as they uphold their covenant with God.

Ishaq, Ibn; *15, 142*

(d. CE 767 or 761). An Arab Muslim historian. He collected oral traditions that formed the basis of the very first biography of the Islamic Prophet Muhammad ﷺ—usually called *Sirat Rasul Allah* (*Life of Allah's Messenger*).

Ismail (Ishmael); *71, 139*

Ismail is a figure in the Torah, the Bible, and the Qur'an. He was Abraham's eldest son, born of his wife Sarah's hand maiden Hagar. Both Jewish and Islamic traditions consider him to be the ancestor of Northern Arab people. The Qur'an views him as a prophet, and as the actual son that Abraham was called on to sacrifice, as opposed to Issac.

Izutsu, Toshihiko; *152, 157*
(d. CE 1993). Author of many books on Islam and other religions. In 1958, he completed the first direct translation of the Qur'an from Arabic to Japanese. His translation is still renowned for its linguistic accuracy and widely used for scholarly works.

Jacob; *71*
The third Biblical patriarch. Jacob was the son of Isaac, and the grandson of Abraham. Jacob sired the twelve Tribes of Israel. He is respected as a prophet by Muslims.

Jafar Sadiq; *3*
(d. CE 765). Highly respected by both Shia and Sunni Muslims for his great Islamic scholarship, pious character, and academic contributions. The 6th infallible *Imam* on the Shia chain. He is also the founder of *Shia fiqh*, known as Jafari jurisprudence. Interestingly enough, he was also the teacher of the famous Abu Hanifa, the founder of *Sunni Madhhab*.

Jahiz; *151*
(d. CE 868). A famous Arab scholar, believed to be of East African descent. He was an Arabic prose writer and author of works on Arabic literature, biology, zoology, history, early Islamic philosophy, Islamic psychology, Mutazili theology, and politico-religious polemics.

James, William; *145*
(d. CE 1910). A pioneering American psychologist and philosopher renowned for his works on the psychology of religious experience and mysticism, and the philosophy of pragmatism.

Jaspers, Karl; *8, 137, 152*
(d. CE 1969). A German psychiatrist and philosopher who had a strong influence on modern theology, psychiatry, and philosophy.

Jesus; *10–12, 14, 28–29, 37, 71, 113, 159*
(d. CE 26–36). Also known as Jesus Christ, he is the central figure of Christianity and is revered by most Christian churches as the Son of God and the incarnation of God. Islam considers Jesus, son of Mary, to be a prophet. Judaism holds the idea of Jesus being God, or part of a Trinity, or a mediator to God, to be heresy.

Jinnah, Muhammad Ali; *139*

(d. CE 1948). An eminent politician and leader of the All India Muslim League in British India. He is universally acknowledged to be the founder of Pakistan and served as its first Governor-General. Jinnah envisioned Pakistan as a secular democratic state, a theme he repeatedly touched upon in his speeches. Nevertheless, this aspect of his ideology never materialized.

Jung, C. G.; *145–46, 154*

(d. CE 1961). As the founder of analytical psychology, Jung has had an enduring influence on psychology as well as wider society. He emphasized understanding the psyche through exploring the worlds of dreams, art, mythology, world religion, and philosophy.

Kabir; *12*

(d. CE 1448). A mystic poet and saint of India. A weaver by profession, Kabir ranks among the world's greatest poets. Kabir openly criticized all sects and gave a new direction to Indian philosophy.

Kant, Immanuel; *49, 121, 152, 157–58, 160, 177*

(d. CE 1804). An 18th century German philosopher. He is considered to be one of the most influential thinkers of modern Europe. His most important work is the *Critique of Pure Reason.*

Khadijah, Bibi; *17, 193, 207*

(d. CE 623). The first wife of Prophet Muhammad ﷺ, as also the first convert to Islam. A prominent business women of Mecca, she initiated the marriage proposal herself. She remained at his side and supported him throughout his mission.

Khaldun, Ibn; *xx, 3, 16, 47, 121, 135, 140, 145*

(d. CE 1406). A famous North African Arab polymath. He was a historian, Islamic scholar, philosopher, social scientist and more. He is best known for his *Muqaddimah*, the first volume of his book on universal history.

Khan, Sir Syed Ahmed; *xvii, xx, 102, 109, 121, 124, 129, 135, 138, 140, 180*

(d. CE 1898). An Indian educator and politician, and an Islamic reformer and modernist. Sir Syed pioneered modern education for the Muslim community in India by founding the Muhammedan Anglo-Oriental College, which later developed into the Aligarh Muslim University. His work gave rise to a new generation of Muslim intellectuals and politicians who comprised the Aligarh movement to secure the political future of Muslims in India.

Khomeini, Ayatollah Ruhollah; *124*

Ayatollah Khomeini (CE 1902–1989), an Iranian, was the charismatic spiritual, and political leader of the successful revolt (1979) against the Westernised regime of the Shah of Iran (Mohammad Reza Pahlavi). A leading scholar and teacher of Shia Islam, he authored numerous writings on Islamic philosophy, law, and ethics. Post revolution, Khomeini became the Supreme Leader of Iran; a post created in the Constitution for the highest ranking political and religious authority of the nation.

Khwaja, Abdul Majeed; *xvii*

(d. CE 1962). An eminent Indian freedom fighter and educationist. He was one of the founders of Jamia Millia Islamia, Delhi, India.

Khwaja, Nizamuddin Auliya; *12, 121*

(d. CE 1325). The pre-eminent Sufi saint of the Chishti Order in India. His shrine is located in Delhi.

Kierkegaard; *137, 152*

(d. CE 1855). A prolific 19th century Danish philosopher and theologian. Much of his work deals with religious themes such as faith in God. Crossing the boundaries of philosophy, theology, psychology, and literature, he is an influential figure in contemporary thought.

Kindi; *3, 140*

(d. CE 873). Is known for his efforts to introduce Greek and Hellenistic philosophy to the Arab world. In mathematics, Al-Kindi played an important role in introducing Indian numerals to the Islamic and Christian world. An Arab polymath, Al-Kindi was a master of many different areas of learning and is considered to be one of the greatest Islamic philosophers.

Krishna, Bhagwan; *12*

Avatar. He is worshiped by Hindus from a variety of different perspectives. The most famous scripture portraying Krishna is the *Bhagavad Gita.*

Kung, Hans; *123*

(Born, CE 1928). Swiss Catholic priest, theologian, and prolific author. Kung has written extensively on Judaism, Christianity, and Islam. He speaks forcefully against the clash of civilizations and for peace through interreligious dialogue. He is the author of *Islam: Past, Present and Future.*

Lat; *68, 165*
A pre-Islamic Arabian goddess who was one of the three chief goddesses of Mecca. Her idol was kept inside the sanctuary. In the Qur'an, she is mentioned along with Uzza and Manat in *surah* 53:19–23.

Lings, Martin; *xvii, 143*
(d. CE 2005). A Sufi and a student and follower of Frithjof Schuon, and a prolific and well-regarded author on Islam and comparative religion. Written in 1983, his biography of the Prophet Muhammad ﷺ has been hailed as the "best biography of the Prophet in English."

Mahatma Gandhi/Gandhiji; *See* Gandhi

Maharishi Mahesh Yogi; *12*
(d. CE 2008). Founded and developed the Transcendental Meditation technique and related programs. He became known in the Western world in part due to interactions with The Beatles and other celebrities.

Manat; *68, 165*
A pre-Islamic Arabian goddess who was one of the three chief goddesses of Mecca. Her idol was kept inside the sanctuary. In the Qur'an, she is mentioned along with Uzza and Lat in *surah* 53:19–23

Marcel, Gabriel; *68, 165*
(d. CE 1973). French philosopher, leading Christian existentialist, and author of about thirty plays.

Marx, Karl; *121, 142, 175*
(d. CE 1883). German social philosopher, and father of the world Communist movement.

Mary (mother of Jesus); *28, 37, 71, 159*
Revered as the ideal women in Islam. Her story is related in the Qur'an in great detail.

Maududi, Mawlana Abu Ala; *xx, 124*
(CE 1903 –1979). Prominent Pakistani journalist, theologian, Muslim revivalist leader, and founder of *Jamat-e-Islami*, the Islamic revivalist party (1941, British

India). The modern conceptualization of the "Islamic state" is attributed to Maududi. His influence was widespread. The Egyptians Hassan al Banna and Sayyid Qutb were deeply influenced by him.

Mian Mir; *12*
(d. CE 1635). Indian Muslim Sufi saint of Lahore and symbol of the interfaith movement.

Moore, G.E; *158*
(d. CE 1958). An influential English philosopher, best known today for his defense of ethical non-naturalism, his emphasis on common sense in philosophical method, and the paradox that bears his name.

Moses (Prophet); *14, 28–29, 59–60, 71, 143*
Moses is mentioned more often in the Qur'an than any other individual. He is defined in the Qur'an as both a prophet (*Nabi*) and a messenger (*Rasul*), which means he was one of the few prophets who brought both a scripture and a law to his people.

Muslim ibn al-Hajjaj, also known as *Imam* Muslim; *134*
(d. CE 874/875). A renowned scholar. He traveled widely to compile a collection of about 4000 *hadith*. Sunni Muslims consider it to be the second most authentic collection of its type.

Muhammad, Prophet of Islam; *xvii, 1–2, 4–6, 10–12, 14–15, 17–18, 23, 45, 48–49, 51–53, 73–77, 103, 107, 111, 113, 116, 118–19, 123, 125, 129–34, 139–40, 142–44, 146–47, 149, 160, 164, 166–67*
(d. CE 632). He is the central human figure of the religion of Islam and is revered by Muslims as the final messenger and Prophet of God.

Nanak, Guru; *11, 137*
(d. CE 1539). The founder of Sikhism. Guru Nanak believed in a personal and merciful God. He endeavored mightily to remove ignorance and superstition from the minds of people.

Nehru, Jawaharlal; *139*
(d. CE 1964). A pivotal figure in the Indian independence movement and the first Prime Minister of the Republic of India. A life-long liberal, Nehru was an advocate

for Fabian socialism. His long tenure was instrumental in shaping the traditions and structures of independent India.

Naim, Abdullah Ahmed; *123, 126*
An independent minded intellectual, Naim was born in Sudan in 1946. His works include *Toward an Islamic Reformation: Civil Liberties, Human Rights and International Law* and, more recently, *Islam and the Secular State: Negotiating the Future of Sharia.*

Niebuhr, Reinhold; *177*
(d. CE 1971). A Protestant theologian best known for his study of the task of relating the Christian faith to the realities of modern politics and diplomacy. During his pastorate, Niebuhr was troubled by the demoralizing effects of industrialism on workers. He became an outspoken critic of Henry Ford and allowed union organizers to use his pulpit to expound their message of workers' rights.

Nietzsche, Friedrich Wilhelm; *152*
(d. CE 1900). He wrote critical texts on religion, morality, contemporary culture, philosophy, and science. Nietzsche's influence remains substantial within and beyond philosophy, notably in existentialism and postmodernism.

Noeldeke, Theodor; *149*
(d. CE 1930). In 1859 his history of the Qur'an won for him the prize of the French Académie des Inscriptions et Belles-Lettres. Noldeke's range of studies were wide and varied, but the main focus of his work was Semitic languages, and the history and civilization of Islam.

Uthman Ibn Affan; *10, 20, 21, 22, 148, 149*
(d. CE 656). As an early convert to Islam and Muhammad's ﷺ son-in-law, he played a major role in early Islamic history, most notably as the third Caliph of the Muslims. The compilation of the Qur'an was completed under his supervision.

Otto, Rudolph; *177*
(d. CE 1937). An eminent German Lutheran theologian and scholar of comparative religion.

Pickthall, Marmaduke; *xvii*
(d. CE 1936). A British convert from Christianity to Islam, author of the famous translation *The Meaning of the Glorious Koran.*

Plato; *121, 175*

(d. 347 BCE). A classical Greek philosopher, who, together with his mentor, Socrates, and his student, Aristotle, helped to lay the foundations of Western philosophy.

Pratap, Raja Mahendra; *94*

(d. CE 1979). A freedom fighter, journalist, writer, and revolutionary social reformist of India.

Qutb, Sayyid; *124*

Sayyid Qutb (CE 1906–1966) was an Egyptian poet, author, educator, Islamist theorist, and the leading member of the Egyptian Muslim Brotherhood in the 1950s and 1960s. He is best known for his 30-volume commentary on the Qur'an, *Fi zilal al-Qur'an* (*In the Shade of the Qur'an*), as also his book, *Milestones*. Views on Qutb vary widely. Admired by some in the Muslim world, Qutb also has numerous critics. His writings are said to have inspired Osama bin Laden.

Rama; *12*

The legendary king of Ayodhya in ancient India. In Hinduism, he is considered to be an *avatar* of Vishnu. Rama is referred to within Hinduism as *Maryada Purushottama*, literally, the Perfect Man. The majority of details concerning Rama come from the *Ramayana*, one of the two great epics of India. The legend of Rama is deeply influential and popular in the societies of the Indian subcontinent and across South East Asia.

Ramadan, Tariq; *123, 126*

Born in 1962, in Switzerland. Tariq is an eminent academic, poet, and writer. He advocates that Western Muslims should study and re-interpret core Islamic texts, while taking into account cultural differences between modern Europe, America, and the traditional Muslim majority cultures. He is both, admired and distrusted, because of his close family ties to the founders of the Egyptian Muslim Brotherhood.

Ramakrishna, Paramhansa; *12, 138*

(d. CE 1886). Premier saint of modern India and spiritual father of the Ramakrishna Mission of Bengal.

Raman, Maharishi; *12, 138*

(d. CE 1990). Indian saint and yogi.

Renan; *142*
(d. CE 1892). A French philosopher and writer. He is best known for his influential historical works on early Christianity and his political theories.

Robinson, John Arthur Thomas; *177*
A New Testament scholar, notable author and former Anglican Bishop. He played a major role in shaping liberal Christian theology. Wrote the controversial book *Honest to God.*

Rosenthal, Franz; *16, 135*
(d. CE 2003). Professor Emeritus of Arabic, scholar of Arabic literature and Islam. He was born in Germany.

Rumi, Jalaluddin; *12, 121*
(d. CE 1273). Renowned Persian poet and Sufi. Rumi's importance is considered to transcend national and ethnic borders. His poems have been widely translated into many of the world's languages. BBC News has described him as the "most popular poet in America."

Rushd, Ibn; *xx, 3, 140, 177*
(d. CE 1198). Better known in European literature as Averroes. He was a Muslim philosopher, physician, and polymath. He has been described as the founding father of secular thought in Western Europe.

Russell, Bertrand; *158*
(d. CE 1972). A prolific writer, he was an acute mathematical thinker and a commentator on a large variety of topics.

Sadi; *12*
(d. CE 1292). A major Persian poet of the medieval period. He is recognized not only for the quality of his writing, but also for the depth of his social thought.

Sarmad; *12*
(d. CE 1659/1661). He arrived in India during the 17th century. Of Jewish and Armenian origin, Sarmad was known for espousing and ridiculing the major religions of his day, but he also wrote beautiful mystical poetry in the form of quatrains. The Mughal emperor Aurangzeb beheaded Sarmad for poetry deemed heretical.

Sartre, Jean-Paul; *137, 152*
(d. CE 1980). A French existentialist philosopher, playwright, novelist, screen-writer, political activist, biographer, and literary critic. He was the leading figure in 20th century French philosophy. In 1964 he was awarded the Nobel Prize for Literature, but he declined it.

Satan; *See* Iblis/Devil

Schimmel, Annemarie; *xii, xvii, 135, 142*
(d. CE 2003). German religious thinker and eminent scholar of Islam.

Shafai, *Imam*; *3*
(d. CE 820). An Arabic jurist. He was active in juridical matters, and his teaching eventually led to the Shafai school of *fiqh* (or *Madhhab*) named after him. Hence he is often called *Imam al-Shafai*.

Shankar, Ravi; *138*
A leading Indian instrumentalist of the modern era. His collaborations with vio-linist Yehudi Menuhin, film maker Satyajit Ray, and the The Beatles have added to his international reputation.

Shariati, Ali; *124*
Ali Shariati (CE 1933–1975) was educated in Iran and the Sorbonne Univer-sity, Paris. He was an influential Iranian sociologist and political activist who attempted to explain and provide solutions for problems faced by Muslim socie-ties, by interweaving traditional Islamic teachings with the insights of modern sociology, and philosophy.

Shibli Nomani; *135, 173*
(d. CE 1914). An Indian poet and scholar of Islam. He collected much material on the life of Prophet Muhammad ﷺ, but could write only the first two volumes of the planned work, *Sirat-un-Nabi,* during his lifetime.

Sina, Ibn; *xx, 3, 140, 177*
(d. CE 1037). Commonly known as Avicenna. An eminent figure in Islamic learn-ing, he is considered to be the father of early modern medicine. His most famous works are *The Book of Healing* and *The Canon of Medicine.*

Sivananda, Swami; *138*

d. CE 1963). A Hindu spiritual teacher and a well-known proponent of *Yoga* and *Vedanta*.

Smith, Huston; *7, 143*

He is among the preeminent religious studies scholars in the United States. His work *The Religions of Man* (later revised and retitled *The World's Religions*) is a classic in the field, with over two million copies sold.

Sundarlal, Pandit; *12*

(d. CE 1981). Indian social reformer, interfaith leader, and close associate of Gandhi.

Tagore, Rabindranath; *12*

(d. CE 1941). Bengali poet, Indian thinker, sage, and patriot. Winner of the Nobel Prize for literature in 1913.

Tillich, Paul; *177*

(d. CE 1965). A German-American theologian and Christian existentialist philosopher. One of the most influential Protestant theologians of the twentieth century.

Toynbee, Arnold; *135*

(d. CE 1975). Eminent British historian of world history and civilizations.

Tufail, Ibn; *3*

(d. CE 1185). An Arabic writer, novelist, Islamic philosopher, theologian, physician, vizier, and court official. He is most famous for writing the first philosophical novel, *Hayy ibn Yaqdhan*, also known as *Philosophus Autodidactus* in the Western world. As a physician, he was an early supporter of dissection and autopsy.

Umar, ibn al-Khatab; *3, 20, 22, 93, 132–34, 149, 173*

(d. CE 644). A righteous companion of the Prophet ﷺ. He became the second Caliph following the death of Abu Bakr, and is thus regarded by Sunni Muslims as one of the *Rashidun* (four righteously guided Caliphs).

Uzza; *68, 165, 200*

A pre-Islamic Arabian goddess who was one of the three chief goddesses of Mecca. Her idol was kept inside the sanctuary. In the Qur'an, she is mentioned along with Manat and Lat in *surah* 53:19–23.

Waraqah ibn Nawfal; *17*

(d. CE 610). He was the parental cousin of Bibi Khadijah, Muhammad's ﷺ first wife. According to Muslim tradition, Waraqah was a Christian monk living in Mecca, who when told of Muhammad's ﷺ first revelation immediately recognized him as a prophet.

Watt, Montgomery; *xvii, 135, 142*

(d. CE 1979). British religious thinker and eminent biographer of Prophet Muhammad ﷺ.

Whitehead, Alfred; *156*

(d. CE 1947). English mathematician who became a world famous philosopher.

Wittgenstein, Ludwig; *152, 158, 182*

(d. CE 1951). An Austrian philosopher who worked primarily in logic, the philosophy of mathematics, the philosophy of mind, and the philosophy of language. As one of the twentieth century's most important philosophers, his influence has been wide-ranging.

Yogananda; *12, 138*

(d. CE 1952). Indian yogi, thinker, sage, and founder of interfaith centers in the USA. Yogananda taught his students the need for direct experience of truth, as opposed to blind belief.

Zayd bin al-Hareth; *17*

(d. CE 630). A prominent figure in the early Islamic community. As an adopted son of Muhammad ﷺ, he was an early convert to Islam and, later, a military leader.

Index of Subjects

adversarial relationship 178

"*Ajami*" distortions of Islam 145

American Constitution xii, 121, 176

amoral politics 121

angels 10, 15–16, 21, 28, 34, 37, 44, 47, 60, 73, 75, 82, 85, 94, 112, 115, 118, 128, 140, 144–47, 149, 151–52, 154, 165, 173–74

anthropomorphism 145

apologetics xix, 8, 13, 97, 103

apostasy 5, 107, 114, 168

atheists 6, 100, 105, 137, 171, 177

authentic conscience 8, 177

authentic integrity 81

awakened soul 8, 11

beautiful fellowship 87, 169–70

blaming others 161, 171

booty 132

Boston Brahmans 97

bracketing of Qur'an and *hadith* 5, 92, 125

Buddhism 11

capacity for receiving revelation 147

character of Prophet Muhammad 2, 11, 48–49, 116, 130, 135, 142

Christians xii, xiii, xiv, 9–12, 17, 24, 29–30, 52, 61, 70, 73, 78, 102–3, 105, 117, 120–21, 136–38, 141, 151, 166–68, 171, 177–78

chosen people 172

class interest 175

compulsion in religion 53, 84, 113, 163

conceptualization 7, 19, 48, 119

conceptual evolution 5–6, 125

conceptual frame xix, 4, 21, 25, 110, 137, 140–41, 144–45, 147, 161

conscientious objection 97, 170, 176

core of Islamic faith 15, 21–22, 24, 147, 160

core of Qur'anic piety 79–81

core of Qur'anic vision 51–54

"Countenance of the Lord" 81, 153

creative fidelity 13, 99, 123, 132, 179

cultural fruits 7

Day/Day of Judgement 9, 24, 28–30, 37, 45, 54, 58, 60–61, 81, 87, 89, 112–14, 118–19, 125, 146, 153, 160, 163–64, 166, 171

dead wood 98–99

deconstruction 136, 167, 179

demythologize 140, 147

Devil (*Iblis*) xiii, 10, 46, 53, 60, 115, 118, 146, 170, 174

distress loans 99

Divine attributes 12, 14, 30, 48, 116, 119, 140, 145

elliptical style of expression 27

embryonic idea 175

empathy xiii, 3, 50, 80, 102, 104, 125

equality of opportunity 4, 95, 120, 175

erotic fancies 96–97

eternity of the Qur'an 151

evaluative verses of the Qur'an 25, 28, 30, 155

About the Author

Jamal Khwaja was born in Delhi in 1928. After doing his M.A. in Philosophy from the Aligarh Muslim University, India, he obtained an Honors degree from Christ's College Cambridge, UK. Later he spent a year studying the German language and European existentialism at Munster University, Germany. At Cambridge he was deeply influenced by the work of C.D. Broad, Wittgenstein, and John Wisdom, apart from his college tutor, I.T. Ramsey who later became Professor of Christian Religion at Oxford. It was the latter's influence, which, taught Khwaja to appreciate the inner beauty and power of pure spirituality. Khwaja was thus led to appreciate the value of linguistic analysis as a tool of philosophical inquiry and to combine the quest for clarity with the insights and depth of the existentialist approach to religion and spirituality.

Khwaja was appointed Lecturer in Philosophy at the *Aligarh Muslim University* in 1953. Before he could begin serious academic work in his chosen field, his family tradition of public work pulled him into a brief spell of active politics under the charismatic Jawahar Lal Nehru, the first Prime Minister of India. Nehru was keen to rejuvenate his team of colleagues through inducting fresh blood into the *Indian National Congress*. He included young Khwaja, then freshly returned from Cambridge, along with four or five other young persons. Khwaja thus became one of the youngest entrants into the Indian Parliament as a member of the *Lok Sabha* (Lower House) from 1957 to 1962. While in the corridors of power he learned to distinguish between ideals and illusions, and finally chose to pursue the path of knowledge rather than the path of acquiring authority or power. Returning to his *alma mater* in 1962, he resumed teaching and research in the philosophy of religion. Ever since then Khwaja has lived a quiet life in Aligarh. He was Dean of the *Faculty of Arts* and was a member of important committees of the University Grants Commission and the *Indian Council for Philosophical Research* before retiring as Professor and Chairman of the *Department of Philosophy* in 1988. He was a frequent and active participant in national seminars held at the *Indian Institute of Advanced Study*, Shimla.

He was invited to deliver the *Khuda Bakhsh Memorial Lecture* in Patna. He was one of the official Indian delegates at the *World Philosophical Congress, Brighton*, UK, in 1988, and also at the *International Islamic Conference Kuala Lumpur*, Malaysia, in 1967, and the *Pakistan International Philosophy Congress, Peshawar*, Pakistan, in 1964.

About the Author

Khwaja's written works include:

1. *Five Approaches to Philosophy: A discerning philosopher philosophizes about the philosophy of philosophy with wisdom and clarity* (1965)
2. *Quest for Islam: A philosophers approach to religion in the age of science and cultural pluralism* (1977)
3. *Authenticity and Islamic Liberalism: A mature vision of Islamic Liberalism grounded in the Qur'an* (1986)
4. *Living the Qur'an in Our Times: A vision of how Muslims can revitalize their faith, while being faithful to God and His messenger* (2009)
5. *Essays on Cultural Pluralism: A philosophical framework for authentic interfaith dialogue* (2011)
6. *The Call of Modernity and Islam: A Muslim's journey into the 21st century* (2011)
7. *The Vision of an Unknown Indian Muslim: My journey to interfaith spirituality* (2011)

For more information about the author and his works visit:
www.JamalKhwaja.com